Heaven

YOUR REAL HOME . . .
from a Higher Perspective

EXPANDED EDITION

JONI EARECKSON TADA

**ZONDERVAN
BOOKS**

ZONDERVAN BOOKS

Heaven
Copyright © 1995, 2018 by Joni Eareckson Tada

Published in Grand Rapids, Michigan, by Zondervan. Zondervan is a registered trademark of The Zondervan Corporation, L.L.C., a wholly owned subsidiary of HarperCollins Christian Publishing, Inc.

Requests for information should be addressed to customercare@harpercollins.com.

ISBN 978-0-310-35305-8 (softcover)
ISBN 978-0-310-35308-9 (audio)
ISBN 978-0-310-35306-5 (ebook)

Library of Congress Cataloging-in-Publication Data

Tada, Joni Eareckson.
    Heaven : your real home / Joni Eareckson Tada.
       p.   cm.
    Includes bibliographical references.
    ISBN: 0-310-21919-1 (softcover)
    1. Heaven—Christianity. 2. Spiritual life—Christianity. I Title.
  BT846.2.t33
  1995236'.24—dc20   95-12441

Published in association with Wolgemuth & Associates, Inc.

Cover design: James W. Hall IV
Cover photo: Jeja / Getty Images
Interior design: Kait Lamphere

Printed in the United States of America

24 25 26 27 28 LBC 20 19 18 17 16

Joni is a friend of mine who has been leading people with love and courage for decades. God uses the most unlikely guides to take us up the rugged terrain in our faith. God's plan is pretty simple. He wants us to spend forever with Him. This life is just practicing for eternity. Will we face difficulties and setbacks? You bet. In this updated book, Joni has taken us once again to the high places, and she's done so from her chair.

BOB GOFF, author of the *New York Times* bestsellers *Love Does* and *Everybody Always*

Drawing from her work with persons who have disabilities, Joni Eareckson Tada has given us some of the most poignant images of heaven: a place where she will be on her feet dancing, a place where her mentally challenged friends will receive, at last, completed minds. Now, in *Heaven*, she gives a full treatment to one of the most important yet sadly overlooked doctrines of the Christian faith.

PHILIP YANCEY, author of *Where Is God When It Hurts?* and *The Jesus I Never Knew*

Although Joni Eareckson Tada is no stranger to suffering, she radiates a contagious joy that has impacted countless lives. Now, in her updated version of *Heaven*, Joni has shared the source of her hope by painting an irresistible picture of our eternal home.

JIM DALY, president of Focus on the Family

For more than half a century, without the use of physical legs, Joni Eareckson Tada has scaled heights and witnessed vistas most only dream of. Her life has given us glimpses of the joy found in the presence of our Savior. She has shown us what it looks like to keep pressing on, seeing and savoring Christ by faith until we are home with Him forever. Joni has given us an exquisite depiction of what lies ahead for those who have set their sights and hearts on the Summit.

NANCY DEMOSS WOLGEMUTH, author, teacher/host of *Revive Our Hearts*

When I researched in preparation to write my book *Heaven* years ago, I read 150 books on the topic, some of them hundreds of years old, literally every book I could find. I've often been asked which was my favorite, and my answer is always the same: Joni's. I'm delighted that this already great book has been updated and will reach a new generation of readers! I personally look forward to reading it again. Thank you, Joni, for your great heart for God and your infectious anticipation of heaven as our home.

RANDY ALCORN

Not merely in spite of but actually *because* of her own suffering, Joni is able to give to us her keen vision of heaven's joy.

THE LATE ELISABETH ELLIOT, author and speaker

As long as I've known Joni Eareckson Tada, her heart has been set on heaven. She pores over the biblical promises with an expectant heart. Her conversation, songs, and messages reflect a heavenly preoccupation. Joni has collected her thoughts on heaven in this moving book, filled with contagious expectation, rich biblical insight, and the warm glow of heaven itself. Joni, always a gifted artist, paints such a vivid picture of heaven that you'll get the sense she has lived half her life there.

DR. JOHN MACARTHUR, pastor-teacher, Grace
Community Church, Sun Valley, California

My first words to Joni when I met her in July 1999 were, "I'm reading your book, *Heaven*, because my daughter just went there." I was so grateful to know that my daughter, Hope, was in heaven, but it just felt so far away from me. Reading *Heaven* helped me to focus on all that Hope had gained rather than only on what I had lost. It increased my own anticipation of heaven and loosened my grip on this world. My copy is worn and underlined and treasured. This book is filled with godly wisdom and perspective for living this life in anticipation of the life to come.

NANCY GUTHRIE, author and Bible teacher

Joni Eareckson Tada has a unique gift for stating the profoundest wisdom in the vividest and most warmhearted way, and in *Heaven* she outshines herself. Theologically, spiritually, and humanly, her modeling from her wheelchair of healthy hope for the Christian's homeland is pure gold, as powerful as it is poignant. Don't miss it!

J. I. PACKER, theologian and author of *Knowing God*

Having ministered to college students for many years, I've experienced the generation gap firsthand. After mentioning something from my childhood, be it a favorite book or treasured toy, I get a blank stare that tells me the student has no idea what I mean. Thankfully, the lessons learned in suffering have no expiration date, and God's truths are everlasting. It is my joy to commend this book to those who haven't heard Joni's story or gleaned from the treasures she has found in dark places. My mentors introduced me to her writings, which has shaped and strengthened my love for Jesus, who is the centerpiece of heaven. I'm pleased to introduce her to younger generations in the hope that God will do the same for them.

AIMEE JOSEPH, Campus Outreach San Diego and Women's Ministry director at Redeemer Presbyterian Church, Encinitas

What a wise and warm and wonderful book! It will build up many people's faith and hope and love for God and heaven.

DR. PETER KREEFT, professor of philosophy, Boston College

There is a lot to find in this book—a lot of Scripture, a number of great stories, a series of prayers, and a host of important insights. But here's what I found above all else: hope. I was struck time and again by how much Joni has invested in heaven—and how much I ought to have invested in heaven. This is a book for people who are ready to take heaven seriously. I was encouraged, rebuked, and comforted.

KEVIN DEYOUNG, senior pastor of Christ Covenant Church, Matthews, North Carolina, and assistant professor of systematic theology, Reformed Theological Seminary-Charlotte

In the season after a near-fatal stroke changed our lives forever, we received so many books offering a picture of hope for our new normal. There was none more influential than this one as it lifted our eyes toward the hope of heaven with Joni's hard-won wisdom. It's a deep well of healing for every hurting heart.

KATHERINE AND JAY WOLF, coauthors of *Hope Heals*

I don't know of anyone I'd rather learn about heaven from than Joni Eareckson Tada. From the surprising platform of a wheelchair, Joni has radiated joyful courage and gospel hope for more than fifty years. She longs for the world to come, but even more, she longs for the King who came. "The first thing I plan to do on resurrected legs," Joni will often say, "is drop on grateful, glorified knees." Believers who read this powerful book won't just learn about their future home; they'll long for it.

MATT SMETHURST, managing editor of The Gospel Coalition and author of *1–2 Thessalonians: A 12-Week Study*

Step back for a moment, focus your eyes of faith, and then come with Joni Eareckson Tada into a world you've heard about from your youth but have never seen: heaven. You'll learn what heaven is like and who will be there—and how you can prepare your heart on earth for the reality of heaven. You just may discover that heaven is closer—and more real—than you've ever thought. My friend Joni is one of God's choice servants of today.

THE LATE CHUCK COLSON, Prison Fellowship

Though Christian culture is awash in bland thinking about heaven, Joni Eareckson Tada's *Heaven* is not like that. It is the product of decades of meditation on biblical teachings about a new earth more real than this one, with streets, rivers, and things to rule. Many will be surprised to know that God has crowns and rewards in store for those who did not drink the Kool-Aid of complacent theology but who allowed suffering to be a purifier and preparer for the next life.

ANDRÉE SEU PETERSON, author, writer for *World* magazine

Those who have suffered the most earthly pains for the longest time are often best fit to prepare us for heavenly joys—that is, if their suffering has been shaped by God's Word. And few have suffered as much for as long—and clung so tightly to Christ—as this remarkable woman. I cannot think of anyone from this century I'd rather read on heaven than Joni Eareckson Tada.

DAVID MATHIS, executive editor of desiringGod.org;
pastor of Cities Church, Minneapolis/St. Paul;
author of *Habits of Grace*

Heroes are people who give us hope. In this book, one of my heroes will deepen your understanding of the future hope that our soon coming King has prepared for all of us who have believed. Brace yourself for more hope for what is coming and more passion to live in light of that hope today.

TODD WAGNER, pastor of Watermark Community
Church and author of *Come and See*

Also by
JONI EARECKSON TADA

Joni: An Unforgettable Story

Diamonds in the Dust

When God Weeps

More Precious Than Silver

Pearls of Great Price

Finding God in Hidden Places

A Place of Healing

Joni & Ken: An Untold Love Story

Beyond Suffering

Beyond Suffering for the Next Generation

Beside Bethesda

A Spectacle of Glory

When Is It Right to Die? (updated edition)

For Al Sanders—
This world is not his home;
he's just a-passin' through—

and for Margaret,
who makes his journey
as smooth as possible.

CONTENTS

PREFACE TO THE
FIRST EDITION

I t's odd to express appreciation to a wheelchair, but I do. Almost thirty years of quadriplegia, and almost as many studying God's Word, have deepened my gratitude to God for these bolts and bars. The chair has shown me the way Home by heart.

Great writers and thinkers have helped guide my heart toward heaven. Over the years, I have scoured bookshelves for every essay, sermon, or commentary written by C. S. Lewis and Jonathan Edwards, from Bishop J. C. Ryle to contemporaries like Peter Kreeft and John MacArthur. Of course, when I want to reflect on a more poetic view of heaven, I always brush the dust off old favorites like George MacDonald and Madame Jeanne Guyon. I acknowledge here those marvelous philosophers and theologians, many whose fingerprints you will detect on the following pages.

I also express gratitude to a few others—Scott Bolinder of Zondervan who has been saying for years, "We'd love to hear what you have to say about heaven." And John Sloan, my editor, who graciously gave me a free hand and a wide berth to write what is on my heart. Also, Bob Hudson for examining my paragraphs with a magnifying glass. John Lucas, art director at Zondervan, and James Sewell, my art instructor who provided guidance as I worked on the rendering for the cover. And thanks to my friends at Wolgemuth & Hyatt for helping to make it all happen.

I thank Judy Butler and Francie Lorey for graciously serving as my "hands" on this project. And Steve Estes for reviewing the manuscript to keep me on the scriptural straight and narrow. I offer special thanks to the women who come to my home on different days to get me up, dressed, sitting in my wheelchair and ready to face the tasks at hand: Irene Lopez and Carolyn Simons, Patti Guth and Francie Lorey, Donna Condon, Judy Butler and Karen Crum. These friends make a heavenly investment every time they patch my pressure sores, scrub my teeth, or give me bran and orange juice. Of course, I can't miss saying "thank you" to my husband, Ken, who tolerated more than his share of Mexican take-out platters while I worked late on the manuscript.

Lastly, I'm so grateful that the Lord Jesus moved on the hearts of so many prayer warriors who faithfully interceded. Bunny Warlen, Mary Lance Sisk, Jean Kenoyer, Pam Rosewell Moore, and my Wednesday night prayer group at church. Also, the Joni and Friends staff who gather together every morning before work to pray.

One more thing. I thank you for taking the time to join me on this journey toward heavenly glories above. And who knows. Perhaps before you finish reading, you'll discover you know the way Home by heart too.

PREFACE 2018

The longer you journey with your eyes on heaven, the more you begin to see. And that's why I've put together an updated version of my 1995 book, *Heaven: Your Real Home*.

Nearly twenty-five years ago, I poured my heart into that book. I had been dreaming of heaven and longing for heaven almost since the beginning of my quadriplegia. When the opportunity came to write about my heart's desire, it filled me with excitement. How wonderful to capture in paper and ink so many of my reflections and long hours of searching the Scriptures. And thank God, the book did well. It was warmly received and has had a healthy readership through the years.

I was content with that . . . until I recently read the book again. And it gave me the feeling of a partially told story or a song half sung.

I'm in a very different place in my journey now. In body, soul, and spirit, it feels like I have come a great distance. Why do I feel that way? Perhaps it's because I've outlived my life expectancy. Perhaps it's the added years of dealing with the effects of remorseless gravity on an aging, paralyzed body. Maybe it's because of the life-threatening, tooth-and-nail battle with stage III cancer. Quite certainly it relates to year after year of living with mind-bending chronic pain.

My earthly life looks different to me now. And so does heaven. I've seen more, studied more, suffered more, endured more, learned more, prayed more.

Most important, I've fallen more in love with Jesus.

That's the nub right there. That's the beating heart of what I want to say.

In the original book, I make the point that heaven isn't so much a Place as it is a Person. But I didn't say nearly enough. Yes, Jesus said, "I am going there to prepare a place for you" (John 14:2). But it isn't the mansion or celestial condo or quarter acre of heavenly real estate that really matters to me.

It's Him. Truly.

If He's there—wherever there is—it's heaven. If He's not, then it's not.

All of the suffering and hurt and longing of the past quarter century hasn't focused my heart on twenty-four-karat avenues or tree-lined crystal rivers. Yes, of course I long for the "better country" of Hebrews 11:16, and a new body that runs, dances, swims, and embraces loved ones on the other side. But what I really want is Jesus. The Son of God who loved me and gave Himself for me. The Bridegroom. The Friend closer than a brother. The King. *My* King.

Prolonged suffering gives focus, and as the days slip by, my focus is more and more on my Rescuer and Companion.

In my late sixties now, I'm much closer to heaven than I was in my midforties. And that means I will soon—soon!—hear His voice, look into His eyes, and feel His embrace. And He will say, "Welcome home, Joni."

At the end of each chapter in this revised book, I've included some additional reflections that speak to where I am now, further along on life's winding trail and higher up on the hill of perspective. I've called these thoughts "Climbing Higher," and that's my invitation to all who make this journey with me.

It may have been long ago and far away, but I can still remember hiking with my family, sometimes along switchbacks that zigzagged up the side of a long, steep incline. Stopping to occasionally catch our breath, we would look back at where we had been and where we were headed—constantly surprised to realize how much more you can see with a little more altitude. Sometimes we could make out the tiny figures of hikers way back on the trail, struggling up the slope just where we had walked a half hour before. And it was encouraging to say to each other, "We've made good progress! It won't be long now."

That's what I hope these chapter-ending thoughts will do. Together, we'll stand at a few vistas, looking back on the faithfulness of God to get us where we are. And we will also look ahead to see Someone waiting at Trails End.

Or maybe we should say, at the real Trailhead.

Though I spend my mortal lifetime in this chair,
I refuse to waste it living in despair.
And though others may receive
Gifts of healing, I believe
That He has given me a gift beyond compare . . .

For heaven is nearer to me,
And at times it is all I can see.
Sweet music I hear
Coming down to my ear;
And I know that it's playing for me.

For I am Christ the Savior's own bride,
And redeemed I shall stand by His side.
He will say, "Shall we dance?"
And our endless romance
Will be worth all the tears I have cried.

I rejoice with him whose pain my Savior heals.
And I weep with him who still his anguish feels.
But earthly joys and earthly tears,
Are confined to earthly years,
And a greater good the Word of God reveals.

In this life we have a cross that we must bear;
A tiny part of Jesus' death that we can share.
And one day we'll lay it down,
For He has promised us a crown,
To which our suffering can never be compared.

NANCY HONEYTREE,
"JONI'S WALTZ"
(used by permission)

What's So Great
ABOUT HEAVEN?

I t was a dark and windy night.

Before returning to the warmth of the house, I huddled against the cold air to listen to my neighbor's whistling pine trees and gaze at the thin slice of moon smiling on the horizon. My eyes scanned the canopy of stars above to locate the constellation Ursa Major—I knew the Big Dipper was part of it, but having only recently memorized it from a book, I had never seen the whole thing.

I searched and searched, and suddenly, there it was, the familiar arrangement of stars spread out grand and glorious across one-fourth of the sky. I had no idea it was so *big*. Nor had I realized how beautiful it was.

I shivered, feeling small and swallowed up underneath the starry dome that seemed to reverberate with a song. Yes, I could have sworn I heard a song. Was it the faint tune of a hymn in my heart? Was it the morning stars singing together? I don't know, but the song struck a chord in me, like a tuning fork resonating in my soul. The stars and music took my breath away, and before the cold drove me indoors, my heart broke with joy, and I whispered toward the sky, "Jesus, I'm coming home; I belong up there."

I wheeled out of that moment, through the garage door and into the kitchen. The fluorescent lights made me squint as I nudged the door shut. I breathed in the aroma of dinner cooking. The house was warm and softly lit; the television was droning in the living room; and my husband, Ken, was in the hallway talking to a friend on the phone.

For a long minute, I sat in the kitchen, letting the warmth caress my icy cheeks. Outside I had touched a moment of great happiness and wisdom, but I knew I was incapable of holding on to that heavenly moment. Few are skilled at holding themselves in a state of listening to heaven's music. Ordinary things—like kitchen pots clattering, telephones ringing, and TV commercials about frozen foods and dishwashing detergent—drown out the song. It is too delicate to compete against mundane things. The music and the moment fades, and we become our ordinary selves, leaving the child outside and shelving our fascination with the moon, the stars, and the night wind. We consign heavenly thoughts to some other time.

Yet we live in the powerful memory of those moments.

Whether we are adults or children, our best memories are usually the sort that, like a tuning fork, strike a resonant chord in our souls. It's a song we never quite forget and recognize immediately whenever we catch its echo. We recognize it because it is so full of heartbreaking beauty. Like deep calling to deep, it is stamped with His imprint; and since we bear His image, the memory is sealed in that deepest, most profound part of us. Such moments cast soundings and plumb the real depths of who we are. And what we hear is a heavenly echo.

We may hear the haunting echo under a night sky or even in a symphony or a poem, or catch it in a painting. In fact, it is singers, writers, and painters who most often try to capture the echo, this heavenly music that compels us to sing, write, or paint something truly beautiful.

I know because I'm an artist. I have to confess, though, that I've never succeeded in painting a picture of heaven. People have asked me why, and I haven't come up with a good answer except to say that heaven defies the blank canvas of the artist. The best I can offer are scenes of breathtaking mountains or clouds that halfway reflect something of heaven's majesty. I'm never quite able to achieve the effect.

And neither is earth. Actual mountains and clouds are exalting, but even the most beautiful displays of earth's glory— towering thunderheads above a wheat field or the view of the Grand Canyon from the South Rim—are only rough sketches of heaven. Earth's best is only a dim reflection, a preliminary rendering of the glory that will one day be revealed.

Trouble is, we rarely let that fact sink in. That is, until we are stopped short by one of those brilliant nights when the air is clear like crystal and the black sky studded with a million stars. It takes such a moment to make us pause, watch our breath make little clouds in the night air, and think, *"What is your life? You are a mist that appears for a little while and then vanishes"* (James 4:14).

Then we rush indoors to catch the six o'clock news or referee an argument between our kids. The heavenly moment is lost, and we think, *Life doesn't seem like a mist that quickly vanishes.*

We really don't believe it's all going to end, do we? If God hadn't told us differently, we'd all think this parade of life would go on forever.

But it will end. This life is not forever, nor is it the best life that will ever be. The fact is that believers *are* headed for heaven. It is reality. And what we do here on earth has a direct bearing on how we will live there. Heaven may be as near as next year, or next week, so it makes good sense to spend some time here on earth thinking candid thoughts about that marvelous future reserved for us.

I love thinking and reading about heaven. But I've noticed as I've flipped through the pages of Scripture—our best resource about heaven—that its language is cryptic. You almost have to crack heaven's hieroglyphics before any of it makes sense.

What's more, I've gotten lost in the chronological chaos, wondering how Jesus' return to earth connects with the millennium, the rapture, the judgment, and the bowls, scrolls, and trumpets in the book of Revelation. How can we pursue heaven through so much confusion or consider our future "marvelous" if we keep stumbling over word pictures of crowns and thrones?

These things only *seem* to be deterrents. They are actually incentives. The symbols that Scripture uses of palms, crowns, streets of gold, and seas of glass are just that—symbols. They never quite satisfy our curiosity about heaven, and they're not meant to. They are only shadowy images of the real thing, as well as guides and signposts that point us in the right direction to show us the way home.

That's what the following pages are—guides and signposts to point you to heaven, the real home of our heart and spirit. I want to tap on your heart, open up a map, and show you the way home. The thoughts contained here are for those whose hearts break for heavenly joy, or at least would like to have their hearts break for heaven. It's even for those who don't have the faintest idea about heavenly joy but are haunted with curiosity.

True, heaven may defy the printed page of the author, but words and even paintings can sometimes strike a resonant chord, helping us hear the ancient and heavenly song that the morning stars sang together. Rather than let that song retire in the presence of mundane things like scratchy AM radios and grinding dishwashers, I hope the following pages will help you tune into heaven's melody.

Like stealing a tiny sip of stew before dinner, it's meant to be a foretaste of what to expect when you get to the banquet table.

It's meant to point you to the sky and help you see something far, far beyond the constellation of Ursa Major.

Let's not get too settled in, too satisfied with the good things down here on earth. They are only the tinkling sounds of the orchestra warming up. The real song is about to break into a heavenly symphony, and its prelude is only a few moments away.

A FIRST HINT *of* HEAVEN

The first time I heard that haunting heavenly song, so ancient and so new, was in the summer of 1957. My family and I had packed up, piled into our old Buick, and were heading west through the country roads of Kansas. Daddy pulled the car over onto the gravel shoulder to stop by a roadside ditch so my sister could go to the bathroom. I jumped out of the sweltering back seat and wandered beside a barbed wire fence along the road. It was a chance to dry the sweat off my back, as well as to explore.

I stopped and picked up a piece of gravel, examined it, and then heaved the stone beyond the fence far out into the biggest, widest, longest field I had ever seen. It was an ocean of wheat, waves of golden grain rippling in the wind, all broad and beautiful against a brilliant blue sky. I stood and stared. A warm breeze tossed my hair. A butterfly flitted. Except for the hissing sound of summertime bugs, all was quiet, incredibly quiet.

Or was it?

I can't remember if the song came from the sky or the field, or if it was just the sound of crickets. I tried hard to listen, but instead of actually hearing notes, I felt . . . space. A wide-open space filling my heart, as if the entire wheat field could fit into my seven-year-old soul. I rolled my head back to look up at a hawk circling overhead. The bird, sky, sun, and field were lifting me in some heavenly orchestration, lightening my heart with honesty and clarity like an American folk hymn in a major key, pure, upright, and vertical. I had never felt—or is it, heard?—such a thing. Yet as soon as I tried to grasp the haunting echo, it vanished.

I was only seven, but standing there by the barbed wire fence in a Kansas wheat field, I knew my heart had been broken by God. No, I didn't actually know Him at the time, but I wasn't so young that I couldn't sense the occasional stirrings of His Spirit. I kept staring while humming an old Sunday school favorite: "This world is not my home, I'm just a passing through." For me, the moment was heavenly.

Daddy honked the horn, and I ran back. Our family drove away with a slightly changed little girl in the back seat.

I can recount handfuls of similar moments when my heart seemed to be a beat ahead of my body and very much in rhythm with the Spirit. One such moment was a few years after the 1967 diving accident in which I became paralyzed. I was just beginning to get my spiritual act together with Jesus, having been pressed up against a wall that caused me to seriously consider His lordship in my life. Those were times I spent long evenings by the fireplace with my friend Steve Estes as he pored over his open Bible.

He was guiding me through the Word of God to help me learn about heaven. Immediately, he had my attention. Everybody wants to go to heaven. We are all curious to know where it is, what it looks like, who's there, and what they wear and do. I'm no exception.

I was fascinated to discover that one day I would no longer be paralyzed but have a new glorified body. Immediately I began imagining all the wonderful things I would do with resurrected hands and legs. Swim a couple of laps. Peel a few oranges. Sprint across fields and splash into waves, scale a few rocks and skip through meadows. Such thoughts enraptured me, and sitting there, in a wheelchair and unable to move, I began to sense a longing, a rising echo of that heavenly song about to stretch wide open my heart's capacity for joy. I could tell my heart was, once again, ready to break for joy.

Sensing my wonder with it all, Steve pointed me to a passage in Revelation 21. I couldn't wait to read all about this future God was reserving for us. I picked it up with the first verse:

"Then I saw 'a new heaven and a new earth' . . ."

Okay, I'll buy that. This old planet is in bad need of repair.

". . . for the first heaven and the first earth had passed away . . ."

Wait a minute, you mean everything about this earth will disappear and pass away? But there are lots of things I like. Chili dogs with cheese. The NBA playoffs. Bridalveil Fall in Yosemite National Park.

". . . and there was no longer any sea."

What! No sea? But I love the ocean. The waves. The wind. The smell of salt in the air. What about splashing in the breakers? What about digging my toes in the sand? To me, heaven has to have oceans in it.

"I saw the Holy City, the new Jerusalem, coming down out of heaven from God, prepared as a bride beautifully dressed for her husband."

No seas? No sand dunes? No Great Barrier Reef? No fields of wheat or sequoia trees? That does it! I hate cities, even if they are holy. Who wants sixteen-story housing projects in the center of heaven? Some people may like perfect urban planning, but not me, brother.

My friend closed his Bible. He sensed my disappointment. He knew that as quickly as the wonder of heaven had risen in my heart, it had disappeared. This was *nothing* like the sensation of gazing out over that Kansas field as a kid. Something was terribly wrong, either with me or with the Bible's descriptions of heavenly glories above.

Sound familiar?

Be honest. Be like any red-blooded, right-thinking Christian with both feet planted firmly on earth. Haven't there been times when word pictures of heaven from the Bible fall flat and boring next to the breathtaking sight and thunderous roar of Niagara Falls? Or scanning the serene Colorado plains from the pinnacle of Pikes Peak? Or swaying with the motion of acres of rippling waves of golden grain? Do you sense that sometimes the musical notes of God's creation almost eclipse Ezekiel's footnotes describing things in heaven as wheels that intersect other wheels and also move in four directions? "Their rims were high and awesome, and all four rims were full of eyes all around" (Ezekiel 1:18). *Whhaat?*

Reading about heaven in Scripture can almost sound like bad copy in a AAA TourBook:

> A large set of pearl-studded gates will welcome you to heaven, but be careful of slippery roads that are paved with gold. Don't bother looking for interesting local cuisine, as there is no need to eat while in heaven; you won't need to look for lodging either, since comfortable beds, crisp sheets, and downy pillows have no purpose.
>
> Topping the list of scenic points is a sea of glass. However, local conditions preclude sunsets, sunrises, or full moons. Do not miss the spectacular new Jerusalem, a striking city of the future, employing award-winning architectural design. Marvel at its twelve foundations. Stand amazed before its twelve gates, each made of a gigantic, single pearl. For sheer spectacle, the new Jerusalem eclipses even the Emerald City of Oz.

"This is upsetting. I don't understand," I said to Steve.

For encouragement, he flipped to Jesus' words in John 14:1–4: "Do not let your hearts be troubled. You believe in God; believe also in me. My Father's house has many rooms; if that were not so, would I have told you that I am going there to prepare a place for you? And if I go and prepare a place for you, I will come back and take you to be with me that you also may be where I am. You know the way to the place where I am going."

My friend tried to excite my imagination, explaining that if Jesus is presently preparing heaven, it must be out-of-sight. It only required seven days for Him to create the earth; and, hey, He's had almost two thousand years to work on my room in His mansion.

A clever maneuver, but it dive-bombed. I could only think of the times I had become bored with the most beautiful hotel rooms in less than a week. He tried again, explaining that all this stuff about mansions and rooms was probably allegorical anyway. I gave him a puzzled look, wondering how that idea improved on the previous.

You can understand why, at least in the beginning, I preferred thinking about heaven from the edge of a cliff overlooking a stormy ocean rather than from the edge of Revelation 21.

WHY DO HEAVEN'S SYMBOLS SOUND SO NEGATIVE?

I don't mean to poke fun, but like you, I'm struck that heaven is often described in terms of "no this" and "no that." No more sea. No more night. No more time. No more moon or sun. And what about food, marriage, sex, art, and great books? Do Ezekiel and the writer of Revelation assume that all the other benefits in heaven should outweigh the "no this" and "no that"? Sitting in a wheelchair for decades has loaded me with a lifetime of glorious memories, everything from feeling my fingers on the cool ivory keys of a piano to the euphoria of diving through the breakers at high tide. Such memories flood every nerve and fiber of my being and, thus, my imagination. It's awful to think that the best stuff of which memories are made will have no place in heaven. I'm sure you could say the same.

"However," Steve challenged, "as it is written: 'No eye has seen, no ear has heard, no mind has conceived what God has prepared for those who love him.' Your imagination can't begin to picture all that God has in store."

"Well, then," I fumed, "God can't expect us to get very excited about heaven. If I've got to stomp underfoot all the wonderful things I enjoy about earth just so heaven can come off looking better, then count me out."

It was lost on me how so much of heaven's happiness could be described in negative terms. Why did God seem to talk about heaven in terms of what it will *not* be rather than what it will be?

That's not all. I was also struck that the positive descriptions about what heaven *is* seem clumsy and ungraceful. Rainbow thrones? Streets of gold? Pearly gates? A glittering city 1,400 miles in length and as wide and high as it is long, with walls two hundred feet thick and made of jasper? It more closely resembled Minnesota's monolithic Mall of America. I was embarrassed to admit it, but even the descriptions about everlasting peace and eternal felicity seemed boring.

My friend sighed and gave one more stab at it. "Joni, you know the Bible well enough to realize it won't steer you wrong. So rather than put us off, shouldn't such descriptions ignite our hearts? Aren't you just a little relieved that heaven can't be reduced to terms we can manage?"

I looked at him blankly.

"Doesn't it console you to think that its marvels defy description?" He paused for a long minute and then added, "Simply put, there are no words for heaven." Now it was his turn to look at me blankly.

What he was saying was, as someone put it, darkness to my intellect but sunshine to my heart. He was right. I wanted those streets of gold and pearly gates to ignite my heart, not throw ice water on it. My heart wanted heaven to be the tuning fork that God strikes. I wanted the deepest part of me to vibrate with that ancient yet familiar longing, that desire for something that would fill and overflow my soul.

I smiled. Then we both smiled. We knew that God had not brought us this far only to disappoint me with mere negatives. I was not about to be daunted. There must be positives. The Bible was a book to be trusted, so there *must* be more behind the rainbow throne than met the eye. All this stuff about golden cities and seas of glass had to be clues in some amazing mystery. And if Psalm 25:14 was correct—if "the LORD confides in those who fear him"—then it's a mystery that God intends to stimulate me to seek, to rouse and stir my interest, until I grasp what heaven is about.

I felt recharged. I decided to tell Steve about that long ago and faraway summer afternoon by the wheat field in Kansas. "I was only a little girl, but heaven seemed so close to me then, so real," I sighed. I described the joy and the wonder, the feeling of space and the sound of music. I then told him I wanted heaven to feel like that. I wanted a kind of map back to that wheat field.

"But your longings about heaven have to hang on something," my friend warned. "You can't ignore streets of gold and rainbow thrones just because they don't thrill you at first glance. They're the images God gave us—the symbols that Scripture invites us to ponder. They're not deterrents to your faith; they're incentives."

I knew he was right on this point too. If I skirted the glittering celestial city with walls two hundred feet thick and made of jasper—just because I didn't like the idea of urban planning in heaven—I'd have nothing to hang my faith on but my imagination. And that could be dangerous, if not a little New Agey.

"Joni, don't mistake signs in the Bible for the reality they only represent. It's like this: Suppose we're driving down the road and see a green highway sign that reads, 'Chicago: 50 miles.' In no way would we mistake that road sign for Chicago, right?"

"Right."

"We both understand it's pointing us fifty miles down the road to a reality far, far beyond a five-by-eight-foot green sign with white lettering."

This was easy to track.

"In the same way, don't walk up to a wall 1,400 miles high made of sparkling jewels and stop there. Don't get down on all fours to examine whether the gold streets are 18 karats as opposed to 24 karats. These things are only pointing to a mind-boggling reality far beyond mere symbols."

Slowly the light dawned. The problem lay not with the Bible's descriptions of heavenly glories, but with the way I was looking at those symbols.

Steve charged ahead. "Since you seem less than enthusiastic about the new Jerusalem, consider this: Its walls are said to be the same height, width, and length. The city is a perfect cube of 1,400-mile proportions. What do you think that means?"

"That heaven's ugly," I replied.

"Aha! Watch it or you'll smack your face on a Chicago road sign," he laughed. "If you stop with only the symbol, you're right—it's not a pretty sight. But symbols point away from themselves to something else."

We turned to the Old Testament description of King Solomon constructing the Most Holy Place in the ancient temple in Jerusalem, the room where the ark of the covenant rested. First Kings 6:20 reads, "The inner sanctuary was twenty cubits long, twenty wide and twenty high."

"You see," he said, "the proportions are identical, only heaven is said to be about a quarter of a million times larger. Since the book of Revelation insists that no temple is found in heaven, the idea is probably that Paradise is all temple. Just as God's dazzling presence filled the Most Holy Place, so it will fill that Holy City. Only more intensely."

"Hmmm, that's something to think about," I mused.

"Exactly! You *have* to think. When you take time to ponder Scripture, your faith has something to hold on to. Something that's factual and true. Your faith has something to feed on, something from which your dreams about heaven can take root."

I didn't realize it at the time, but Steve Estes had just shown me how to read the map, how to understand the legend and symbols that would show me the way home to heaven. For when it comes to heaven, there is no limit to what the Lord will confide to those whose faith is rooted in Scripture.

SEEING HEAVEN *through* EYES *of* FAITH

The Bible provides the symbols. But it is faith that makes the hieroglyphics of heaven come alive. And heaven *has* to come alive! After all, you're a citizen of the kingdom of heaven, and according to Philippians 3:20, you're supposed to be eagerly awaiting it. Heaven is your journey's end, your life's goal, your purpose for going on. If heaven is the home of your spirit, the rest for your soul, the repository of every spiritual investment on earth, then it must grip your heart. And your heart must grip heaven by faith.

Heaven has been, and always shall be, a matter of faith. "Now faith is confidence in what we hope for and assurance about what we do not see," reads Hebrews 11:1. Stop and pick that verse apart. Faith means believing in realities that go beyond sense and sight. It is being sure of something you hope for, that is, sure about unfulfilled things in the future. And it's being assured of something you can't see, that is, being aware of unseen divine realities all around you. To put it another way, faith not only

makes you sure that heavenly streets of gold really exist, but it
helps you see something beyond the earthly streets of asphalt that
exist in the here and now.

Now, it takes no more than a mustard seed–sized grain of
faith to be sure of unfulfilled things in the future. It takes no great
faith to be aware of unseen divine realities all around us. If you
are aware of realities you can't see, and if you're certain there are
many more realities yet to be fulfilled, you are halfway to solving
the mystery!

Let's try it out on a few word pictures in the book of Ezekiel.

The prophet is sitting by a riverbank when suddenly—in a
flash—he squints at the heavens opening above him: "I looked,
and I saw . . . an immense cloud with flashing lightning and
surrounded by brilliant light. The center of the fire looked like
glowing metal, and in the fire was what looked like four living
creatures . . . Their faces looked like this . . ." (Ezekiel 1:4–5,
10). Then Ezekiel goes on to describe four heads with eyes, ears,
noses, and mouths of oxen and men, lions and eagles.

My heart goes out to Ezekiel. He was just minding his own
business by the river when, without warning, God pressed his
eyes smack-flat against the brilliance of heaven, a brilliance that
the ordinary faithful see from a distance, and then, only through
a glass darkly. The prophet strained to find words to describe
what he witnessed, but after hunting through his dictionary for
adequate nouns and adjectives to draw a picture of heaven, he
had to fall back on language that was old and familiar. Thus, the
strange pictures of beasts with weird faces and wheels that science
fiction writers would dream up.

Ezekiel courageously plunged ahead and put it into writing.
God revealed to him something supernatural—a whole bunch of
unseen divine realities—but God didn't give the prophet a thesaurus of supernatural words. So Ezekiel had to rely on the language
of resemblance. The center of the fire looked *like* this . . . and the

faces looked *like* that. In fact, the closer Ezekiel got to the burning throne, the less sure his words.

You can almost hear Ezekiel stutter and stammer, starting with verse 26 of chapter 1:

> Above the vault over their heads was what looked like a throne of lapis lazuli, and high above on the throne was a figure like that of a man. I saw that from what appeared to be his waist up he looked like glowing metal, as if full of fire, and that from there down he looked like fire; and brilliant light surrounded him. Like the appearance of a rainbow in the clouds on a rainy day, so was the radiance around him.
>
> This was the appearance of the likeness of the glory of the LORD.

Did you count all the "looked likes" and "like that ofs" and "what appeared to bes" and "as ifs"? Poor guy. The throne wasn't anything like King David's; the piece of furniture Ezekiel observed was more like *the appearance* of a throne. And the Lord who was sitting on it? He could only be described as *the appearance* of the likeness of a man.[1]

The same is true for the apostle John scrambling to write down his heavenly vision as he sits on the beach on the island of Patmos. Thus, it is the apostle's best effort to describe what looks like rivers of glass, streets of gold, and gates of pearl.

My point? Were Ezekiel and John sure of what they hoped for? Of course. Were they certain of things they had never seen? You bet. They witnessed far into the future something yet to be fulfilled, and when the Lord pulled back the curtain so they could actually see the unseen realities, they trusted Him to bring it to pass. Their faith about heaven may have been hazy in days gone by, but once their eyes were opened, realities with a small *r* became Realities with a capital *R*.

Now it's true they had a slight advantage. When they saw heaven, it was a little like standing in front of an arc light without sunglasses on. They couldn't miss it. They saw with their eyeballs what they had been hoping for all their lives. But before you envy them, remember that "hope that is seen is no hope at all. Who hopes for what they already have?" (Romans 8:24–25).

Ezekiel and John saw their hope. We cannot. And this is why the heavenly song is still an echo. It's a yearning, something that is unfulfilled. A longing that is still an ache. But that's not such a bad thing. We may strain and squint to see heaven through a glass darkly, but when we, the ordinary faithful, catch a glimpse, we may be in a more blessed state than even that of a prophet. How so? Jesus commends the faith of people like you and me in John 20:29 when He elevates us, saying, "Blessed are those *who have not seen* and yet have believed" (emphasis added).

Jesus says there is a special kind of blessedness, a unique happiness reserved for people like you and me who dig through earth's dirt to decipher heaven's hieroglyphics. When it comes to heaven, if you can move beyond the symbols and be sure of what you hope for, as well as certain that what you do not see is *there*, then you are edging close to the fellowship of prophets and apostles. For although a rainbow throne was emblazoned on their eyes, you can glimpse what the throne symbolizes, and you can see what's beyond, albeit through a glass darkly.

WHY HEAVEN IS HARD
to UNDERSTAND

There is something else we can learn from Ezekiel and John. As weird and strange as the word pictures are, they convey one thing for certain: The whole scene in heaven is very real. There's nothing wispy or vaporous about the exact measurements of a twelve-layered foundation of precious stones.

It's real, but it's entirely alien to anything that people have heard of on earth.

God has good reasons for describing it this way. You see, if Ezekiel or John or even we were able to break down the infinitely high wall that separates "everything that is spiritual" from "everything that is not spiritual," if we were able to scale that wall with the ropes and grappling irons of human understanding, then, good grief, our faith wouldn't mean very much.

God designed both heaven and humans so that a cloud of mystery prevents you and me from fully grasping heaven with language and logic. The apostle Paul, like Ezekiel and John, saw heaven with his own eyes; but unlike them, he was not only unable to describe the sights; he wasn't permitted to! The mystery is *supposed* to remain intact. We cannot fashion heaven solely out of the Lincoln Logs of our logic. Even if we could, we would merely be illuminating the sun with a flashlight. We are only allowed to break through the glass darkly by faith.

I'm thankful heaven is grander than human language. And as for those "clunky" sights in that AAA TourBook, faith removes the clunkiness. Trying to grasp heaven without faith is like trying to admire the outside of a huge great cathedral with grand windows. Standing outside, you see an impressive but imposing structure. The building is striking, but has no real glory. But if you go inside the cathedral—which is a little like looking at heaven through eyes of faith—you are breathless as you stand awash in glorious colors from the light that streams through the window.[2]

Faith takes us beyond the imposing and impressive language of golden cities and thrones and reveals the better, brighter glory inside the walls of the new Jerusalem. Faith takes the descriptions of 24-karat asphalt and big pearls swinging on hinges and makes us certain that what we hope for is far, far better than here.

How much better?

LOOK BEYOND *the* NEGATIVES

Remember how I soured on all the "no this" and "no that" descriptions in heaven? No food, no marriage, no moon, no need for good books? *Faith reminds us that every negative is only the reverse side of a fulfilling.* A fulfilling of all that God intended our humanity to be. True, we may enjoy a good charcoal-broiled steak or a night of romance with our husband or wife under a full moon, but faith tells us these things are inklings of better tastes and enraptured delights yet to come. They won't be negated, no; rather, the whisper of what they are on earth will find complete fulfillment in heaven.

Don't assume that if there is no marriage in heaven, we will be forced to embark on an eternal abstinence. Don't chew on the idea that with no charcoal grills in heaven, we will be compelled to take nourishment in gray tasteless pills.

Use your eyes of faith. Think of it in terms of "future divine fulfillments." See that every negative is just a reverse side of a fulfilling. Because what is no longer needed for biological purposes, such as procreation or digestion, may serve a far higher, more beautiful function.

This is one of those realities that goes beyond sense or sight. Consider where it says, "Blessed is the man that endureth temptation: for when he is tried, he shall receive the crown of life" (James 1:12 KJV). From a verse like this we can infer that when we curb our appetites on earth and refuse to let lust and gluttony ruin wonderful things like marriage or food, our victories gain glory and splendor in heaven. If we controlled our hormones on earth, then fidelity in marriage will serve us in eternity as a triumphant weapon with which we defeated temptation. All of this will bring greater glory to God.

I broached this subject of "controlling hormones" on another one of those pleasant evenings around the fireplace with Steve.

It was the big question everybody wonders about heaven sooner or later. I was only a teenager and embarrassed to use the word *sex*, so I casually remarked, "What's this stuff about 'no marriage in heaven' supposed to mean?"

He seemed to read my mind, and smiling, he said, "Joni, things like procreation and digestion are physical functions necessary for our life here on earth. When it comes to heaven, I don't think we'll become genderless or never sink our glorified teeth into a juicy peach. It's just that heaven promises something far, far better. Far better than even the pleasure that people enjoy in marriage."

I looked at him with skepticism. "I'm not married, but that's pretty hard to imagine."

"No, it's not *hard* to imagine; it's impossible. Absolutely impossible. We have no idea what God is preparing. But look at this verse in Psalm 16:11," he said as he flipped back to the Old Testament: "'You will fill me with joy in your presence, with eternal pleasures at your right hand.' Faith tells us that the pleasures and the privileges people enjoy in marriage are only hints and whispers of greater delights yet to come."

I gave him a doubtful grin. I decided, though, that he was right. My questions about intimacy and food would have to be shoved to the back burner for the time being. I would have to cultivate faith that every negative is only the reverse side of a fulfilling. A fulfilling of all that God intended our humanity to be.

Not only will there be no need for procreation and digestion, there will not—I repeat, *will not*—be a sun or a moon in heaven. Revelation 21:23 reads, "The city does not need the sun or the moon to shine on it." But don't grieve. Heaven won't be less than the wonder you experience over a glorious sunrise or a glowing moonlit night, "for the glory of God gives it light, and the Lamb is its lamp." Even light will have its future divine fulfillment, for it will be a better light, "not as a candle flame that is put out but as a candle flame which becomes invisible because someone has pulled up the blind, thrown open the shutters, and let in the blaze of the risen sun."[3]

Faith tells us not to grieve. We will not lose in heaven. We will gain. The Lord who has planted the seed of future divine fulfillments in almost every good thing on earth will carry it on to completion until the day He arrives and makes crystal clear all the unseen divine realities. God won't throw any good thing away. As C. S. Lewis writes, "The old field of space, time, matter, and the senses is to be weeded, dug, and sown for a new crop."[4]

SEE INTO *the* POSITIVES

May I pose a question that will explain something else about all those negatives in heaven? Do you know why a photographer uses a negative to take your photo? He uses it to show us a positive image. It's the same principle when I paint at my easel. Sometimes I choose not to outline a shape, such as a leaf, with a brush, but rather I paint the sky all around the leaf, which then defines its shape. It's called "negative space" painting, and it's a way—some would say a better way—of giving definition to the shapes of leaves against a sky. The artist helps you see by painting what you don't see.

The principle is the same when it comes to heaven: *The negatives are used in order to show us the positive.* On earth, we know all too well what the negatives are: suffering, pain, and death. Show us their opposites, the positive side, and we will have the best possible idea of the perfect state. For instance, there may be no moon, no marriage, and no need to eat in heaven, as suggested in Revelation 21, but there are also some pretty *good* negatives we can relate to, and curiously, they're all listed in Revelation 21 too.

- no more mourning
- no more crying

- no more pain
- no more curse
- and, praise God, no more death

Selah. Pause. Think of that.

We'd all admit that the sum of human misery on earth vastly outweighs the sum of human happiness. Job said, "Mortals, born of woman, are of few days and full of trouble" (14:1). David the psalmist expresses this in Psalm 55:6, 8: "Oh, that I had the wings of a dove! I would fly away and be at rest . . . I would hurry to my place of shelter, far from the tempest and storm."

I'm with Job and David: Get me outta here!

Have you ever felt that way? I can't tell you how much sorrow I've held at bay over the years. Tears could come easily if I allowed myself to think of all the pleasures of movement and sensation I've missed. Diving into a pool and feeling my arms and legs slice through the water. Plucking guitar strings with my fingers. Jogging till my muscles burn. Cracking steam-broiled Maryland crabs with a mallet. Throwing back the covers in the morning and hopping out of bed. Running my hands across my husband's chest and *feeling* it. To think that one day we will hear these words uttered that haven't been spoken since Adam was thrust out of Eden: "There shall be no more sorrow."

FAITH *to* FIND YOUR WAY HOME

Do you see it? Are your eyes of faith focusing better? Or rather, can you hear it? The faint echoes of some distant heavenly song? It's whispering that heaven will not be an *unmaking* of all the good things we know, but a new and vastly improved version. Heaven will also be an *undoing* of all the bad things we know as God wipes away every tear and closes the curtain on pain and disappointment.

In fact, I'm going to correct something I wrote earlier. Remember the comment made during one of those fireplace discussions: "There are no words for heaven"? It should be, "Heaven is too specific, too real, for language."[5] If we've learned anything from the prophet Ezekiel and the apostle John, it's that heaven is real. It's not a state or a condition, but a place. A place with streets, gates, walls, and rivers. We are wrong in thinking that heaven is wispy, thin, and vaporous. It is earth that is like withering grass, not heaven.

What it takes to know the place that Jesus has gone ahead to prepare is faith. Faith in what God has to say about heaven from His Word. For when God chose to talk about heaven, He did so using the nouns and verbs, the syntax and grammar, of the Bible. And although He mainly expounded on heaven in highly symbolic books like Ezekiel and Revelation, these symbols are meant to be motivation for our minds and fodder for our faith.

Faith that focuses not *on* the scriptural symbols, but *inside* and *beyond* them.

Faith that develops the skill of holding on to that heavenly moment.

Faith that shows us the way home.

This kind of faith will bring heaven forward into vivid reality. It will bring into vital contact with your heart the things that people call invisible and distant. It will involve your heart and your eyes. If the apostle Paul were here, he would repeat Ephesians 1:18: "I pray that the eyes of your heart may be enlightened in order that you may know the hope to which he has called you, the riches of his glorious inheritance in his holy people."

Step back for a moment, focus your eyes of faith, and then walk with me into a world you've heard about from your youth but have never seen: heaven. What will we be like there? What will we do? Where is this place called heaven, and why is it called "home"? Look with me through a glass darkly, and you just might discover that Home is closer—and more real—than you ever thought.

CLIMBING HIGHER

In his letter to the Colossians, the apostle Paul tells us, "Let heaven fill your thoughts; don't spend your time worrying about things down here . . . Your real life is in heaven with Christ and God" (Colossians 3:2–3 TLB).

For years I've been trying to do that. With all my heart I *want* to think about my "real life" with God's Son and the place He is preparing for me. But I don't often succeed—not nearly as much as I would like to. For so much of the time, so many other things fill my thoughts: worries, regrets, fears, frustrations, and all sorts of earthly, here-and-now, Joni-centered things.

But there are moments.

Something I see, hear, dream, or remember will open my spirit like a shutter. In those breathless intervals, I slip from my temporary earthbound citizenship to my true and rightful one. For several heartbeats, I catch a glimpse of another Reality, inhale the fragrance of a Better Country, and sense a moment in time that's somehow beyond time.

And it feels like home.

Always, when something like that would happen, I would try to capture the experience, bottle it up, tuck it away in a secret place, or even slip it into a Ziploc bag (to open and experience all over again). But I was never able to do it.

All that changed when I read something in C. S. Lewis's last book. He made a passing reference to the poet William Blake and spoke about joy and how we must "kiss it as it flies."[6]

I had to look that up to see what it meant. The actual four-line poem goes like this:

He who binds to himself a joy
Does the winged life destroy;
But he who kisses the joy as it flies
Lives in Eternity's sun rise.[7]

I'm not positive what Blake or Lewis meant by that, but here's what occurs to me. You can revel in heart-melting moments of beauty, inexpressibly lovely dreams, and even happy times of companionship with Jesus, but you can't freeze time to hold on to them. If you tried to wrap your fingers around them, capture them in a golden cage, or encase them in amber, you would only kill them.

What do you do with those rare golden moments of life when you are swept into wonder or joy bubbles up in your heart like an artesian spring?

You savor them.

You humbly thank God for them.

And you let them go.

At the beginning of this chapter, I wrote about a time out on my back porch on a clear cold night. After searching the stars to find Ursa Major, I simply let my spirit soar. That was when I had the unworldly experience of hearing some faint, mysterious strain of music. It wasn't from the neighbor's house, and it wasn't the TV in the family room. It was in the moment; it was in the heavens; it was for my ears only; and it created a deep, unspeakable, half-joyful, half-sorrowful longing for heaven.

It broke my heart, and it healed my heart, and then it was gone.

I couldn't cling to that moment, and to this day I can't recall a single note of that celestial music. As much as I treasure the memory of those few seconds, nothing quite like that has ever happened to me again.

I have a friend who described his first raft trip down a wild river in the remote backcountry of Oregon. As the raft swept along in the rapid current, he would fill his eyes with a rugged vista unlike anything he had ever seen. Keeping his eyes pinned on the sight, he would soon find himself facing sideways and then backward as the beautiful tableau swept by. But facing backward to see what was now departing behind him, he realized that he was missing the *next* beautiful scene around the *next* bend in the river.

He couldn't stop the river. He couldn't freeze the moment. And he soon realized that he had to taste and treasure each scene as it filled his eyes . . . and then quickly let it go.

So it is with those heart-lifting moments when the Lord allows you the tiniest glimpse into your future home. Heaven fills your thoughts, as Scripture says, but it's not like a snapshot you can put on your refrigerator. It's not like a shrine that you come back to.

It's just a shaft of grace through a quick opening in the clouds.

And there will be more.

FIND YOUR TRAIL

1. In Acts 1:7–11, the writer paints a somewhat comical scene. Why were the disciples staring at the sky? What did it take to turn them back to the Lord's words and the urgent business at hand? How does this incident speak to us about moving forward in our walk with Christ?
2. In the midst of work, relationships, and dozens of competing priorities, how do we follow Paul's command in Colossians 3:2 to let heaven fill our thoughts?

A HIKER'S PRAYER

Lord Jesus, thank You for the nudges, whispers, confirmations, and bright, fleeting glimpses of heaven that remind me that I belong to You, that this life on earth isn't everything, that You are at this moment preparing my room in the Father's house, and that a vast, unspeakable joy awaits me just over the horizon.

PART ONE

What Will Heaven Be Like?

Different people through the years have written books and gone on speaking tours talking about briefly dying, visiting heaven, and then miraculously returning to resume their lives on earth. I don't want to refute what these people say they have experienced. Who knows? Maybe the Lord in His mercy gave them a vision, a hint, or a little foretaste of glories ahead. Even so, I hold to the words of Scripture: "No eye has seen, no ear has heard, and no mind has imagined what God has prepared for those who love him" (1 Corinthians 2:9 NLT).

Reading any of these contemporary claims of heavenly visits sound titillating, but it will inevitably result in one thing: disappointment. What they describe is still encased in time and in two-dimensional terms, and we think to ourselves, *That's it? That's what it will be for all eternity?* We feel let down by the pale, diminished, lukewarm realm they describe.

When the apostle Paul was caught up to the third heaven and then returned, he refused to give his readers any details at all (2 Corinthians 12:2). He said, in effect, "I really can't talk about it." And he never did. But one thing for sure: For the rest of his life, he couldn't wait to go back. He could say, from actual experience, "I desire to depart and be with Christ, which is better by far" (Philippians 1:23). In so many words, he told his friends, "I'll stick around here as long as I'm needed and as long as the Lord wants me to. But if I see that door of heaven crack open again, if I hear the Lord's call—just get out of my way, because I'm out the door!"

And in this section, "What Will Heaven Be Like?" I hope I can crack the door for you just a tad. Just enough to help you take Scripture, logic, a little imagination—and get a small glimpse of what God is preparing for those who love Him!

One

Who Are We

IN HEAVEN?

I've been thinking about my heavenly home for years. Naturally, you can understand why: My earthly body doesn't work. That's one reason I dream about heaven all the time.

I can't say my dreams are Technicolor versions of pearly gates and streets of gold; rather, they're more like rough sketches or dim reflections, as when my "eyes will see the king in his beauty and view a land that stretches afar" (Isaiah 33:17). Like the rolling vista of a Kansas wheat field . . .

. . . Except for one extraordinary heaven dream I had one night in a hotel in Stavanger, Norway. My quiet time that week centered on Revelation 21:21, where the apostle John writes, "The great street of the city was of gold, as pure as transparent glass." It didn't make sense. Gold is not transparent, and it's nothing like glass because you can't see through it. It was another one of those heavenly images gone gawky. I shrugged my shoulders and closed my Bible.

That night, as the cold Norwegian wind rattled my bedroom window, I snuggled down and slipped into the most amazing dream. I saw myself standing in a bright yellow bathing suit at the edge of a pool. This was astonishing, since I rarely dream about being on my feet. Usually I can't see or feel my body from the shoulders down; my torso and legs are always hazy and unfinished, like the half-completed edges of a painting. But not in this dream.

I stretched my arms above my head, arched my back, and gracefully dove into the water. When I came up and slicked my hair with my hands, I was stunned to see them glow, all rose-red wet and honey-ivory, bathed in life, beauty, and well-being. I pressed my palms to my nose. They smelled wild and sweet. Some might have mistaken me for an angel, but I never felt more human, more a woman. I cocked my head and admired my outstretched arms and then looked around. This is hard to describe, but the water and air were brilliant, ablaze in light, like pure gold, as transparent as glass.

Each breath was piercing to my lungs, but with a sweet sting that made me want to breathe deeper. I looked down to see the pool water shimmering like diamonds. You know how we say "the water sparkles"? In my dream, it was doing exactly that. The air was sparkling too. Everything was flashing, clear and golden.

I saw a friend sitting poolside, relaxing in a chair under a white cabana and watching me. Oddly, he looked awash in light too. He seemed more real, more a man, than ever before. He was my old friend, but a thousand times more himself, and when our eyes met, youth infused my heart. I wondered if he felt the same. I smiled, waved, and then began swimming, smoothly parting the water with long, powerful strokes. The ripples felt cool and slick, more like satin than water. After a while, my friend dove in. He touched my shoulder, and it burned, but in a painless way. There was no need to talk; our smiles said that we were friends for the first time again. We swam together stroke for stroke. And the longer we swam, the stronger we grew. Not weaker, but stronger.

It was the most remarkable dream I've ever had. When I woke up, I had no doubt it was a dream about heaven. I was convinced that "gold, as pure as transparent glass" existed. It wasn't a gawky image. I saw it with the eyes of my heart.

NEW BODIES

One day the dream will come true.

One day, if I should die before Jesus returns, my soul will be reunited with my body. Pause and dream with me . . .

One day no more bulging middles or balding tops. No varicose veins or crow's feet. No more cellulite or support hose. Forget the thunder thighs and highway hips. Just a quick leapfrog over the tombstone, and it's the body you've always dreamed of. Fit and trim, smooth and sleek.

It makes me want to break into giggles right now! Little wonder that "we eagerly await a Savior from [heaven], the Lord Jesus Christ, who, by the power that enables him to bring everything under his control, will transform our lowly bodies so that they will be like his glorious body" (Philippians 3:20–21).

Our lowly bodies . . . will be like His glorious body. Astounding. Like Jesus in His resurrected body, we will have hands and arms, feet and legs. We won't be spirit beings, floating around like angels who have no bodies.

A promise like this, though, almost raises more questions than answers. Does a glorified body translate into glorified digestive systems? What about sleeping? What if we prefer our teeth a little crooked rather than perfect and straight? Will we look the same? And if we do, will we recognize each other? Will my husband be "Ken Tada," and my mother, "Margaret Johanna Eareckson"? Will I wear a bright yellow bathing suit in heaven if I want to and take a swim with a friend if I wish?

Another thing. What about people who died in the ocean

centuries before, whose bodies long ago became fish food? Or people who were blown to smithereens in bomb blasts, or pioneers who perished on the prairies, whose bodies dissolved into dust that was scattered to the four winds? Will God vacuum up the winds, collect and sort everyone's body particles, and divvy out the correct DNA?

These questions became real to me in the summer of 1990 when my ninety-year-old father passed away. He had led a cowboy roughrider life, trading with Native Americans, riding fast horses, and scaling the highest peaks of the Rockies. So it wasn't an unusual activity that summer for my family and Ken and me to drive to the top of Pikes Peak to scatter my father's ashes.

We found a private place near the edge of a cliff. Thousands of feet beneath us spread a green valley patchworked in sun and cloud shadows. The icy wind whipped our hair, and we held on to our wool hats. An eagle hang glided above our heads. Ken opened the *Book of Common Prayer* and read:

> Forasmuch as it hath pleased Almighty God, in his wise providence, to take out of this world the soul of our beloved father, John Eareckson, we therefore commit his body to the ground; earth to earth, ashes to ashes, dust to dust; looking for the general Resurrection in the last day, and the life of the world to come, through our Lord Jesus Christ; at whose second coming . . . the earth and the sea shall give up their dead; and the corruptible bodies of those who sleep in him shall be changed, and made like unto his own glorious body.[1]

Ken closed the book and read a final verse from Romans 8:11, which assured us that "if the Spirit of him who raised Jesus from the dead is living in you, he who raised Christ from the dead will also give life to your mortal bodies because of his Spirit who lives in you." With that, my mother stepped closer to the edge, took her husband's ashes in her hand, and threw them to the wind. I watched with wet eyes as a gust carried my father's ashes up and beyond the clouds.

Ashes to ashes, and dust to dust.

Later that afternoon, we talked about how God would resurrect our dad's body. We didn't get into details, but our faith assured us that somehow it would happen. That night in bed, I wondered *how* will it happen? Billions and billions of people have lived on earth and have probably shared the same dust and ashes. For all I know, my father's ashes settled on some field in that green valley, providing fertilizer to feed the next generation. It seems silly, but how will John Eareckson's molecules remain distinct from the rest?

Others have wondered the same. The apostle Paul framed their thoughts in 1 Corinthians 15:35 when he wrote, "But someone will ask, 'How are the dead raised? With what kind of body will they come?'"

Paul then cuts those big scary questions down to size when he writes, "How foolish!" In other words, "Guys, get real. Open your eyes." And starting with verse 36, he sketches a few lessons from nature: "What you sow does not come to life unless it dies. When you sow, you do not plant the body that will be, but just a seed, perhaps of wheat or of something else. But God gives it a body as he has determined, and to each kind of seed he gives its own body."

HOW ARE *the* DEAD RAISED?

Have you ever seen those nature specials on public television? The ones where they put the camera up against a glass to show a dry, old lima bean in the soil? Through time-lapse photography, you watch it shrivel, turn brown, and die. Then, miraculously, the dead shell of that little bean splits open, and a tiny lima leg-like root sprouts out. The old bean is shoved aside against the dirt as the little green plant swells. The lima plant came to life because the old bean died.

Not even a PhD in botany can explain how life comes out of death, even in something as simple as a seed. But one thing is for sure: it's a lima bean plant. Not a bush of roses or a bunch of bananas. There's no mistaking it for anything other than what it is. It has absolute identity—positively, plain as day, a lima bean plant. It may come out of the earth different than when it went in, but it's the same.

So it is with the resurrection body. We'll have absolute identification with our body that died. I will be able to positively recognize my dad as John Eareckson. The "Daddy" I meet in heaven will be my dad; he won't be neutered in my eyes, stripped of all the trappings that made him my father. He may come forth from the earth different than when he was buried, but he won't be mistaken for anyone else.

And what about his dust and ashes scattered to the winds? How many of my father's molecules are required to be reassembled before he can be raised? Very little, I suspect. I once read that if all the DNA were collected from the seven billion or so persons now inhabiting the earth, it would approximate the size of two 5-grain aspirin tablets. The "who" you are and the "who" I am is not that big. It's actually very small.[2]

Besides, how much of that old lima bean was the "seed" out of which life miraculously came forth? The best botanists in the world can't answer that one. No one knows how much of that seed is required, or even how life can spring from a dead seed. It's one of God's miracles of nature.

So it will be with the resurrection. God will not have to use every part of your body in order to resurrect it. Anyway, you do not possess today any particle of your body that you had a few years ago. We learn in Biology 101 that human cells are being replaced every seven years. The flesh and blood that make up "you" today is not the same flesh and blood you had in your teens. Yet, somehow, the particular person that you are carries on.

Obviously, God is not as hung up as we are on DNA. Jesus gives a simple biology lesson in John 12:24: "Very truly I tell you, unless a kernel of wheat falls to the ground and dies, it remains only a single seed. But if it dies, it produces many seeds." It is no more difficult to believe in the resurrection than it is to believe in the harvest.

WHAT KIND *of* BODY?

What about the second question, "With what kind of body will they come?" True to the apostle Paul and his lessons from nature, all we have to do is open our eyes and look around. "You do not plant the body that will be, but just a seed . . . If there is a natural body, there is also a spiritual body . . . And just as we have borne the image of the earthly man [Adam], so shall we bear the image of the heavenly man [Jesus]" (1 Corinthians 15:37, 44, 49).

You do not plant the body that will be. I learned this lesson on one of those blustery November afternoons when I tend to get thoughtful and meditative. I glanced outside my window and spied a fat, furry squirrel doing his autumn ritual of collecting acorns. I watched him sniff each one, inspecting them in his paws and then stuffing his cheeks with the tastiest nuts. Others he dropped on the ground.

The acorns he discarded rolled around in the stiff breeze. I knew most of them would blow away. Others would remain on the dirt to dry in the chilly air. And a few, just a few, would take root under the soil. They would be the ones next season to sprout forth green shoots of new life. These were the acorns destined to be trees.

I shook my head in amazement. If you were to tell the tiny

acorn that one day it would be as tall as a building, with heavy branches and thick, green leaves, a tree so great it would house many squirrels, that nut would say you were crazy. A gigantic oak tree bears absolutely no resemblance to an acorn. The two, although related, seem as different as night and day. Somehow, somewhere, within that acorn is the promise and pattern of the tree it will become.

Somehow, somewhere within you, is the pattern of the heavenly person you will become, and if you want to catch a glimpse of how glorious and full of splendor your body will be, just do a comparison. Compare a hairy peach pit with the tree it becomes, loaded with fragrant blossoms and sweet fruit. They are totally different, yet the same. Compare a caterpillar with a butterfly. A wet, musty flower bulb with an aromatic hyacinth. A hairy coconut with a graceful palm tree.

It's no wonder you and I get stymied thinking about our resurrection bodies—whether or not our teeth will be straight or our digestive systems intact. First Corinthians 15:42–44 only touches on it: "The body that is sown is perishable, it is raised imperishable; it is sown in dishonor, it is raised in glory; it is sown in weakness, it is raised in power; it is sown a natural body, it is raised a spiritual body." *It* is sown . . . *it* is raised. We may not be able to describe the changes, but we know it's the same "*it*." You and what you will one day be are one and the same—yet different.

Trying to understand what our bodies will be like in heaven is much like expecting an acorn to understand its destiny of roots, bark, branches, and leaves. Or asking a caterpillar to appreciate flying. Or a peach pit to fathom being fragrant. Or a coconut to grasp what it means to sway in the ocean breeze. Our eternal bodies will be so grand, so glorious, that we can only catch a fleeting glimpse of the splendor to come. C. S. Lewis marveled: "It is a serious thing to live in a society of possible gods and goddesses."[3]

Lima beans. Kernels of wheat. Peach pits. Acorns and oak trees. Examples in nature are what the Bible invites us to use, since "what we will be has not yet been made known" (1 John 3:2). One of the best ways to understand the resurrection is to take a field trip after the apostle Paul's lesson in nature: go find an acorn on the ground, look up into the billowy skirts of the tree from which it fell, and then praise God that "so will it be with the resurrection of the dead" (1 Corinthians 15:42).

Can you now see why I enjoy dreaming about heaven?

Somewhere in my broken, paralyzed body is the seed of what I will become. The paralysis makes what I am to become all the more grand when you contrast atrophied, useless legs with splendorous resurrected legs. I'm convinced that if there are mirrors in heaven (and why not?), the image I'll see will be unmistakably "Joni," although a much better, brighter "Joni." So much so, that it's not worth comparing. There's no way I can comprehend it all, because I'm just an "acorn" when it comes to understanding heaven. But I'll tell you this: whatever my little acorn shape becomes in all its power and honor, I'm ready for it.

I'm ready to have this lowly body transformed. That means I won't merely be revived from the dead, like Lazarus when he came out of his tomb. People who return from the dead—whether from the tomb or from off the operating table—aren't, like Jesus, able then to appear and disappear, walk through walls, or transport themselves through time and space with a single thought.

No, I will bear the likeness of Jesus, the man from heaven. Like His, mine will be an actual, literal body perfectly suited for earth *and* heaven. Whether flinging a Frisbee or flying past Ursa Major. Scaling walls or walking through them. Speaking with friends or conversing with angels. Whether trout fishing in the Crystal Sea or going for seconds at the Wedding Supper, at all times and in all places, we will be perfectly fitted for our environment in the new heaven and new earth.

A NEW HEART

Please don't assume that all I ever do is dream about springing out of this chair, stretching glorified fingers and toes, and pole-vaulting over the pearly gates. However much I relish the idea of leaving this wheelchair behind, that is still, for me, not the best part of heaven.

I can put up with legs and arms that don't obey. For me, hands that refuse to pick up things, no matter how much my mind commands them to move, are a fact of life. I can cope with this.

However, there is something that I can't cope with. In fact, the older I get and the closer to heaven I draw, the less I'm able to adjust to it. I am sick and tired of combating my flesh—that is, "the law of sin at work within me" that just won't do as I command: "Although I want to do good, evil is right there with me. For in my inner being I delight in God's law; but I see another law at work in me, waging war against the law of my mind and making me a prisoner of the law of sin at work within me. What a wretched man I am!" (Romans 7:21–24).

That's why the best part of heaven will be a completely purified heart.

I'm reminded of this every time I recite those beautiful words in the General Confession from the *Book of Common Prayer*:

> Almighty and most merciful Father; we have erred, and strayed from thy ways like lost sheep. We have followed too much the devices and desires of our own hearts. We have offended against thy holy laws. We have left undone those things which we ought to have done; and we have done those things which we ought not to have done; and there is no health in us . . . miserable offenders.[4]

I love those words. And I hate those words. I'm weary of constant confession. I despise sinning. It pains me to keep erring and straying, to do things that I shouldn't do, to always fall face-flat in the dirt, grieving that I miserably offend the God I love. My heart is soiled and stained, and that drives me to the Lord on my knees (at least, metaphorically). What's odd is, the closer I draw to Jesus, the more intense the heat of the battle.

Never do I feel more on the frontlines of this battle than when I offer praise to God. Right in the middle of adoring Him in prayer or singing a praise hymn, my heart will start wandering off into some wicked thought. I have to grab my heart by the aorta and jerk it back in line time and again!

"Who will rescue me from this body that is subject to death? Thanks be to God, who delivers me through Jesus Christ our Lord!" (Romans 7:24–25). One day, Jesus will come back to complete the salvation He began when I first believed. One day, He will release me from the presence and influence of evil. That's why the bad news of Romans 7 is followed by the good news of Romans 8: "We ourselves, who have the firstfruits of the Spirit, groan inwardly as we wait eagerly for our adoption to sonship, the redemption of our bodies" (Romans 8:23).

Right here is the highest and most exalted reason that "flesh and blood cannot inherit the kingdom of God" (1 Corinthians 15:50). Entrance to heaven requires a redeemed body. The body must be rid of the law of sin at work in its members. At this present time, the spirit is willing, but the flesh is weak. The day is coming, however, when instead of being a hindrance to the spirit, the body will be the perfect vessel for the expression of my glorified mind, will, and emotions. Right now, we wear our souls on the inside. But one day, we will be clothed with righteousness as we wear our souls on the outside, brilliant and glorious.[5]

I can't wait to be clothed with righteousness. Without a trace of sin. True, it will be wonderful to stand, stretch, and reach to the sky, but it will be more wonderful to offer praise that is pure. I won't be crippled by distractions. Disabled by insincerity.

I won't be handicapped by a ho-hum halfheartedness. My heart will join with yours and bubble over with effervescent adoration. We will finally be able to fellowship fully with the Father and the Son.

For me, this will be the best part of heaven.

A NEW MIND

I look forward to heaven because I've got a lot invested there. A new body. A new heart free of sin. But I have some other friends who have just as much, if not more, invested.

I encountered these friends in a Sunday school class a while back where I shared my testimony. They were young adults who had mental disabilities, some because of Down syndrome, others who had autism or various brain injuries. It was pretty tough getting their attention. A few were looking out the window, others were drumming their fingers on their desks, and some were ambling around at the back of the room. The teacher clapped her hands and directed the class's attention my way.

One or two of them leaned on their elbows and studied me in my wheelchair with casual curiosity. I caught their interest when I flailed my useless arms and told them that the guys who run Six Flags Magic Mountain wouldn't let me ride the giant water slide. They felt bad. Some booed. Then I told them that one day, when I get my new body, I'd not only master the water slide, but also snow ski the Cornice Bowl at Mammoth Mountain or run the New York City Marathon if I wanted to (a few of them laughed when I told them I really didn't want to).

"It's going to be great having a new body." I smiled at the men and women who were now looking with intense interest. The guys in the back found their seats, and the others quit throwing spitballs and drumming pencils on their desks. Everybody wanted to hear about heaven.

"They say that the gates of heaven are made from a single pearl," I said with wide eyes.

"Na-a-ahh!" a teenager with Down syndrome said in unison with a couple of his buddies. They giggled and covered their mouths. "No pearl that big!" he scoffed.

"Oh yes there is," I teased. "And can you guess how big the oyster will be that makes that pearl?" By this time, half the class was spreading wide their arms, trying to size up how large of an oyster was needed to produce a pearl the size of a gate.

I had their attention. I challenged them to come up with other neat things I'd do with a new body. They thought it would be great for me to walk into McDonald's and stand in line. I'd be able to unwrap a Snicker's bar. I could flush a toilet (that got more giggles). One girl wanted to know if I'd still have my plastic arms in heaven. I looked at her a little funny because there's nothing plastic about my arms; but I grinned, shrugged my shoulders, and said wistfully, "No, no more plastic in heaven. I'll have a real body, and I'll be able to do all kinds of things, even go swimming if I want."

My comment drew a new level of empathy. One girl came up, patted my arm, and said, "Be careful next time, okay?"

"Okay," I promised. The class wanted to talk more about heaven. They invented all sorts of wild and wonderful heavenly activities. Riding giraffes. Going on a picnic with Jesus. Petting sharks. Earning lots of money. Shaking hands with Kareem Abdul-Jabbar. I reminded them that was only possible if Mr. Abdul-Jabbar knew Jesus. It was then suggested that someone should pray for the LA Lakers.

As their enthusiasm mounted, I finally blurted out, "Hey, guys, I may have a new body, but one day, you will have . . . new . . . *minds!*" The entire class jumped to their feet and wildly applauded. Amidst whistles and cheers, I went on to say, "You will be able to think better than your teacher here. And you will show your sister how to do her homework, even the hard stuff like math and things. You will think high-powered, supercharged thoughts and know just about everything there is to know. Your brain will burn rubber! Most of all, you and Jesus will be together, and you'll have lots of things to talk about."

By the time the Sunday school session ended, the class was well on their way to setting their hearts and minds on heavenly glories above. They were looking out the window to see if Jesus was coming back, clapping their hands, and jumping up and down. I thought I had taught them a lesson about heaven, but they had taught me what it meant to "have the mind of Christ" (1 Corinthians 2:16).

A new mind!

First Corinthians 13:12 describes it this way: "For now we see only a reflection as in a mirror; then we shall see face to face. Now I know in part; then I shall know fully, even as I am fully known." We will have the mind of Christ. No need to worry about feeling dumb or not knowing the answers. *We will know as we are known*, and our present knowledge will increase beyond belief. What's more, the shine of our best thoughts and memories will be made more resplendent as they are magnified through our new mind.

But what about the sad thoughts left over from earth? Isaiah 65:17–18 reads, "See, I will create new heavens and a new earth. The former things will not be remembered, nor will they come to mind. But be glad and rejoice forever in what I will create." This, at first, looks like a snafu. Didn't we just read that we will fully know *all* things? Are bad things excluded?

Our ignorance or imperfect thoughts and memories won't be erased so much as eclipsed, like the stars are mitigated by the rising of the sun. Something so dazzling is going to happen in the world's finale that its light will obscure every dark memory. We won't forget so much as have no need or desire to remember.

Bad things will not come to mind, as Isaiah observes, for they will be blocked out by the brilliance of the knowledge of God.

Only good things will come to mind. Our thought processes will no longer connive; we won't devise nasty words or scheme wicked plans. We won't battle against idle daydreams or lustful fantasies. Rather, our thoughts will be gloriously elevated, for "when Christ appears, *we shall be like him*, for we shall see him as he is" (1 John 3:2, emphasis added).

Think of perfect obedience to the Ten Commandments. Having no other gods before the Lord? Easy, we will be one with Him. I don't know about you, but I would love to tiptoe alongside the ranks of the seraphim and harmonize as they constantly proclaim day and night, "Holy, holy, holy is the Lord God Almighty" (Revelation 4:8).

Jealousy? You and I will have nothing but admiration for whomever is selected to sit on the right and left hand of Christ.

Keeping the Sabbath? We will have entered God's seventh and final day, the Sabbath rest of peace and joy for eternity.

Adultery? I will love everyone as perfectly as Christ loves, and I will never be grieved with the thought that I am slighted by those I love or that their love is not fully and fondly returned. I will find in every person that facet of the Lord's loveliness that only he or she can uniquely reflect—I'm going to be in love with a mountain of people, both men and women!

Coveting? We will be co-heirs with Christ. We'll have everything.

Bearing false witness? The father of lies will be dead. The flesh will no longer entice us to lie. Only truth will spring from our heart.

Misusing the name of the Lord? Only praise will be on our lips. Never a hurtful thought.

Oh, happy day, we will have the mind of Christ!

And with the mind of Christ, we will "know fully." Not halfway, but fully. While we were on earth, we only sort of knew or partially understood the "all things" that God kept working together for our good and the good of others, especially in the midst of painful trials. Most of the time, we scratched our heads and wondered how the matted mesh of threads in Romans 8:28 could possibly be woven together for our good. On earth, the underside of the tapestry was tangled and unclear, but in heaven, we will stand amazed to see the upper side of the tapestry and how God beautifully embroidered each circumstance into a pattern for our good and His glory.

This will be one of those fringe benefits not essential for our eternal happiness, but simply nice to know. The parents of the little girl paralyzed in a drunk-driving accident will understand. They will see how her accident touched the lives of friends and neighbors, sending out repercussions far and wide. They will see how God used the prayers of people halfway across the country, and how those prayers reached relatives and friends of relatives, rippling out farther than they ever dreamed. They will see how God's grace cradled their daughter, forging her little character with nobility and courage. They will see that nothing—absolutely nothing—was wasted, and that every tear counted and every cry was heard. "Record my misery; list my tears on your scroll—are they not in your record?" (Psalm 56:8).

My sister Linda will understand why God took her five-year-old daughter Kelly through brain cancer. My friend Diane will see how her multiple sclerosis safeguarded her from falling into spiritual indifference. My coworker Greg will realize the measure of mercy God poured out to him after his divorce. You will marvel at the time you scolded yourself for making a wrong left-hand turn at a traffic signal, a wrong turn by which you narrowly missed a terrible accident—an accident that never happened.

We will lift our hands and glorify God when we see how He used the hundred dollars we invested at the missions conference to reach many hundreds in Brazil. We'll see how many times

He engineered the right places and the right moments so that we'd meet just the right people—and the happy marriages and friendships that resulted.

We will understand how everything fit. Everything counted. Nothing was wasted. "The LORD works out everything to its proper end—even the wicked for a day of disaster" (Proverbs 16:4). Every jot and tittle of life will give supreme glory to our all-wise and all-powerful God.

PERFECTION *of* BODY *and* SOUL

Perfection of body and soul can, to some, sound boring.

I have two friends, John and Mike, with whom perfection just doesn't click. They are wonderful brothers in Christ, but they are the robust sort who would rather tackle the work of the kingdom on earth and not get sidetracked with future things. They'll do their God-appointed job here and let heaven take care of itself. Anyway, their picture of heaven is static—a never-ending do-nothingness in which there are no more things to achieve or goals to accomplish. For them, heaven is literally the end. The idea of a "never-ending relationship at the feet of Jesus," though comforting, doesn't get them stoked.

Perfection? Nah, they savor the spice of a good argument now and then. "Who wants a friend, or even a wife, who always agrees with you?" they say.

These guys would rather help pave the streets of gold with titanium monster trucks, backhoe loaders, and steamrollers. They'll take kayaking on the River of Life any day, and would rather take Joseph and Daniel fly-fishing than sit around and listen to them explain dream therapy.

I'm not about to fault these friends of mine. Frankly, I hope they take me fly-fishing too. They're just being left-brained. They're into logic and explanations and—watch it—clunky earthly symbols. Perfection of body and soul has nothing to do with casting the perfect fly or playing the perfect round of golf. (Although I remember the time an eighth grader once told me he couldn't understand how anyone would ever score in a heavenly game of basketball if the offense was as perfect as the defense, to which I replied, "Well, if there are going to be different levels of giftedness and skill in heaven—and I think there will be—you'll just have to find a few saints to play with whose perfect layup isn't as classy as yours!")

But even with that eighth grader, we've got to watch it. We can't construct heaven with the Lincoln Logs of our logic. We can't forget that what we imagine turns clunky when we rely on earthly images.

To appreciate the perfection of our bodies and souls, we must begin to get our hearts and minds somewhat in tune for heaven. Heaven is a prepared place for prepared people. Otherwise, heaven is a turnoff.

It's like this. I love listening to Mozart. That's because Mozart was a master at composing perfect music. I'm told that he arranged his notes flawlessly in every bar of every page and even employed certain numerical progressions that reflect absolute order and symmetry in tone and balance. Mathematicians study this composer. He's perfect.

Now if I were to play his *Magic Flute* for a couple of home-boys from a high school down the road, they'd guffaw and turn up the volume on their boom box. Hip-hop and death rap are more their speed. But it's a far, far cry from perfect music. You have to spend a lot of time listening to perfect music before you can appreciate it.

My point? You have to spend time doing the "be perfect . . . as your heavenly Father is perfect" thing here on earth before you can enjoy the idea of heavenly perfection (Matthew 5:48). To John and Mike, this may at first chill rather than awaken their desire for heaven. But whether left-brained or right-brained, whether macho or meditative, each of us must never avert our eyes from those elements of heaven that seem puzzling or repellent, for it is precisely the puzzlement of perfection that conceals what we do not yet know and yet need to know.

"Duh, what was that?" I can hear my macho friends now.

The closer we draw to the Lord Jesus and the more we set our hearts and minds on heavenly glories above, the better prepared we will be for heaven's perfection. Fellowship won't mean sitting at the feet of Jesus and fighting back boredom while everyone else is enraptured. No. Fellowship will be the best of what earthly friendship merely hinted at.

I would like to tell John and Mike, "Hey, don't forget, Christ knows better than you do what it means to be human. He sailed on the seas, hiked mountains, and slept under the stars by a rushing brook. He realizes what gets your heart pumping. Remember, He made you. You won't stop being human. Rather, you'll enjoy the full richness of all that your humanity was designed to be. You, with all your propensity for chumming it up around the campfire, will be a better . . . you!"

And a better you is a perfect you.

PERFECT PEOPLE *in* PERFECT FELLOWSHIP

Heaven's wedding supper of the Lamb will be the perfect party. The Father has been sending out invitations and people have been RSVPing down through the ages. Jesus has gone ahead to hang the streamers, prepare the feast, and make our mansion ready. And like any party, what will make it sweet is the fellowship.

Fellowship with our glorious Savior and with our friends and family.

There are countless people I'm waiting to see—Queen Esther,

Daniel, Jonah, and, of course, Mary and Martha. What's amazing is that I'll immediately recognize these people and all the other redeemed whom I never met on earth. If the disciples were able to recognize Elijah and Moses standing next to Jesus on the Mount of Transfiguration—saints they had never laid eyes on—then the same is true for us. I can't wait to meet them all!

However, one person I'm particularly eager to see in heaven is Steve Estes, my friend whom I mentioned in the introduction. He's a small-town pastor of a country church in Pennsylvania. And next to my husband, he's my dearest friend. Ken is the first to understand and accept my affection for Steve. After all, Ken realizes that in the sixties, the Lord used this young man to lift me out of my suicidal despair. Steve understood nothing about wheelchairs, but he loved Christ with a passion, and he wanted me—his depressed neighbor fresh out of the hospital—to find help and hope in God's Word. So we made an arrangement: I would provide plenty of RC Cola and he would come to my house on Friday nights with his Bible to help me painstakingly piece together the puzzle of my suffering. Yes, I found the help and hope he talked about. And the rest is history.

That was a long time ago, and even though we only visit occasionally over the phone, our friendship remains strong and secure. Still, whenever I miss "the good ole days" or wish I could see him more often, these longings are tempered by one amazing thought: *we will be forever friends.*

Our friendship is no coincidence. God has something eternal in mind for me and Steve. How do I know? In Acts 17:26, the apostle Paul writes, "From one man he made all the nations, that they should inhabit the whole earth; and *he marked out their appointed times in history and the boundaries of their lands*" (emphasis added).

Did you catch that? Of all the billions of possibilities, of all the millions of people with whom I could be friends, the Lord chose Steve for me. A few more miles between our houses or a few more years between our ages, and chances are, we would have never encountered each other. But for Christians, as C. S. Lewis says, there are no such chances. "Christ, who said to the disciples, 'Ye have not chosen me, but I have chosen you,' can truly say to every group of Christian friends 'You have not chosen one another but I have chosen you for one another.'"[6]

This has powerful implications for eternity. Friendship initiated on earth barely has time to get started; we only scratch its surface in the few short years we reside on earth. Its greater and richer dimension will unfold in heaven. God has a plan for Steve and me in eternity, and together we will play an intimate role in carrying out that special plan. I will love him as I never thought possible on earth. Wow, if I think my husband and Steve and others I hold dear bring me joy in the here and now, just think what's in store for us in heaven!

How it will pan out is yet to be seen, but this I know: All the earthly things we enjoy with our friends here will find their more exalted expression in heaven. I'll never forget one night when, sitting by the fireside, Steve opened his Bible and took me through a study on heaven. My heart burned as bright as the coals in the fireplace as I caught glimpses of heavenly joy, especially the excitement of a new glorified heart, mind, and body. It was a moment both human and divine. In fact, our joy was so great that we raced outside onto the front lawn to sing and howl at the midnight moon. We just had to *do* something human to express our divine joy. And minus the howling at the moon, I'm assured heaven will be much like that. It'll be a place where we *do* things with our friends for the sheer joy of being together and blessed by God.

Heavenly fellowship with friends won't be some ethereal do-nothingness where we yawn, sit around on clouds, and ogle angels. Because heaven is the home of redeemed humans, it will be thoroughly "human" in its structure and activities. As one theologian once wrote, "Its joys and its occupations must all be rational, moral, emotional, voluntary and active. There must be the exercise of all faculties, the gratification of all tastes, the development of all talent capacities, the realization of all ideals. The reason, the intellectual curiosity, the imagination, the aesthetic instincts, the holy affections, the social affinities, the inexhaustible resources of strength and power native to the human soul, must all find in heaven exercise and satisfaction."[7]

Oh, the things we will do! You and your friends will rule the world and judge the angels. Together, friends will eat the fruit of the tree of life and be pillars in the temple of God. Together, we will receive the morning star and be crowned with life, righteousness, and glory. Most of all, together we will fall on our faces at the foot of the throne and worship our Savior forever.

Note how many times I've used the word *together*. Heaven is by no means a hangout for mavericks roaming the universe and doing their own thing. It's a place of sweet togetherness, and maybe that's why the Bible says we all live in a city, the new Jerusalem. We won't be speckled here and there in rural cottages isolated from one another, but we'll live in harmony in a city. A *nice* city. A holy city!

Dreaming about this makes missing Steve—and many other dear friends—more bearable. It even makes my relationship with friends who have died and gone on to glory sweet and close.

The same is true for you. Read Acts 17:26 again, and rejoice that it's no accident that you are living in this decade, in your part of the country, and in your town where you enjoy your best friends. These dear ones in your life are no coincidence. You could have been born in another time and another place, but God determined to "people" your life with these particular friends.

These special ones strike a resonant chord in your heart; there is something about them, some aspect of beauty or goodness, that reminds you of God. I have an inkling that when you see the face of God in heaven, you will say, "Yes, I always knew You!" It was Him all along that you loved whenever you were with that treasured person. In friendship, God opens your eyes to the glories of Himself, and the greater the number of friends with whom you share deep and selfless love, the better and clearer the picture of God you will have.

WHAT I'LL DO WHEN I GET *to* HEAVEN

I grew up in a little Reformed Episcopal Church where the gospel was preached, the liturgy was read, the hymns were sung, and the prayers were said from bended knee. Banners and candles, processionals and recessionals, were a part of regular worship. Sunday morning worship was serious business, and I learned as a child what it meant to bend my knee before the Lord. Yes, kneeling felt hard on the knees, but what it did for my heart felt better.

I don't intend to make an issue of kneeling. God listens when His people pray as they stand, sit, or lie prone or prostrate. What's my point about kneeling? It's just that I wish I could do it. It's impossible for me to bow in worship.

Once at a convention, the speaker closed his message by asking everyone in the large room to push their chairs away from the tables and, if they were able, to kneel on the carpeted floor for prayer. I watched as everyone in the room—maybe five or six hundred people—hiked up their cuffs and got down on their knees. With everyone kneeling, I certainly stood out. And I couldn't stop the tears.

I wasn't crying out of pity or because I felt awkward or different. Tears were streaming down because I was struck with the beauty of seeing so many people on bended knees before the Lord. It was a picture of heaven.

Sitting there, I was reminded that in heaven I will be free to jump up, dance, kick, and do aerobics. And although I'm sure Jesus will be delighted to watch me rise on tiptoe, there's something I plan to do that may please Him more. If possible, somewhere, sometime before the party gets going, sometime before the guests are called to the banquet table at the wedding feast of the Lamb, the first thing I plan to do on resurrected legs is to drop down on grateful, glorified knees. I will quietly kneel at the feet of Jesus.

To *not* move will be my chance to demonstrate heartfelt thanks to the Lord for the grace He dispensed year after year when my legs and hands were limp and motionless. To not move will be my last chance to present a sacrifice of praise—paralyzed praise.

And after a while, I will spring to my feet, stretch my arms, and shout out to anyone within earshot of the whole universe, "Worthy is the Lamb, who was slain, to receive power and wealth and wisdom and strength and honor and glory and praise!" (Revelation 5:12). I wonder if at that point, my Episcopalian roots will have me clap my hand over my loud mouth. If so, at least for me, the party will have gone up a notch. It will be a dignified celebration of worship, eloquent and regal.

It has been decades since I've been able to kneel. Those long-ago Sunday mornings at our little church seem so far away. I didn't appreciate then the privilege of Psalm 95:6: "Come, let us bow down in worship, let us kneel before the LORD our Maker."

I sure appreciate it now. And the day is drawing near when I'll be able to kneel again. I know it, I can feel it. Heaven is just around the corner. So do me a favor. Do what so many of us who are paralyzed or too lame or old *can't* do. Flip open your Bible to Psalm 95:6, read it aloud, and take its advice. And when you kneel in prayer, be grateful for knees that bend to the will of God. Be grateful you're destined for heaven, for a new heart, mind, and body.

Our risen heart, sin-free will be
pure passion poured
purely
Adore!
He will give us this heart free
to love for the first time again.
Our risen body, light, bright
clothed with righteousness,
blessed with glowing flesh
that feels, really feels, for the first time again.
But now we wait
wait
wait for our Risen Lord,
who will reward we who weep,
yet still seek Him above all
so . . .
stand we tall together
for the first time ever,
then fall, please, on grateful knees . . .
Eternity is ours.

JONI TADA

CLIMBING HIGHER

I used to think that once I arrived in heaven, God would kick my wheelchair out of the celestial city and into the pit of hell. *Good riddance to bad garbage . . . it was nothing but a painmaker anyway!* Actually, I assumed that my old Everest & Jennings, with its clunky gears and dusty battery box, wouldn't even make it past the pearly gates. That's what I *used* to think. But then I met Robin.

My friend Robin has lived with Down syndrome for more than sixty years. In so many ways, she has prospered. Her intellectual disability has helped foster her incredibly sweet spirit and happy countenance. Robin *loves* to worship, sing praise songs, and pray for people. Her disability has helped shape her into the exceptional follower of Jesus that everyone knows her to be. Those of us who know her well love and value Robin exactly the way she is!

How will it all work out in heaven? God knows. But here is what I wonder. Robin's disability has helped her grow in Christ by leaps and bounds. But does that mean her chromosomal deficiency will accompany her into heaven? Will it be there when she first opens her eyes in the fresh celestial air of her Father's "better country"? Will it define her new glorified body? Robin would say that her disability is part of who she is; it's what makes her "Robin."

So . . . will disabilities somehow follow us to heaven?

Even a casual reading of the Bible will tell you *no*. There is no multiple sclerosis, spinal cord injury, osteogenesis imperfecta, or Down syndrome in heaven. Disabilities, infirmities, and chromosomal deficiencies are all a result of the fall of mankind, but heaven will see a complete restoration of all things. Heaven will be a place where the presence of sin and all its results—*including disabilities*—will be eradicated forever.

But what does that mean for Robin? Does it mean that she can't be "who she is," and still be part of eternity? What will her body and mind be like? For that matter, what about my quadriplegia? What will happen to my wheelchair, the very tool God chose time and again to refine my faith and make me more like Jesus?

I think the apostle Paul leaves a clue for us in Philippians 3:21 (TLB): "[Jesus] will take these dying bodies of ours and change them into glorious bodies like his own, using the same mighty power that he will use to conquer all else everywhere."

Consider those words "like his own." The resurrected Christ, God's mighty Son, is recognized as a deity whose hands, feet, and side bear the visible wounds of grace. For all of eternity, those wounds will call to mind our Savior's great mercy and loving-kindness. And we will praise Him again and again.

Will we, like our Lord, somehow display our marks of suffering in heaven?

I realize that Christ's wounds are utterly unique and incomparable, and that nothing can be likened to the marks that bought our redemption. In heaven, they will be markers, endless sources of wonder, reminding us and innumerable legions of angels of how He endured suffering for our sakes.

Even so, I can't help wondering. Could there be markers or reminders for us as well, pointing to our own suffering—now forever healed?

You see, I have always called my quadriplegia a "strange, dark companion." It is strange and dark in that quadriplegia has caused me many overwhelming challenges and often extreme pain. It has been messy and inconvenient to say the very least. Yet this same dark companion has served as God's choicest tool in shaping God's character within me. My disability is "part of who I am" in that it has pushed me to the Father's throne every morning—sometimes every hour—where I find help and grace for the day. It is like a stern schoolmaster teaching me many spiritual lessons, as well as refining my character.

That means it is a gift. My life of disability was *given* to me by God (Philippians 1:29). It is a gift because of every good thing God has done *in* it and *through* it.

And if God has given me my disability as a gift, I think it is fair to say that it may appear as a gift in heaven. Yes, it will be somehow transformed, perhaps almost unrecognizable from what it was on earth, but a gift nonetheless. Philippians 3:21 says that everything about me that is dying, that is weak and mortal, will be changed in heaven. Will the scars of my disability also be transformed? Since my disability is the tool that primarily fit me for heaven, I believe I will forever be connected to its merits and virtues.

No, I will not be a quadriplegic. My resurrection body will be raised in power and glory (1 Corinthians 15:43). It is still true that there will be no wheelchairs or crutches or walkers in heaven. But my quadriplegia may well be seen to be the companion it was on earth, no longer strange and dark, but forever pointing to the glorious outcomes that only came about through the sanctifying work of the Holy Spirit in my earthly suffering.

And who knows? Maybe Robin and I will wear our disabilities as badges of courage. Or like a royal sash. Or a medal of honorable endurance. Or perhaps even a jewel or two in our crowns. All I know is that every good thing that God has ever given will last for all eternity—including the best part of every affliction.

For these, too, were gifts from God.

Find Your Trail

1. Look at Philippians 3:19–21. The marketing minds in today's media are pushing countless products to hide the effects of old age or ease the symptoms of disease or ill health in our bodies. How is that different from what Jesus will accomplish in us on the day we enter heaven?
2. In what sense can suffering be considered a gift of God (Philippians 1:29)?

A Hiker's Prayer

Dear Lord Jesus, thank You for Robin and countless men, women, and children like her. Thank You for those who display such faith, courage, dignity, and kindness in the face of huge obstacles, limitations, and heartbreaking physical pain. I don't understand why You choose to reveal Your grace through people in such difficulty, but I praise You that You do. Please let Your radiant beauty shine through my life somehow, even in those times when I'm not at my best and brightest and don't even feel like facing the world. Do it for Your sake . . . for mine . . . and for those who observe me.

Two

What Will We Do

IN HEAVEN?

I can still hardly believe it. I, with shriveled, bent fingers, atrophied muscles, gnarled knees, and no feeling from the shoulders down, will one day have a new body, light, bright, and clothed with righteousness—powerful and dazzling.

Can you imagine the hope this gives someone who has a spinal cord injury, like I do? Or someone who has cerebral palsy, a brain injury, or multiple sclerosis? Imagine the hope this gives someone who has bipolar disorder. No other religion, no other philosophy, promises new bodies, hearts, and minds. Only in the gospel of Christ do hurting people find such incredible hope.

It's easy for me to "be joyful in hope," as it says in Romans 12:12, and that's exactly what I've been doing for the past fifty-odd years. My assurance of heaven is so alive that I've been making dates with friends to do all sorts of fun things once we get our new bodies—like the following conversation I had with a girl in a wheelchair I met at a conference.

"Since we've been sitting here talking about heaven," I said, "would you like to make a date to get together up there?"

The girl, sitting twisted and humped over, gave me a funny look and asked, "And do what?"

"What would you like to do?"

"Uh, I'd like to be able to knit," she said hesitantly.

"Then let's make a date to meet in a cabin, pull up a couple of rocking chairs by the fireplace, and reach for our knitting needles, okay?"

My friend in the wheelchair scoffed, "You're just saying that. Heaven's not going to have cabins and rocking chairs. That stuff's only on earth."

I looked at her in all seriousness and said, "I believe heaven will. Heaven is by no means ambiguous. Isaiah 65:17 says that God is planning 'new heavens and a new earth.' Did you get that? Heaven has our planet in it. A new earth with earthly things in it. Nothing clunky, no gawky images—just warm and wonderful things that make earth . . . *earth*."

"How can you be so sure of what the new earth will be like?"

"'Cause I don't think God is going to switch dictionaries on us and suddenly redefine what *earth* is. If there are streets, rivers, trees, and mountains in the new earth, like the Bible says there will be, then why not all the other good things? Why not rocking chairs?"

She looked at me with a wry smile, and then her skepticism vanished. She started deliberating about which sweater pattern to use. She learned what most people discover after spending a few minutes talking to me. I take heaven seriously.

I take it as seriously as children do. One morning while I was waiting in an airport, I told my five-year-old friend Matthew Fenlason and his little brother, Stephen, to grab hold of the arm of my wheelchair and come with me to look for some kids to play with. We found a couple of little boys sitting with their parents in the waiting area, and I asked if they would like to play a game with us. Within minutes, in the open area of the airport lounge, we started a game of Duck, Duck, Goose. When Matthew tagged me "goose," I raced in my wheelchair around the circle of children, but I couldn't catch him. Feeling bad that I wasn't able to get up and run, he whispered, "Don't worry, Joni. When we get to heaven, your legs will work, and we'll be able to *really* play Duck, Duck, Goose."

He meant it. And so did I.

Rana Leavell and I plan to climb the mountains behind the Rose Bowl. Thad Mandsager and I, both quads, will ski the Sierras. My sisters Linda, Kathy, Jay, and I are going to play doubles tennis. Michael Lynch plans to teach me how to dance the Paso Doble, and my husband, Ken, has already said, "I don't mind who fills up your dance card in heaven, but make sure you save the last one for me." I have a whole circle of Romanian orphans I want to take picnicking on the Hungarian plains, and I can't wait to put my friend Judy Butler on a really fast horse and go racing across Windsor Great Park.

Horses in heaven? Yes. I think animals are some of God's best and most avant-garde ideas. Why would He throw out His greatest creative achievements? I'm not talking about my pet schnauzer, Scrappy, dying and going to heaven—Ecclesiastes 3:21 puts the brakes on that idea. I'm talking about new animals fit for a new order of things. Isaiah foresaw lions and lambs lying down together, as well as bears, cows, and cobras; and John foresaw the saints galloping on white horses. I have no idea where they will fit, but I'm certain they will populate part of the new heaven and the new earth. Again, underline that word *earth*. It just wouldn't be "earth" without animals. So if you want to go horseback riding, meet Judy and me at the statue of the Copper Horse at the end of the bridle path in Windsor.

You can tell I don't take these appointments lightly. I'm convinced these things will actually happen. Goodness, I thought my friend under the white cabana next to the swimming pool was pleased to see me in a glorified state; just think of the pleasure we all will experience to see each other sin-free, with glowing bodies all light and bright. It will be the answer to all our longings.

And not only our longings, but those of Jesus as well.

REWARDS *in* HEAVEN

You are the fulfillment of Jesus' desire.

You can hear the yearning in Jesus' voice in John 17:24: "Father, I want those you have given me to be with me where I am, and to see my glory, the glory you have given me because you loved me before the creation of the world." My heart glows to think of His delight over our joy. I keep picturing His pleasure when He sees us dressed in white raiment for the wedding supper.

In fact, you give Him so much pleasure that somewhere in the midst of the royal heavenly celebration—maybe right before the banquet, or soon thereafter—Jesus will rise, ascend His throne, and present rewards and crowns to all the guests. This is a *most* unusual celebration. For it is not the guests who come bearing gifts, but the Host. The Lord Jesus does all the gift giving.

And these rewards aren't your average party favors.

We shall be given crowns. Second Timothy 4:8 reads like the invitation to a coronation: "Now there is in store for me the crown of righteousness, which the Lord, the righteous Judge, will award to me on that day—and not only to me, but also to all who have longed for his appearing."

Wow, God wants to award me a crown! Maybe some adults pooh-pooh the idea of rewards, but I don't. The child in me jumps up and down to think God might actually award me something. I remember when I took piano lessons as a kid and would squirm with delight on my bench whenever Mrs. Merson pasted gold crowns on my sheet music for a job well done. I wasn't so much overjoyed with my performance as I was with pleasing Mrs. Merson. My focus wasn't on what I did; it was on her approval. Sophisticated adults aren't into such whimsy, but children sure are.

Nothing is so obvious in a heavenly-minded child of God as their undisguised pleasure in receiving a reward—a reward that reflects the approval of the Father. C. S. Lewis wrote, "To please God . . . to be a real ingredient in the divine happiness . . . to be loved by God, not merely pitied, but delighted in as an artist delights in his work or a father in a son—it seems impossible, a weight or burden of glory which our thoughts can hardly sustain. But so it is."[1]

So for all the children whom Jesus said were best fit for the kingdom of heaven, get ready for God to show you not only His pleasure, but His approval.

What does a crown in heaven look like? Does it look like the shah of Iran's with spotted ermine, studded with pearls and diamonds, or the kind Queen Victoria wore with a cross on top? Watch it, I have a sneaking suspicion we're edging close to earthly imagery again.

Psalm 149:4 gives a hint as to what kind of crown God means: "For the LORD takes delight in his people; he crowns the humble with victory." Aha! God probably doesn't mean a literal crown, because victory isn't something you put on your head. Heavenly crowns must represent something He does, something He gives, as when He crowns us with victory, with His salvation. Anyway, this is more resplendent and illustrious than any old hunk of platinum with a lot of sparkly things in it.

There's also the *crown of life* in James 1:12, reserved for those who persevere under trial. This means God awards us with life eternal.

There's the *crown of rejoicing* in 1 Thessalonians 2:19, given to believers who introduce others to Christ. This means God awards us with joy that lasts forever.

The *eternal, incorruptible crown* in 1 Corinthians 9:25, presented to those who are found pure and blameless on the judgment day. Nothing God gives will ever perish, spoil, or fade.

And in 1 Peter 5:4, there's the *crown of glory*, reserved for Christian leaders who have guided others. God awards us glory that will never diminish, but only increase.

And my favorite, the *crown of righteousness* mentioned in 2 Timothy 4:8 for those who are itching to have Jesus come back. God will award us a right standing with Him that never changes.

Get ready for crowns!

THE JUDGMENT SEAT *of* CHRIST

The apostle Paul writes, "For we must all appear before the judgment seat of Christ, so that each of us may receive what is due us for the things done while in the body, whether good or bad" (2 Corinthians 5:10).

Uh-oh, all of a sudden this doesn't sound like a coronation celebration. This sounds scary. Especially the "whether good or bad" part. Surely the party will turn sour once everyone sees all the bad things you did on earth. They'll wave you off and groan, "*Now* I know what he was *really* like all those years on earth. Boy, am I disappointed in him!"

I used to feel the same way about heaven back in high school. I never could understand why Christians longed to go there. To me, heaven was a place where not only God would know all and see all, but my friends and family would too. Upon passing through the pearly gates, I saw myself standing under a marquee of a theater: Now Showing: the Uncensored Version of *Joni*. I pictured myself walking down the aisle and passing people I respected, like my ninth-grade teacher, my hockey coach, and my Sunday school leader. On each aisle I spotted others like the boy with disabilities in school I made fun of and the girl down the street I beat up in a fistfight. I pictured reaching the first row, sinking into a seat, and cringing as God rolled the movie of my life for all to gawk at. Talk about guilt and judgment!

I'm inclined to believe that the real judgment seat of Christ will be quite different.

Just consider 1 Corinthians 4:5: "Therefore judge nothing before the appointed time; wait until the Lord comes. He will bring to light what is hidden in darkness and will expose the motives of the heart. At that time each will receive their praise from God."

Read that one more time. *Each will receive their praise from God.* When Christ ascends His throne and sits at the judgment seat, I don't believe He'll roll an uncut, uncensored version of your life. He won't wear the scowl of a rigid and inflexible judge who bangs the gavel and reads aloud your sins for the court record. No, that already happened at another judgment. The judgment at the cross. It was there the Father slammed down the gavel and pronounced His Son "Guilty!" as He became sin for us. It went on record in the courts of heaven, and then the indictment was canceled with the words "Paid in Full," written not with red ink but red blood. Anyway, "If you, Lord, kept a record of sins, Lord, who could stand? But with you there is forgiveness, so that we can, with reverence, serve you" (Psalm 130:3–4).

Your sins will not condemn you in heaven. Psalm 103:10–12 promises that God "does not treat us as our sins deserve or repay us according to our iniquities. For as high as the heavens are above the earth, so great is his love for those who fear him; as far as the east is from the west, so far has he removed our transgressions from us." If you have placed your trust in Christ for having borne your transgressions on His cross, then you have nothing to fear. He did away with it. Erased it. Sin no longer has power to wound or to inflict remorse and regret.

The judgment seat of Christ is different. It's not a trial to determine whether you are guilty or innocent; it's more like a judging stand to ascertain your capacity to serve God.

The following analogy may be too simple for a seminary student, but I like to picture a judge's stand at a housing contractors' convention where rewards are distributed to all the architects, builders, supervisors, and construction crews. The judge examines the quality of each person's work. Each receives praise for what they have built and how they have built it. Praise, not condemnation. It's true that the praise doled out to some contestants will be greater than others, but each will receive his reward. And the prize? The judge will say, "Well done! You've accomplished much with these few buildings; now we will put you in charge of a big development." Thus, the architects and supervisors are awarded larger and more elaborate contracts. And the builders get to roll up their sleeves and tackle the newest and best homes on the market. Each person walks away from the convention happy, heartened, and with an increased capacity to serve the industry.

It's a little like this for Christians. While we're on earth, we have a chance to "store up . . . treasures in heaven" (Matthew 6:20) and to send ahead, so to speak, building materials so that something of eternal worth can be constructed. That's why "each one should build with care. For no one can lay any foundation other than the one already laid, which is Jesus Christ. If anyone builds on this foundation using gold, silver, costly stones, wood, hay or straw, their work will be shown for what it is, because the Day will bring it to light. It will be revealed with fire, and the fire will test the quality of each person's work. If what has been built survives, the builder will receive a reward. If it is burned up, the builder will suffer loss but yet will be saved—even though only as one escaping through the flames" (1 Corinthians 3:10–15).

I'm constructing with an eye toward eternity, and so can you. Every day we have the opportunity to roll up our spiritual sleeves and apply our spiritual energies toward building something that lasts—in our lives and in the lives of others. We are warned to be careful and choose as our building materials gold, silver, and costly stones—that is, to render service out of a pure heart, a right motive, and an eye for God's glory. Or we can choose wood, hay, or straw—doing things out of impure motives and an eye to our own glory.

We will bring to the judgment seat of Christ all that we are and all that we've done. One look from the Lord will scrutinize the quality of what we've built, and selfish service will be consumed in a fiery flash. Although it's true that no child of God will be scolded, some will walk away scalded from the heat; their only reward will be their eternal salvation.

This is sobering. I can't help but see myself coming away a little singed on the edges. Don't get me wrong, I believe I will bask in God's approval for my service on earth, but pride and impure motives may well have sullied a lot of it. Burnt away will be those times I gave the gospel out of puffed-up pride. Up in flames will go any service I performed for "performance's sake." Reduced to charcoal will be manipulative behavior and lies dressed up like truth.

But, hey, even if a lot of people survive the judgment seat by the skin of their teeth, keeping only their crown of salvation, that's plenty of cause for rejoicing. Look at all the people who trusted Christ on their deathbed, with barely time to say yes to Jesus, let alone build anything for eternity. Think of being snatched from the jaws of hell seconds before one dies. Such joy would be hard to beat.

One look from the Lord will consume worthless service. But it will illuminate God-honoring service. Like gold and precious stones, pure service will easily survive the test. It is *this* for which we will be commended. We will drop to our knees in front of the judgment seat with the words of our Master ringing in our hearts, "Well done, good and faithful servant! You have been faithful with a few things; I will put you in charge of many things. Come and share your master's happiness! . . . For whoever has will be given more, and they will have an abundance" (Matthew 25:23, 29).

I'm dying to hear those words. Literally. I want to put to death every selfish motive and prideful pretense so that when the Lord's eyes scan my service, what I have built will stand the test. I want to be careful how I build and realize that every smile, prayer, or ounce of muscle or money sacrificed is a golden girder, brick, or two-by-four. I want everything I do here to be an eternal investment, a way of building something bright and beautiful there. That's how much things down here count.

And no one will be left out. Each will receive their reward. Each of us will have a capacity to serve in heaven. We will all have something to do.

ETERNAL WORSHIP THAT IS NEVER BORING

I can just see my two macho friends, John and Mike—the ones who hated the idea of doing nothing in heaven—as they stare open-mouthed and wide-eyed after the judgment seat. While on earth, they always knew they were sons of God, but they also knew "what we will be has not yet been made known" (1 John 3:2). But now, in heaven, they are sons of God in the fullest sense. What power, what privilege! And God has crowned them as proof.

I picture them grabbing each other, jumping up and down, and exclaiming, "Oh boy, now we get to *do* something! We get to serve." They rub their hands together, roll up the sleeves on their white robes, and ask, "Okay, Lord, what are our jobs? Just point us in the right direction, and we're ready to go!"

Jesus may then repeat His own words from John 4:23 and

say, "Yet a time . . . has now come when the true worshipers will worship the Father in the Spirit and in truth, for they are the kind of worshipers the Father seeks."

Our first assignment is *praise*. Our most important service to God in heaven is *worship*. Heaven is a place of eternal, loving worship. Our service will be to continually praise God without interruption.

"Huh?" I can just see my guy friends respond.

And if God weren't able to read their thoughts, they might dare think, *This is great, and I'm all for it and everything, but isn't this going to get a little tedious after a while? Won't we run out of Scripture choruses and praise songs after a few millennia?*

Again, I used to feel the same way about heaven. To me, anything changeless had a high boredom factor. Anything, even a great vacation at the beach, always had a hidden potential to be boring if it went on for too long. I was always happy for good things to come to an end after a time.

But in heaven, praise will never become boring.

First, the only reason we find even the best things monotonous after a while is because of . . . *a while*. In other words, because of the passage of time. Eternity is not changelessness (which is boring), because changelessness means that time passes while everything stays the same. It's not like that in heaven at all. Eternity is not many millennia. It's not even a billion millennia or a trillion. Time doesn't pass in heaven; it just *is*.

Next, I can hear my macho friends retort, "Yeah, but you can only be enthralled over truth, goodness, beauty, and the purity of heaven for so long. There's something stifling about arriving at perfection; we almost preferred the thrill of getting here rather than arriving. Heaven is so, so . . . final!"

You could only say this if you conceive of truth, goodness, or even eternity and heaven as static and abstract. It's not. Truth and goodness, eternity and heaven—yes, God Himself—are not static, but dynamic. Not abstract, but concrete. More real than anything we've ever touched or tasted on earth. Remember, we are wrong in thinking heaven is wispy, thin, and vaporous. It is *earth* that is like withering grass, not heaven.

In C. S. Lewis's *The Great Divorce*, there is a dialogue between a confused ghost from hell and a heavenly spirit who is trying to teach him about the concreteness of eternity. The heavenly spirit begins, "Will you come with me to the mountains?"

The ghost replies, "Of course I should require some assurances . . . an atmosphere of free inquiry."

The heavenly spirit then says, "No . . . No atmosphere of inquiry, for I will bring you to the land not of questions but of answers, and you shall see the face of God."

In response, the ghost says, "Ah, but we must all interpret those beautiful words in our own way! For me there is no such thing as a final answer . . . To travel hopefully is better than to arrive . . . You must feel yourself that there is something stifling about the idea of finality? Stagnation, my dear boy, what is more soul-destroying than stagnation?"

The spirit answers, "You think that, because hitherto you have experienced truth only with the abstract intellect. I will bring you where you can taste it like honey and be embraced by it as by a bridegroom. Your thirst shall be quenched."[2]

In heaven, praise won't be inert and abstract, like the impression you have when you hear a musty old hymn sung by a handful of stone-faced worshipers in a huge cathedral. Or like the feeling you get when singing a praise chorus for the hundredth time. Even the most beautiful Scripture choruses wear out after a while, and you moan, "We've sung that a zillion times. Can't we sing something new?" Our heart really doesn't care if the song itself is new—some of the oldest hymns of the church are still fresh—but our hearts cannot tolerate words or songs of praise that have dug ruts over the passage of time. If joy and satisfaction aren't in your worship, then you know you're missing the mark. You want to offer something fresh that hits home in the heart of God.

In heaven, praise will never be empty or fall short of its target. Worship won't be suspended between us at point A and God at point B. This kind of praise may be endured on earth, but it's hanging in the breeze when it comes to heaven.

Praise in heaven will have substance.

We will eat from the tree of life.

Taste hidden manna like honey.

Smell truth like a flower.

Wear righteousness like light.

Hold the morning star like a scepter.

Shine like the stars of the heavens.

Enter into the joy of the Lord.

There's nothing inert or abstract about those verbs. Everything in heaven will have more substance than we ever dreamed.

In eternal praise, the thrill of getting there will be more than matched by what we see, hold, taste, and wear when we arrive. For John and Mike, the thrill will include not only climbing the mountain, but enjoying the view from the top, and doing both at the same time. We shall travel hopefully and arrive, as it were, all at the same moment—we will no longer desire our God who is absent, but rejoice in our God who is present.

WHY WE WILL PRAISE HIM FOREVER

Next, our worship of God will never end. It's like the excitement I used to feel as a child when my father would read me a story. To me, the beginning was always the most fascinating part. It was fresh. That's because the beginning touches something timeless that no events in time can tarnish. Unfortunately, as the story progressed, my interest frittered away, along with my wonder.

Except for one fairy tale. In C. S. Lewis's *The Last Battle*—the conclusion of *The Chronicles of Narnia* series—there wasn't the usual "and they lived happily ever after." Instead, on the last page, after scores of exhilarating adventures and journeys in all the previous books, C. S. Lewis wrote that now he had come to the beginning of the real story. All the previous chapters of adventures in Narnia had only been the cover and the title page. The real "Chapter One of the Great Story" was about to begin, a story no one on earth had ever read, which would go on forever and ever, with each chapter better than the last.[3]

As a child, I remember thinking, *You mean all that's happened up until now has only been the preface to the real story? All the good stuff was only foreshadowing a greater story?* The wonder was back. I was at the beginning again.

Most people wish it were like that in real life. Just as in a story, people labor through chapter after chapter of their lives, and the fascination and wonder they felt as a child fade as the years go by in a succession of events. We grow tired and weary, never able to grasp the dreams that enthralled us at the beginning. The state that we long for is never quite embodied. And so our interest fritters away.

But for Christians, all the things that stir our interest about eternity *will be embodied*. We shall behold the Lamb. Savor purity. Touch truth. Be clothed with righteousness. Like a grand story, it will always be an enchanting beginning. Or better yet, the end *and* the beginning, as God is both Alpha and Omega, the First and the Last, the Beginning and the End (Revelation 21:6).

Little wonder that flesh and blood cannot inherit heaven. To be at both the beginning and the end, or to wear righteousness like a bright raiment, requires a complete metamorphosis. Like a caterpillar becoming a butterfly or a peach pit becoming a blossoming tree. Our earthly bodies would never be able to contain the joy or express the praise. Our fleshly hearts and minds could never hold it all. Heavenly worship would split the seams and break the human container. We're not talking shedding snakeskins here; we're talking radical transformation. We little caterpillars and peach pits need to go from death to life so that our glorified bodies and hearts are fit for the filling and overflowing of ecstatic praise. As Jesus declared, "Very truly I tell you, no one can see the kingdom of God unless they are born again" (John 3:3).

No, praise will not be something we will be assigned or commanded to do; it will be natural. Rather, a supernatural, effervescent response of the born-again creature, new and fit for heaven. Professor E. L. Mascall put it this way: "We do not praise God because it does us good, though no doubt it does. Nor do we praise Him because it does Him good, for in fact it does not. Praise is thus strictly ecstatic in the sense that it takes us wholly out of ourselves; it is purely and solely directed upon God. It takes our attention entirely off ourself and concentrates it entirely upon Him."[4]

I can't wait! I get so sick and tired of thinking about myself. I sometimes feel like the self-absorbed woman in the movie *Beaches* who says to her friend, "Enough talk about me . . . let's talk about you. Tell me, what do *you* think about me?" Ever feel that way? Well, in heaven, self-forgetfulness will be second nature; thus, nothing will be tedious. Praise would only be boring if we were able to stop and look at ourselves to see how we were doing, how we were sounding or performing, but such self-consciousness will be foreign in heaven. The crowning glory for us will be in losing ourselves and yet finding ourselves in the Alpha and the Omega. This is pure praise. Total preoccupation with God.

Finally, because we will be one with Him and full of light as He is, our bright, dazzling bodies can't help but be shot through with the glory of God. After all, "glory" is the reflection of God's essential being, whether holiness, justice, compassion, or mercy.

Whenever He reveals Himself in any of these qualities on earth or in heaven, we say that He is "glorifying Himself." And in heaven, we, like diamonds, will give off prism-like praise as every facet of our being reflects His Shekinah glory. It will be impossible *not* to praise Him. Daniel 12:3 turns on the light switch when it says, "Those who are wise will shine like the brightness of the heavens, and those who lead many to righteousness, like the stars for ever and ever."

Remember my dream in which everything—the air, water, and my body—dazzled with light? I don't think my dream is that far off from the real heaven. Heaven will shine by the Lamb who is the Lamp. Light will so much *be* in heaven that "the moon will be dismayed, the sun ashamed; for the LORD Almighty will reign on Mount Zion and in Jerusalem, and before its elders—*with great glory*" (Isaiah 24:23, emphasis added). God's glory and His light go hand in hand. Heaven is a place full of glory, light, and praise.

My macho guy friends will, with every other redeemed person, happily transcend the time warp to be a part of that "great multitude that no one could count, from every nation, tribe, people and language, standing before the throne and before the Lamb. They were wearing white robes and were holding palm branches in their hands. And they cried out in a loud voice: 'Salvation belongs to our God, who sits on the throne, and to the Lamb'" (Revelation 7:9–10).

Who can find words for such worship? What thesaurus has the nouns or adjectives to convey "eating" life like fruit from a tree or "tasting" the bread of heaven? I want to lift up my hands and whisper, "Oh, the depth of the riches of the wisdom and knowledge of God! How unsearchable his judgments, and his paths beyond tracing out! . . . For from him and through him and for him are all things. To him be the glory forever! Amen" (Romans 11:33, 36).

SERVING GOD *by* REIGNING *with* HIM

I have a confession. I'm more like my friends John and Mike than I've admitted. Just spend a few weeks with me, and you'll understand. I love rolling up my sleeves down here on earth and pouring myself into serving God. I'm less of a human being, and more of a human *doing*. Visiting hospitals, advocating on issues, shopping for dinner, traveling in ministry, relating in marriage, painting at my easel, writing at my computer, working on radio programs, counseling on the phone, helping with Sunday school, and on and on, ad infinitum.

I'm also a perfectionist. If a painting is not up to par, it's shoved aside. If an article is not up to snuff, it's dumped in the trash. If a friendship is injured, it's painstakingly repaired. If my marriage is hurting, everything else gets canceled and Ken gets priority. If I feel that a speech I gave fell flat, I berate myself endlessly, thinking, *Why did I say that? . . . Why didn't I say this?* There have been days when I've thrown up my hands and sighed, "What's the use? I've blown it again!"

A lot of this pressure, because it is self-imposed, is unnecessary. However, some of it is real and needed. That's because God imposes pressure when He knows I've approached service to Him with a lazy, nonchalant attitude.

But in heaven, there will be no failure in service. No disappointment in doing. We will never struggle with failing to do the task God puts before us, as in a failed marriage or mission. We will never fall short of meeting our responsibilities.

And, boy, will we *do*! John and Mike will be on cloud nine, but only for a short time, because they will be busier than they ever were on earth. No idling away eternity strolling the streets of gold. No passing time while plucking harps by the glassy sea. We will have jobs to do. I can hardly hold back the tears thinking of my friend Cornelius, who has been bedridden for fifteen years, unable to lift a finger to do an ounce of work. I can just see this man in his glorified body, leaving John and Mike in the dust as he tackles all the labor he missed out on those many years on earth. We will serve God through worship and work—exciting work we'll never grow tired of.

For me, this will be heaven. I love serving God. And if we've been faithful in earthly service, our responsibility in heaven will increase proportionately. No, I take that back. It won't be increased in proportion. God's too generous for that. Our service will increase *completely out of proportion*. It doesn't take a rocket scientist to read the formula Jesus gives in His heaven parable in Luke 19:17: "'Well done, my good servant!' his master replied. 'Because you have been trustworthy in a very small matter, take charge of ten cities.'"

Stop and read that again. Ten cities? In exchange for faithfulness in a very small matter? Whoa! When it comes to blessing us, Jesus goes beyond basic math and gets into calculus. Those who are faithful in a few minor things will be put in charge over multitudinous things.

Were you faithful in your marriage or a mission? Even if only in a small way? God is already thinking exponentially, as in His "ten cities" equation. He generously raises your capacity for service to the nth degree. The more faithful you are in this life, the more responsibility you will be given in the life to come.

Please note that Jesus doesn't say, "Because you've been successful in a very small matter," He says, "Because you've been *trustworthy*." God is not scrutinizing the success of your marriage or judging the results of your mission. You might have spent forty-five years in marriage, forty of which you were hanging in there by a promise and a prayer. You might have invested twenty-five years in sharing the gospel in the outback of Mozambique, with only a handful of converts to show for it. When it comes to the judgment seat, God won't pull out the return-on-investment charts and do a cost-effectiveness analysis of your earthly service. Every Christian is on the same playing field. Success isn't the key; faithfulness is. Being bigger and better is not the point; it's being obedient.

The more trustworthy you've been, the greater your service in eternity. Here's where our two buddies will shine!

Here's where we get to serve and be busier than we ever were on earth. For we not only get to praise God forever, but we get to reign with Him forever. "To the one who is victorious, I will give the right to sit with me on my throne, just as I was victorious and sat down with my Father on his throne" (Revelation 3:21). Can you believe it? We will sit with Christ on His throne and reign with Him. We will be given a sphere of authority and oversight of God's eternal kingdom.

We get to reign with Him, plus more.

We are *more than* kings? Yes, we are children and heirs. Romans 8:17 elevates us to an incredible position: "Now if we are children, then we are heirs—heirs of God and co-heirs with Christ." Just imagine, we will sit with Christ on His throne, and we will join Him in overseeing His and our inheritance. We inherit what our elder Brother inherits. And Psalm 2:8 reads like His title deed: "Ask me, and I will make the nations your inheritance, the ends of the earth your possession." We're not talking a few acres on the back of the farm. Our sphere of authority will be heaven and earth.

We get to reign over earth with Christ!

RULING *over* EARTH

I wish I understood the specifics, but God hasn't revealed them all. A hint is whispered in Revelation 20:6, where we are "priests of God and of Christ and will reign with him for a thousand years," and in Isaiah 11:4, where "with righteousness he will judge the needy, with justice he will give decisions for the poor of the earth."

Time and again, the words *inheritance*, *earth*, and *reign* appear together. Flip through the Old Testament, and you'll see repeated references to God's Anointed personally administering justice, uplifting the oppressed, or ruling with a rod of iron. The particulars may not be laid out, but there's one hint we're supposed to get: we will reign with Christ over the earth.

It's not clear if it's this earth or what the Bible calls "the new earth." But I do know that the pièce de résistance of God's creation, this jewel of a planet, will not be abandoned. It will not be left to go spinning off into space. God doesn't waste things; He redeems them. And Romans 8:20–21 reveals the Lord's intentions for this beautiful blue marble: "For the creation was subjected to frustration, not by its own choice, but by the will of the one who subjected it, in hope that *the creation itself will be liberated from its bondage to decay and brought into the freedom and glory of the children of God*" (emphasis added).

The whole creation, like us, "is groaning as in the pains of childbirth right up to the present time" (Romans 8:22). I sense this whenever I see smog, a junkyard, and dead raccoons in the road. When I drive the coastal mountains just a stone's throw from where I live and marvel at the jutting, jagged rocks and canyons, I'm vividly aware I'm in the middle of earthquake country (the Northridge quake of 1994 felt like one of those "pains of childbirth"). Mudslides and fires happen all the time around here. These hills are restless. They're also scarred by the improbable palaces of Malibu movie stars who litter the landscape with satellite dishes. My heart breaks for these mountains and trees (and movie stars!) to be liberated from their bondage.

This is the earth that Christ will bring into His freedom and glory. Can you hear the sighing in the wind? Can you feel the heavy silence in the mountains? Can you sense the restless longing in the sea? Can you see it in the woeful eyes of an animal? Something's coming . . . something better.

If you want to know exactly what this "something" is, study Revelation and Isaiah. Delve into the hermeneutics. Scrutinize the eschatology. I have to confess I've never had the benefit of going to seminary, and I can't cut as straight a theological line as I'd like, but I'm satisfied just to know that heaven involves earth, old or new. It intrigues me to think that after Christ comes back for us, we may inhabit this very planet again. The paths that I wheel over in my chair now may well be the same ones my glorified feet will walk on when Christ reigns.

If so, then the mountains of the Sierra will actually be the ones Thad and I will ski. And the rambling mountain paths behind the Rose Bowl will, in fact, be trod by the heavenly feet of my friend and me. That is, if Thad, Rana, or others want a time-out from their thrilling escapades in the far corners of the universe!

The possibilities are endless, as well as exhilarating. Maybe our reign on earth will include lifting up the poor and the needy of Kurdistan, reforesting the hills of Lebanon, helping to judge the wicked, or planting trees along the Amazon. How about clearing the courts of corruption and schooling judges on godly wisdom? How about clearing the slums of Rio de Janeiro or getting rid of nuclear waste? Maybe we'll teach the nations how to worship God, as well as how to redefine *peace* and how to beat their swords into plowshares. Shall we do a patch job on the ozone layer and make the blue Danube absolute azure rather than mud-brown? Cut government fat, get rid of red tape, and show everyone that a theocracy is the only rule in town?

One thing's for sure. There will be no shelters for the homeless (no homeless men and women!). No orphanages or mental hospitals. No abortion clinics. And no nursing homes for old people.

In the midst of it all, the glittering capital city of heaven, the new Jerusalem, will be set like a gleaming pearl. Kings and princes will pour into the Holy City from the far corners of the earth to pay homage. The image blows my mind, but it's laid out as clear as crystal glass in Revelation 21.

I realize this raises more questions than answers. Like, who are all these people who have to be ruled with a rod of iron? After the return to earth of the Lord Jesus and His saints, what are all those other folks still doing on earth? People who are wicked and need to be judged or the poor who have to be lifted up? Why are they still hanging around if heaven has come to earth?

Theologians are the ones who tackle questions like these all the time. Some scholars say that after the dead in Christ are raised at His return to earth, we will reign with Him over the people of this planet for a thousand years. At the close of this period, the devil will incite one last rebellion, which will kick off Armageddon. God's armies will win; the devil will lose; wicked people will be resurrected; the Book of Life will be opened; and the day of judgment will have come. After the final destruction of that old serpent and his wicked hordes, earth will be consumed in fire, cleansed, and made new and fit for eternal habitation. Got that?

Other scholars assert that when the Lord Jesus comes to earth as King of kings, time will end after an immediate Armageddon, the defeat of Satan, the judgment of the dead, and a fiery holocaust that incinerates all of the earth and space beyond. When the smokes clears, the Lord and His saints will set up the eternal kingdom in the new heaven and the new earth.

Whew, I'm glad theologians study these things! How the earth, whether new or old, fits into God's heavenly scheme of things, I can't say for certain. I tend toward the view that we will reign with Christ on this earth for a thousand years, this period being a kind of vestibule to heaven. But all I really need to know is that "we are looking forward to a new heaven and a new earth, where righteousness dwells" (2 Peter 3:13). Heaven will feel like home. I will be a co-heir with Christ . . . I will help rule in the new heaven and the new earth . . . and I will be busier and happier in service than I ever dreamed possible.

And you will be too.

IT'S MORE REAL THAN WE CAN IMAGINE

You know what thrills me most about reigning with Christ on earth? It's concrete. Heaven is not some never-never land of thin, ghostly shapes and clouds. It's not a place where you can poke your finger through people, only to discover that they are spacey spirit beings you can't really hug or hold. No way!

Just writing the last few pages has invigorated my excitement over how like the Rock of Gibraltar heaven is. We shall touch and taste, rule and reign, move and run, laugh and never have reason to cry.

Maybe years ago, I assumed heaven was a misty, nebulous home for angels and—gulp!—humans, but not now. I get tickled thinking about how rock solid real heaven is and how much of a home—much more so than earth—it will be. Every time I want to visualize just how dynamic and definite heaven is, I flip through the pages of C. S. Lewis's *The Great Divorce*, a fantasy in which unredeemed people take a day excursion by bus to the bright borders of heaven. Listen to their words when they take an amazing peek at heaven:

> It was the light, the grass, the trees that were different; made of some different substance, so much solider than things in our country . . .
>
> Long after that, I saw people coming to meet us. Because they were bright I saw them while they were still very distant . . . The earth shook under their tread as their strong

feet sank into the wet turf. A tiny haze and a sweet smell went up where they had crushed the grass and scattered the dew . . . and the robes did not disguise the massive grandeur of muscle and the radiant smoothness of flesh . . . No one in that company struck me as being of any particular age. One gets glimpses, even in our country, of that which is ageless— heavy thought in the face of an infant, and frolic childhood in that of a very old man. Here it was all like that.[5]

A real reign on a real earth.

And our Savior, our King of kings, leading the way.

But watch out. Wait till you see what we do out beyond this planet!

Climbing Higher

As you already know, the driveway leading up to my house is often the scene of many heaven-inspired moments—whether hearing the wind rustling in my neighbor's pine trees or leaning back to locate the constellation of Orion in the starry dome above me. One night not long ago, I stopped to admire a full moon. It was breathtaking in its beauty, and I was struck by an unusual phenomenon—a huge corona encircled the moon, its circumference spanning nearly a quarter of the night sky! I've learned enough about stargazing to understand that a corona is a glowing circle caused by light refracted by water droplets. But the entire thing was so *bright* that I had to learn more.

The next day, I looked up the word *corona* and discovered that it is derived from a Latin word meaning "crown," which in turn came from the ancient Greek meaning "garland" or "wreath." This little fact intrigued me. I recalled writing in my book *Heaven* about the crown of life, the incorruptible crown, the crown of righteousness, and other crowns. Even then, when I wrote about crowns, I always had a hard time picturing gold diadems studded with jewels as the rewards that Jesus gives His followers at His judgment seat. They seemed too clunky and earthly. And now, I wondered if crowns could mean "coronas"—like the glowing halos of light that medieval artists painted around the heads of godly men and women?

The Bible is filled with references to the saints' heavenly garments looking like dazzling light. When Elijah and Moses stood next to Jesus as He was transfigured, they were described as "two men in clothes that gleamed like lightning" (Luke 24:4). Glowing light also characterizes the heavenly city where the saints reside: "And he carried me away in the Spirit to a mountain great and high, and showed me the Holy City, Jerusalem, coming down out of heaven from God. *It shone with the glory of God, and its brilliance was like that of a very precious jewel*, like a jasper, clear as crystal" (Revelation 21:10–11, emphasis added).

Even the throne of the Lamb at the center of the new Jerusalem shines with light: "The city does not need the sun or the moon to shine on it, for the glory of God gives it light, and the Lamb is its lamp. The nations will walk by its light" (Revelation 21:23–24).

Light is *everywhere* in heaven. And perhaps those who will be considered closest to God—such as the martyrs described in Revelation 6:9—glow the most gloriously. How can you get closer to God than under His altar at the brilliant center of the Holy City? The brightest part of the new Jerusalem?

In heaven, those who are nearest to the Lord on His throne—those who perhaps will shine the brightest—will be followers who have lovingly sacrificed the most for the sake of Christ. An anonymous believer (some think he was an African martyr) put it this way:

> I'm part of the fellowship of the unashamed . . . I'm done and finished with low living, sight walking, small planning,

smooth knees, colorless dreams, tamed visions, mundane talking, cheap living, and dwarfed goals.

I no longer need preeminence, prosperity, position, promotions, plaudits, or popularity. I don't have to be right, or first, or tops, or recognized, or praised, or rewarded. I live by faith, lean on His presence, walk by patience, lift by prayer, and labor by Holy Spirit power.

My face is set. My gait is fast. My goal is heaven. My road may be narrow, my way rough, my companions few, but my guide is reliable and my mission is clear.

I will not be bought, compromised, detoured, lured away, turned back, deluded or delayed.

I will not flinch in the face of sacrifice or hesitate in the presence of adversity. I will not negotiate at the table of the enemy, ponder at the pool of popularity, or meander in the maze of mediocrity.

I will not give up, shut up, or let up until I have stayed up, stored up, prayed up, paid up, and preached up for the cause of Christ.

I am a disciple of Jesus. I must give until I drop, preach until all know, and work until He comes. And when He does come for His own, He'll have no problems recognizing me. My colors will be clear.[6]

In short, let your life glow with the fiery passion of sacrificial love and service to Christ—it's the *best* way to shine for Him . . . and draw near to His throne.

Find Your Trail

1. Matthew 6:22 reads, "The eye is the lamp of the body. If your eyes are healthy, your whole body will be full of light." If you do a word study on this topic, you'll find insightful hints on how to keep yourself in the light.
2. Look up Psalm 101:3. What are the "vile" things on which your eyes tend to linger? Will you covenant with God to turn your eyes away the next time the Holy Spirit whispers, "Why are you looking at this?"

A Hiker's Prayer

Lord Jesus, I am done with frivolous living and selfish giving. I want my life to shine with Your righteousness—Your way of living—so I can be as close to You as I can possibly be for all of eternity. I'm no saint with a halo, but I'm telling You now that I don't want to miss out on the chance to turn up the wattage on Your glory in heaven. Keep my face set and my gait fast as I make heaven—as I make You—my goal.

Three

Where Is Heaven

AND WHAT IS IT LIKE?

The shadows of night were deep. Dawn was hardly a hint on the horizon. Suddenly, the stillness of night was shattered as our bedroom window rattled from two thunderous jolts: "Boom! Boom!"

A relaxed smile spread across my face even though I was half asleep. I knew it meant the space shuttle had just reentered earth's atmosphere and the astronauts would soon land at Edwards Air Force Base on the edge of California's Mojave Desert.

I glanced out my window to see the night still ablaze with a parade of brilliant stars, messengers of light kindling bonfires of victory all across the sky. I lay there almost envious of the astronauts who had touched the skirts of space that week. For a while, they had been friends of the stars, tickling the toes of the universe from earth's atmosphere. I yawned a prayer before I drifted back to sleep: "Soon, Jesus, I'll be up there . . . so far beyond . . . and even spacemen won't be able to catch me."

The universe fascinates me. If there's ever a program about stars or space exploration on the Discovery Channel, I'm tuned in. Whenever the space shuttle is in orbit, you can find me fixated on the NASA video feed on cable television—I lie in bed and pray over the nations of the world as a little icon of the shuttle moves slowly across a map of the planet.

I watched CNN when the *Endeavor* astronauts walked in space to make repairs on the Hubble Space Telescope. Beneath their floating figures lay the earth like a gigantic blue marble. I shook my head in breathless wonder to observe a live picture of our planet slowly turning, with Africa and then the Middle East and then India all gradually rolling by. What was more amazing were the conversations radioed between the shuttle commander and his coworkers as they manipulated the cumbersome telescope.

"Hold this wrench here and put—Hey, look over your shoulder. That's Venus behind you." He gave a long, slow whistle. "Man, isn't that beautiful!"

"Watch that screw; it's floating away. Ah, would you look at that. There's New Orleans down there."

"Yep, and look, coming up fast, the west coast of Florida."

Like I said, *amazing*.

Then there were the call-in questions from viewers around the world. They fired question after question at the astronomers and scientists sitting behind the CNN desk. Average people like me, transfixed in front of their televisions, wondered the same thing: after the repairs, what would the Hubble Telescope reveal?

One caller asked, "If Hubble is supposed to photograph the edge of the universe, what will they find on the other side?"

This is staggering, I thought. *Here we are, millions of people across the world, watching earth turn before our eyes and discussing what's beyond the universe.*

The astronomer replied, "People assume there's just empty space beyond the universe. But not so. There's another dimension we can't even dream of."

"Yeah," I said out loud to the television, "and it's called heaven."

Someone else asked, "I hear that this telescope is supposed to help scientists tell the age of the universe. How will they be able to do that?"

A scientist cleared her throat and answered, "The Hubble Telescope will be able to photograph the distances between galaxies as they expand away from each other. When we determine the rate of expansion, we'll just 'run the movie backward' to show when the universe began."

I laughed at her answer. A few years ago, Carl Sagan, the famous astronomer, was touting the universe as the only thing that was, is, and ever shall be—it had no beginning, and it will have no end. That's passé now. With the snap of a finger and a few images from Hubble, astronomers are agreeing that the universe had a beginning. Just like that, Einstein's theory of relativity is proved. And if our complex, highly organized universe had a beginning, it stands to reason that Someone began it. They also agree the universe will have an ending—I wonder if scientists have thought to pick up the book of Revelation for a sneak preview.

I doubt it. That's not the way most of them do things. I began to lose interest in the program after one or two callers failed in their attempt to interject God into the discussion. The scientists sloughed them off. Experts would rather seek out Stephen Hawking or other theoretical physicists to enlighten them on dark and mysterious data. They would rather turn to the cool, rational world of scientific debate for answers. Forget that the heavens hold the home of their hearts' longing. Stick to what is flat and factual, impersonal and rational. And so, newly discovered supernovas are assigned numbers in the galactic registry, and stars are given less-than-romantic names like M31. Yawn.

I flicked off the television.

THE TIME *of* THE END

Several days later, when *Endeavor*'s astronauts held a news conference, I was glad they recounted their romantic experience of gazing at Venus over their shoulders and watching the west coast of Florida pass by. I identified more with them than those unimaginative scientists.

I also identified with my father, who, in 1909, saw the first Ford Model T chug down Howard Street and then, months later, the Wright Brothers fly their plane over the Baltimore Harbor. He told me it was just too much for his brain. The world was simply going by too fast. My father should have lived to see this day. Because now, a little more than a generation later, the world *is* going by too fast. Millions of gallons of information are being poured into our one-ounce brains as we stare at our planet passing before our eyes.

I wish the prophet Daniel could have lived to see this day too. Then again, maybe he did. Perhaps he saw CNN in some prophetic vision and could only watch in wide-eyed wonder. Maybe his brain could only absorb so much, and he turned away just in time to hear God say, "But thou, O Daniel, shut up the words, and seal the book, even to the time of the end: many shall run to and fro, and knowledge shall be increased" (Daniel 12:4 KJV).

Knowledge about our universe is flying at us from right and left. We grasp something new, only to find it obsolete the next time we hear a headliner from some international science conference. Does this proliferation of knowledge mean we've arrived at the time of the end? I wonder if God is unsealing some grand book that has been shut up for centuries in order to reveal, page by page, facts about the heavens that confirm His handiwork.

Scientists used to believe that the universe was full of wandering comets and slow-wheeling galaxies that meandered through space with no rhyme or reason. Now most experts are beginning to acknowledge that a powerful order exists throughout the entire universe, as well as a delicate, yet exact, relationship between forces, fields, and matter. Some dare to call it "beautiful" and "an evidence of a divine mind," but these are largely castigated by the scientific community. Still, there are molecular physicists like Dr. John Templeton who are bold enough to say in print, "As science yields more and more data about the universe, we see that in fact God is revealing himself more and more to human inquiry."[1]

It is this delicate and orderly simplicity in the universe that is tugging on the hearts of experts like Dr. Templeton. He and a handful of others are beginning to turn down the chatter on the scientific debate long enough to hear that haunting echo from the skies.

It is that same song, so ancient and so new, whose notes resound in Psalm 19:1–4: "The heavens declare the glory of God; the skies proclaim the work of his hands. Day after day they pour forth speech; night after night they reveal knowledge. They have no speech, they use no words; no sound is heard from them. Yet their voice goes out into all the earth, their words to the ends of the world." When we gaze at a starry dome in a nighttime sky, scientists, along with you and me, aren't simply "hearing things." It is a haunting and mesmerizing melody. It is the heavens declaring the glory of God.

HOW FAR AWAY IS HEAVEN?

As a child, I wondered where God lived in outer space and how long it would take to get there. Had I been old enough to read an astronomy textbook, I would have discovered a few statistics that would have blown me out of the water. Our solar system has a diameter of about 700 light-minutes. That's eight billion miles. But the galaxy in which our solar system is contained has a diameter of 100,000 light-years. Not minutes, but *years*. Forget doing the math on that one. Our galaxy is humongous. But here's the kicker: our little galaxy, which is 100,000 light-years wide, is just *one* of billions of other galaxies out in the cosmos.[2]

I can't comprehend such gargantuan distances or the breathless enormity of space. Billions of stars and planets, all created by God, most of which the Hubble Space Telescope will never have time to scan. But it's up there on the edge of earth's atmosphere obediently and systematically doing just that—scanning the universe. The Hubble has recently captured images close to the very border of our cosmos, and I think it would knock our socks off if it could photograph the actual edge!

What *is* on the other side?

Scientific Journal may be stymied by that question, but not the Bible. Far beyond intergalactic space, with its billions of swirling nebulae and novas, lies another dimension. Some speculate it's the fifth dimension. You could call it infinity, but wherever it is and however far out, the Bible calls it the highest of heavens. "To the LORD your God belong the heavens, even the highest heavens," reads Deuteronomy 10:14. The outermost reaches of space are not as void and lonely as we think, because the highest part of heaven is the abode of God. It would seem this "third heaven," as Scripture calls it (2 Corinthians 12:2), spreads out into infinity and completely engulfs our expanding cosmos with all its celestial bodies. It is the dimension where "the LORD says: 'Heaven is my throne, and the earth is my footstool'" (Isaiah 66:1).

The dwelling place of God exists in infinity. It is far, far away. That's why I'm amused when the apostle Paul writes so casually in 2 Corinthians 12:2–4, "I know a man in Christ who fourteen years ago was caught up to the third heaven. Whether it was in the body or out of the body I do not know—God knows. And I know that this man . . . was caught up to paradise and heard inexpressible things, things that no one is permitted to tell."

The third heaven? The highest of heavens? C'mon, Paul, how did you arrive there so fast?

Paul wasn't the only one to reach the throne of heaven in a flash. To the dying thief next to Him on the cross, Jesus said, "Truly I tell you, today you will be with me in paradise" (Luke 23:43).

Today? Jesus, Paul, and a dead criminal spanned billions of light-years in the snap of a finger?

How Close Is Heaven?

I've always sensed that heaven was a lot closer than we are led to believe. As any good child in Sunday school, I believed that heaven was "up." In later years, I discovered that the Bible says it plainly: Paul was caught *up* to the third heaven; Jesus *ascended* into heaven; the Lord will catch us *up* into heaven when He returns; and, conversely, "God looks *down* from heaven on all mankind" (Psalm 53:2, emphasis added).

This is the language the Bible invites us to use, much as it encourages us to use other earthbound words like *crowns* or *seas of glass*. And it makes sense. Heaven certainly can't be "down," or we'd dig a hole to China.

Yet even though the dwelling place of God may be a long way up, distances like "up" and "down" lose their meaning when we realize that heaven—even the highest heavens—exist beyond our space-time continuum. Latitude and longitude, as well as directions and distances, are related to time, and time is a part of the fourth dimension. And the fourth dimension is only a small part of infinity. Time there will be swallowed up. Step beyond the edge of outer space, and you enter the fifth dimension, where gargantuan distances light-years long are a snap of the finger to, well . . . to the dying thief who, when he died, instantly appeared in paradise alongside Jesus.

Had I been the dying thief, I would have been dumbstruck to hear Jesus say, "Today you will be with me in paradise." Today? This instant? Like Jesus taking my hand and walking with me through a wall, as He did in the upper room? Or appearing on a beach to cook breakfast for His friends? Or ambling along the road to Emmaus one instant and—flash—arriving in Jerusalem in no time flat? Like being changed in the twinkling of an eye?

Yes, and the Lord gives a clue as to how He does it in Revelation 1:8 when He laughs at time and distance: "'I am the Alpha and the Omega,' says the Lord God, 'who is, and who was, and who is to come, the Almighty.'" Notice that Jesus does not follow the convention of our logic about the way time flows; we time-bound creatures want to change the order to read Jesus *was*, is, and is to come. It sounds more chronological. It's consistent with our sense of the past, present, and future. But Jesus is the great I Am who always lives in the present. He is the God of the *now*.

I think of this every time I read Revelation 22, where Jesus says three times to the waiting church, "I am coming soon!" (To which the church replies three times, "Come, Lord Jesus.") It's interesting He doesn't say, "I will come . . . like, sometime around, oh, a couple of thousand years from now." Jesus puts it in the present tense as though He is but a hairbreadth away, all ready to part the veil of time and distance and step back into our world. It's as though He is on His way back now.

So the kingdom of heaven, over which Jesus *is* and was and ever shall be King, is a place, but more so, a dimension where time and distance are not obstacles. The dying thief wasn't transported at superhuman speed to heaven when he died. Rather, he slipped from one dimension to the next, much like Jesus slipped from one room to another, through walls or whatever.

You cannot be *transported* to heaven. You cannot go there in a rocket ship. You couldn't even go there in a time machine, if there is such a thing. That's because heaven exists beyond even speeded-up time. Traveling at a zillion miles per hour might catapult you instantly to the edge of our universe, but to take a step into the third heaven requires more. It requires something different, for our flesh and blood cannot enter heaven.

You must be born again, or you cannot, as Jesus warned, "see the kingdom of God" (John 3:3). When the dying thief was born of the Spirit, he was given the spiritual "genes," so to speak, of God Himself—Christ who *is*, was, and ever shall be. And we are too when we are Spirit-born. We, like the thief, are fit for eternity. Of course, the fine print in the contract says we must also follow the dying thief in another way and die first.

WHERE IS HEAVEN?

Heaven is close. Perhaps closer than we imagine.

It's a little like saying to an unborn infant in his mother's womb, "Do you realize that you are about to be born into a great big world full of mountains, rivers, and a sun and a moon? In fact, you exist in that wonderful world right now."

"Wait a minute," the unborn baby might say. "No way. My world is the one surrounding me. It's soft, warm, and dark. You'll never convince me that just a few hairbreadths outside this uterus exists this place of rivers, mountains, and a sun and moon, whatever that stuff is."

Dear baby! There he is, safe in his little world, ignorant of the fact that a more glorious world is enclosing and encasing his. A world for which he is being fashioned. Only when he is birthed into it will he comprehend that all along his warm, dark world was within it. This other place of wonderful beauty was present all the time. Only inches away.

Even this earth in all its birth pains is about to give one last grunt and find itself born as a "new earth" in heaven. Actually, this moment, less than a hairbreadth, separates this material world from the spiritual world that is embracing earth. And like an unborn baby, we are being fashioned for the greater world into which we are about to be born (by dying, of all things!). We have a hard time believing that heaven encompasses this world, and so the Bible has to keep prodding us to fix our eyes "not on what is seen, but on what is unseen" (2 Corinthians 4:18). It's a matter of "seeing." Of using our eyes of faith.

Faith assures us that heaven is *transcendent*. It is beyond the limits of our experience; it exists apart from our material universe. Heaven is also *immanent* in that it envelopes all the celestial bodies, swirling galaxies, and the starry hosts. If we believe that God is omnipresent, then we can at least believe that what the Bible in Ephesians 2:6 calls the "heavenly realms" are omnipresent as well. For where God is, the kingdom of heaven is.

As I said, heaven is closer than we imagine, even though we can't see it. I can almost see God laughing at people's propensity to fix their eyes only on that which is seen, when in Jeremiah 23:23–24, He reminds us, "'Am I only a God nearby,' declares the LORD, 'and not a God far away? Who can hide in secret places so that I cannot see them?' declares the LORD. 'Do not I fill heaven and earth?' declares the LORD."

One day, we will take the same trip as the dying thief. We will arrive in paradise. In the meantime, we can say we operate in the realm of our omnipresent and sovereign God. In some respects, we exist in the kingdom of heaven now.

We *have already come* to Mount Zion, to the heavenly Jerusalem.

We *have come* to myriad angels in joyful assembly.

We *have come* to God, the judge of all men. There's a significant part of us, the new creature in Christ who lives in the present tense. Very much like our great I AM.

This fact makes the far and distant so near—oh, so close. When we seize this reality, we understand that the air we breathe is celestial. The ground we tread is sacred. The light we enjoy is divine. Could the rustling in the trees even be the whisper of angel wings? That's touching on romanticism, but as the Bible itself says, "[We] have come to thousands upon thousands of angels in joyful assembly" (Hebrews 12:22).

Literally.

ANGELS, DARK *and* LIGHT

This year I took part in a nationwide prayer rally across Canada that linked Christian audiences by live satellite television. My role was to lead the nation in a time of repentance. I took the responsibility very seriously and asked the organizers if I could visit the auditorium the night before.

I wheeled into the cavernous sports arena and stopped at the edge of the railing on the mezzanine level. The place was echoing with the sounds of workers hammering and ushers rehearsing. We all knew that thousands of intercessors would fill the arena the next morning to shake the heavenly realms with their prayers. But a different kind of work needed to be done that night.

When it came time for my sound check, I wheeled to the microphone on the wooden platform still under construction. "Testing, testing," I said as my voice boomed across the arena. Ushers, technicians, and workers continued their routines as the soundman adjusted his volume knobs.

My eyes scanned the empty seats. I tilted my head back and squinted beyond the dark rafters. While the soundman continued his work, I began to pray into the microphone, "Lord, we know that this arena has been the scene of everything from ice hockey fights to drug deals during rock concerts. There are a lot of fallen angels, a lot of demons, hanging around here, I can sense it."

I paused in my prayer and looked over each level. I felt a keen awareness of the presence of spirit beings. It wasn't angels.

I continued to pray, this time a little louder so my amplified voice would reach the rafters. And as I did, some of the workers stopped their drilling, and most of the ushers took seats and bowed their heads.

"Jesus, You told us in Your Word that whatever we bind on earth will be bound in heaven, and whatever we loose on earth will be loosed in heaven. So in Your name, we ask You to clear this place of evil spirits, and we ask You to dispatch big, powerful angels with swords drawn and shields held high to stand guard over this place. Make this sports arena a house of prayer."

And with that, virtually everyone in the place said, "Amen!"

Some skeptics might wave it off and say that such a prayer is a nice token, but merely conciliatory. They would say, "There really weren't demons hangin' around that place, no more than there were angels. Don't take this stuff about the spirit world so seriously."

Christians know better. We know that not only is heaven close, but another part of the spirit world is too. The "kingdom of the air" is heavily populated with spiritual beings, and although we only have a hint in Ephesians 2:2, or in 6:12, where we read of the "spiritual forces of evil in the heavenly realms," we know they are real, powerful, and present.

But not as powerful as angels. I wish our eyes could be opened to see the heavenly realms all around us. Perhaps the reality of heaven would spring to life for us if we could peel away this layer, which is only as thick as a thin veil, and take a peek.

That once actually happened to someone. The servant of the prophet Elisha went out for a casual stroll along the top of the walled city of Dothan one morning. When he paused to enjoy the tranquil sunrise, what he saw made his blood freeze. The morning sun gleamed and flashed from countless enemy shields, arrows, and spear tips. He was struck with terror at the sight of the massive Syrian force that had come by night to surround the city. Filled with dismay, he scampered back to Elisha's chambers and reported that the enemy army was about to launch an early-morning assault.

Elisha's reply was calm: "Don't be afraid . . . Those who are with us are more than those who are with them" (2 Kings 6:16). And then Elisha prayed that his servant's eyes might be opened to see the heavenly realities all around him. The Lord answered his request, and the servant saw that "the hills [were] full of horses and chariots of fire all around Elisha" (6:17).

What was true for Elisha is true for any believer. When we sing in church, "Open my eyes that I may see / Glimpses of truth Thou hast for me," we wouldn't believe our eyes if God answered our request. Our eyes would pop at all the hosts of angels, chariots of fire, archangels and cherubim, living creatures, and ministering spirits. A few of which are most likely within a hairbreadth next to you now.

HOW WILL WE RELATE *to* ANGELS?

The more heavenly-minded I become, the more convinced I am of the presence of angels in my life, whether it's acknowledging their whereabouts in a sports arena or calling them to surround the bedside of someone who is sick. Their job description has included bringing messages, as they did to the seven churches in the book of Revelation.

They aid in answering prayer, as they did with Daniel. God gets all the credit and glory, but angels mysteriously assist in the process—a case in point being Peter's miraculous deliverance from jail.

Angels bring with them something of the presence of God, as well as help the Lord shape history. They really shine when it comes to protecting or delivering us.

Suffice to say, they're busy.

I'm aware of this every time I drive my wheelchair van. Its steering and braking controls are sensitively torqued to accommodate my weak muscles in my shoulders (it doesn't have a steering wheel, but that's another story). When I cruise the Ventura Freeway at fifty-five miles per hour, I'm keenly conscious of a host of angels surrounding my van, sitting on the bumper, and holding on to the radio antenna. Maybe God has dispatched an extra few because I'm disabled and He knows I need extra protection. How many accidents have I avoided because of those angels? When I get to heaven, I'll find out, and I'll thank them for all the times they "lost a few feathers" in near-misses on my behalf.

One of the best parts of heaven may be getting to know and fellowship with angels. They love God, and they enjoy us. In a parable about sinners gaining entrance into the kingdom of heaven, Jesus said, "I tell you, there is rejoicing in the presence of the angels of God over one sinner who repents" (Luke 15:10). If angels rejoiced so happily over our conversion, how much more will they rejoice over us when we arrive at the foot of God's throne. To the angels, we will be a source of eternal joy. They will see our redemption completed, from beginning to end.

I actually saw an angel once. It was 2 a.m. on a pitch-black night. I was wide awake, propped up in bed and straining my ears to hear the muffled voices of my family in the bedroom directly above me. They were surrounding the bed of my five-year-old niece, Kelly, who was dying of cancer. We knew her passing into heaven could happen at any moment, but I was unable to get up the narrow stairs to say good-bye with the others. Suddenly, a brilliant golden shape that glowed whisked by the large bay window I was facing—it didn't move from left to right, but from bottom to top. I screamed. I then searched to see if there were cars on the street outside. Nothing was there. In the next second, my sister Jay called down the steps, "Kelly's gone!"

A few of the family came downstairs to find out why I screamed.

I told them exactly what I saw. My sisters sank on the edge of my bed in amazement. We knew I had seen a large spiritual being, probably sent from heaven to escort Kelly's soul into eternity.

We will also worship with the angels. They've had a lot of practice at worshiping, and access to heaven's throne as well. They've seen it all. Yet when we arrive in heaven, it will be *their* privilege to worship with us. Just think about what our worship will sound like. In Revelation 5:11–12, angels crowd before the throne, "numbering thousands upon thousands, and ten thousand times ten thousand . . . In a loud voice they were saying: 'Worthy is the Lamb, who was slain, to receive power and wealth and wisdom and strength and honor and glory and praise!'"

Every time I read that verse, I recall a marvelous experience at the Moody Pastors' Conference. I was told that the singing would be out of this world. And it was. When I wheeled onto the platform and parked near Dr. Joe Stowell and the other speakers, I scanned the auditorium of 1,800 men and got the jolt of my life. Somehow it had escaped me that I would be among so many, many men.

The song leader had the men stand up, spread out into the aisles, and fill the stage. When they held hymnbooks high and broke into a rousing chorus, a jet blast of sound hit me head-on. A pastor held a hymnal close so I could sing along, but I only managed to get through half of the first verse. Something forced me to stop, close my eyes, and just listen.

Never had I been so utterly surrounded by sound. It was pure and powerful, clear and deep, enveloping me, resonating through my bones, and shaking the chair in which I sat. A thunderous waterfall of perfect bass and baritone, so passionate that it made my heart break.

Through tears I tried to join in the second verse, but my wispy soprano voice sounded thin and frail. I was a tiny leaf carried helplessly along on a surging current, spilling over and splashing

with joy—all joy and music. It was a moment of ecstasy so seren-
dipitous and God-anointed that I had to step outside myself and
be carried heavenward. I could do nothing but laugh through my
tears and enjoy the ride. If this earthly choir moved me, how much
more when our voices blend with those of the angels!

Angels will also serve us in heaven. Their job description in
Hebrews 1:14 extends beyond just earth. Angels will be subject
to us in eternity. We will reign with Jesus. And if He has been
given authority over all the heavenly hosts, then we will reign over
angels too. Will we govern a few legions or many? What will we
command them to do in faraway galaxies? How will they aid us
on earth to help carry out the kingdom rule? I can't say, but it's
thrilling to imagine. And since I never took ROTC in college or
engaged in military service, I'm sure glad I'll have a glorified mind
to handle it. Strategic leadership will be a cinch for us, and we'll
be able to rally angelic legions, as well as lead the way in doing
God's work in heaven and on earth.

One more thing. When it comes to fallen angels—demons—we
will judge them. If 1 Corinthians 6:2–3 didn't spell it out in black-
and-white, I'd laugh at the improbability of it all: "Do you not
know that the Lord's people will judge the world? And if you are
to judge the world, are you not competent to judge trivial cases?
Do you not know that we will judge angels? How much more the
things of this life!"

Incredible!

A verse like this makes me want to settle my differences with
my husband, Ken, real fast. I'm not joking. This short but powerful Scripture is another one of those exponential statements
that smack of an almost unbelievable increase in our capacity to
serve, as well as of our responsibility in ruling. Once again, God
will blow out all formulas on proportions and put us in charge
of judging fallen angels. I cringe at the idea, because on earth I'm
having a tough enough time deciding who's right in a friendly spat

or who ought to get the last piece of pie or whether justice was served in a local court case.

Me? Judging angels? Again, I breathe a sigh of relief to know that I will have all of God's wisdom at my disposal; otherwise, the job would send me cowering. It's just another way we will rule with Christ in heaven.

Frankly, the idea intrigues me. There are a couple of evil spirits I can't wait to nail. On earth, I have been so harassed by troublesome demons of temptation or evil forces that keep trying to trip me up. I'm not saying "the devil made me do it" on earth; I take full responsibility for my choices and actions. But demons sure haven't helped. I could easily throw the book at them!

Then there are the more heinous powers and principalities of darkness that have incited wicked men to wreak havoc. These are the gruesome chief demons under Satan who for centuries have pushed evil people further into rebellion, murder, torture, and grisly massacres. The Nazi Holocaust. Stalin's pogroms. The Cambodian genocide. The Rwandan genocide. And especially those forces of evil that instigated the treason and injustice behind the crucifixion of God's own Son, even the demons that urged those drunken soldiers to slap and spit on the Second Person of the Trinity.

When I see the news photos of starving children in North Korea, old women wandering the rubble of Syrian neighborhoods, or terrified teens running from gunfire in their schools, I naturally get mad at people who do such things. But when we consider who's behind it all, I don't vent anger at God; I get furious with the devil and his cohorts. The psalmist was speaking of evil people in Psalm 139:22, but I'll throw in fallen angels and say, "I have nothing but hatred for them; I count them my enemies."

These demons have had a heyday on earth for too long. I see their trademark on everything from pornography spewed from the internet to the humanism spouted from elementary school textbooks. Satan's legions have left a dark trace on this earth, which has been gutted and denuded of its resources, leaving ugly scars on mountains and smoky trails in the air. Most of all, it hurts when I see men and women gripped in the claws of spiritism and the occult; Satan has blinded their eyes. And unless the Sovereign Lord opens the eyes of wicked men and women through our prayers and witness, they will be crushed and tormented like grapes under His wrath.

This humbles me before God.

And yes, I hate the devil.

I'm 100 percent behind virtually every sermon that Jonathan Edwards preached about hellfire and brimstone, the place God created for the devil and his followers. I can hardly wait for that glorious—yes, glorious—day when Satan and his legions will be punished and eternally tormented for their procuring the fall of mankind. One day we shall have the pleasure of demonstrating "perfect hatred," as Scripture puts it (Psalm 139:22 KJV), against the rulers, powers, and spiritual forces of darkness.

WILL THERE BE ENVY *in* HEAVEN?

I'm speechless to think that, in addition to giving us the blessings of salvation and eternal life, God should reward us with such superior opportunities to serve Him beyond all reasonable proportion. If we think God is generous with His grace to us on earth, wait until we see Him pull out all the stops to spread far and wide His glory in heaven!

That's why I can't get out of my heart or head this thing about crowns. I am awed and inspired by the fact that what I do on earth will have a direct bearing on how I will serve God in heaven. The apostle Peter echoes this in his second epistle: "If you do these things . . . you will receive *a rich welcome* into the eternal kingdom of our Lord and Savior Jesus Christ" (2 Peter

1:10–11, emphasis added). Our present conduct has a bearing on our entrance into heaven and how rich our welcome will be.[3]

Sometimes I feel like I'm in the minor leagues, working hard to be ensured a spot somewhere in the major leagues in heaven, because what I do here affects everything there. I'm not talking about earning salvation, but about earning reward. It affects everything from how much heart will be devoted to my eternal worship of God to the kind of job I'll be assigned on the new earth. It even affects the way I'll govern angels to my capacity for eternal joy and possibly the extent of my appreciation for all that Jesus has done for me and others here on earth.

I know what you're thinking. *Joni, if you are suggesting that there are degrees of responsibility or even joy in heaven, aren't you inviting a little . . . envy? Won't people get jealous if some have bigger, fancier mansions?*

May I straighten out one thing? I didn't dream up the idea of some people becoming greater in the kingdom than others; Scripture did. One of the very last things Jesus says in the final chapter of Revelation is, "Look, I am coming soon! My reward is with me, and I will give to each person according to what they have done" (22:12). If you're faithful in a few things, watch out; it's "ten cities" coming your way. If it's a couple of talents you invest, lo and behold, the Master more than doubles your investment. God's Word is replete with conditional statements like, "Blessed is the one who perseveres under trial because, having stood the test, that person will receive the crown of life" (James 1:12).

As far as envy is concerned, don't worry. It won't happen in heaven. Remember, we will be totally transformed. Envy will be an impossibility. We won't drool over someone's three-story sprawling mansion and think we only get to live in a shack with a tin roof. No competing and no comparison in heaven. Still, it makes perfect sense that God will exalt those whom He chooses to honor. It's His prerogative. And whatever He decides or whomever He chooses to lift up is fine with me. I'll be more than happy for the godly men and women whom Christ will elevate as the most celebrated pillars in His temple.

Once after a speaking engagement, a woman came over to tell me how much she enjoyed my message. In her enthusiasm, she exclaimed, "You're so wonderful. I wish I could be like you. I'm sure you'll get a great reward in heaven!"

I appreciated her accolades, but I see it differently. God is by no means impressed that I can paint with my mouth, have written books, have traveled all over the world, or was on speaking terms with Billy Graham. When He sees my name on a bestseller's list, He doesn't get all effusive and say, "Boy, am I proud of her! Chalk another one up for the woman in the wheelchair."

I'm not discounting my painting or books or the exciting places I've served; I just feel that I have received a lot of my reward here on earth. I've enjoyed the reward of seeing the gospel go forth because of this wheelchair and of watching believers become encouraged and inspired. It is sheer ecstasy to watch God work through my life, and I'm humbled and honored.

It's just that when it comes to heaven, I'm convinced the highest accolades will go—and should go—to godly people who have labored loyally yet received no recognition. The grand and glorious purposes for my suffering are clear to all, but some dear saints have suffered for no apparent reason. I have a Christian friend named Dorothy who has silently lived with excruciating pain for years—such incredible pain that she has nearly passed out on many occasions. It's been agony, but she has bravely endured. I long to see her suffering atoned for when Jesus hands her a crown of life with extra jewels reserved for the saint who "perseveres under trial."

Yes, some will be greater in the kingdom than others. What a wonderful thought! I can't wait for the Lord to greatly honor the missionary in the back jungles of Brazil who spent fifteen years translating Scripture and then quietly moved on to the next tribe to do the same.

I want to see the Lord richly reward small-town pastors who faithfully preached every Sunday morning, despite meager numbers in the pews. Better yet, pastors in China who are still suffering persecution and haven't seen the light of day from their jail cells in years.

I hope the Lord takes highest delight in elderly grandmothers in nursing homes who didn't dwell on their plight, but who rather prayed for others without fanfare. Godly teens who held fast to their virginity, saying no time and again to peer pressure, intimidation, and their hormones. And moms and dads of children with disabilities who, in the name of Jesus, served the family faithfully, despite the day-to-day routine, isolation, and financial setbacks.

These are the real heroes and heroines over whom we will be exceedingly glad to hear the Lord say, "Well done, good and faithful servant!" When they receive their reward, I'll stand happily on the sidelines, cheering, whistling, and applauding wildly. I may have stood up to the vicissitudes of human hardship like pain and paralysis, but their strength of spirit more than matched, even way surpassed, mine. And do you know what will thrill me most? The obedience of these unsung heroes will raise the wattage on God's glory. He will shine brighter because of them.

I won't be jealous of others with brighter raiment than mine in heaven. Neither will they be envious of anyone, such as the two people picked to sit on the right or left hand of Jesus. You won't be either. And do you know why you will be satisfied with the reward Jesus gives you? First, you'll be pleased with whatever Jesus bestows simply because He's Lord. Second, your perfect sense of justice will be in complete accord with the Lord's judgment. Third, your capacity for joy will be filled to overflowing.

Your reward will be your capacity—your capacity for joy, service, and worship. Jonathan Edwards described these capacities this way: "The saints are as so many vessels of different sizes, cast into a sea of happiness, where every vessel is full; this Christ purchased for all. But after all, it is left to God's sovereign pleasure to determine the largeness of the vessel."[4]

When I think of my vessel, I picture a gallon bucket into which the Lord will pour His joy until it gushes over the brim, bubbling up and effervescing. I'll laugh with delight for others who will have a joy capacity the size of a big bathtub or a tanker truck or a silo. Like me, they will be filled to overflowing, and we all will be as happy as cats with nine tails!

Whether a small vial or a large vase, we shall all be spilling and splashing over with the joy of the Lord, and even those whose capacity is only the size of a thimble won't know jealousy. We shall be fat, sassy, and satiated with joy. Constantly brimming over. Happiness unspeakable in worship and service. Each of us will have complete contentment for the station our Master has allocated to us in eternal life.

So I'm fixing my eyes on Jesus and focusing on things unseen. I'm stretching my heart's capacity for God here on earth to ensure that my bucket for joy in heaven will be deep and wide. I'm searching high and low in my heart to choose the right building materials, whether it be gold, silver, precious stones, or platinum-plated service. I'm down here on earth to win as many crowns as possible.

Uh-oh, you may be thinking, *Joni, aren't you being self-serving here? Isn't focusing on gaining rewards a bit mercenary?*

No. I have a clear conscience in light of 1 Corinthians 9:24–26, which encourages missionaries, prisoners, teens, moms, and dads—all of us in the contest—to "run in such a way as to get the prize. Everyone who competes in the games goes into strict training. They do it to get a crown that will not last; but we do it to get a crown that will last forever. Therefore I do not run like someone running aimlessly."

I always run for the reward harder and faster when I read this encouragement from Jonathan Edwards: "Persons need not and ought not to set any bounds to their spiritual and gracious appetites."[5]

Is it selfish to run hard in order to gain the prize? Is working toward rewards mercenary? Certainly not. Heavenly crowns are not just rewards for a job well done on earth; when your focus is on Jesus, they are the glorious fulfillment of the job itself. Just like marriage is the reward and the happy consummation of love, and a medal of honor is the reward given at the end of a victorious battle, so it will be with heaven's crowns. A reward is the cherry and whipped-cream topping on the pleasure of serving God down here on earth. It is the joy of sticking to the call He gave at the beginning.

Heaven is one big reward. Gift after gift after gift.

In Revelation 2 and 3, God unfolds the rewards He has reserved in heaven for you and me, His overcomers. My friend Margaret Clarkson takes a stab at describing each reward:

> The fruit of the tree of life, the hidden manna—what food that will be for souls that hunger and thirst for God! The white stone, with the new and secret name known only to God and the soul that receives it—what infinite value our God must set on individuality of personality to know each one of His overcomers so personally and so intimately! The white raiment, forever spotless—what a joy after this life of soiling and defeat! The pillar eternally erect—what a strength after this pilgrimage of weakness and failure! To receive the morning star, sweet synonym for the Savior's own person; to be given the holy name of God Himself and the name of His city and the new name of the Lamb—only a God like ours could have designed rewards such as these! And only the Head that was crowned with thorns could fashion such crowns of life, righteousness, and glory . . .

What can we do but fall down before Him who sits upon the throne and worship Him for ever and ever?[6]

I have an idea that when we step into eternity, I won't be the only one who, with new resurrected legs, will drop on grateful glorified knees. Tens of thousands will have the same idea. Our knees will kneel on jade and jasper. Our feet will walk on gold. Our hands will touch walls of sapphires and emeralds. We will feel utterly at home in the golden throne room of the King.

But wait. At home? In a glittering throne room? A mansion made of sardonyx and chrysolite doesn't sound very homey, let alone comfortable. Even after looking at these pictures of what heaven will be like and sensing how it will feel on "that great gettin' up morning" for all of us in the future, one thought may still be nagging us: *Will I fit? Will heaven really be like home?*

CLIMBING HIGHER

Remember Clarence, that quirky angel assigned to watch over George Bailey in the holiday movie *It's a Wonderful Life?* Though Clarence was a bit odd, he was certainly loveable—and just the way we might picture a guardian angel to be.

Last Christmas when Ken and I watched that movie, Clarence piqued my interest in the ministry of angels in our lives. Some of us, when we were little, were even told we had our own guardian angel (and that if we weren't careful, we might wear him out!). Jesus seemed to speak to this when He said to His disciples, "See that you do not despise one of these little ones. For I tell you that their angels in heaven always see the face of my Father in heaven" (Matthew 18:10).

I wondered, *Who are these little ones? Young boys and girls? And what about "their angels"? Are they harried, amiable fuss-budgets like Clarence?*

When I asked a pastor about these things, he took the time to point me to the context of the Lord's remarks in Matthew 18. In that passage, Jesus was talking about His followers who become *like* children. So, in effect, Jesus is saying, "Don't look down on other believers, because their *angels* [plural] always see the face of My Father."

We followers of Jesus have a mighty entourage camped around us. Remember when Jacob was given the ability to actually see his angelic escort in Genesis 32? And these very angels have the unspeakable, preeminent privilege of standing in the glorious presence of Almighty God!

So even the most unimpressive, simple, weak-in-the-faith follower of Christ is a child of God. And because of that relationship, wherever he or she goes, a powerful escort surrounds them before and behind—divine emissaries of immense strength and beauty. And as Jesus said, we should not look down on another believer, if for no other reason than the impressive company of radiant heavenly beings in tow.

This is no elderly, fumbling Clarence in a lace nightshirt. Yes, it may sound cozy to imagine that God has assigned us a single guardian angel—one spiritual watchman with big feathery wings—to keep vigil over us. But consider Psalm 91:11: "He will command his angels concerning you to guard you in all your ways." So don't picture the framed print in the hallway of your grandmother's house—the one showing a lovely feminine angel in flowing robes striding protectively behind a little girl.

It's a nice picture, but that's thinking too small.

Scripture tells us that angels are "ministering spirits sent to serve those who will inherit salvation" (Hebrews 1:14). In other words, angels—all angels—are specifically sent by God to serve and help followers of Jesus Christ. Everything that angels do, everywhere in the world and at all times, is for the good of Christians.

Does that mean we will never experience harm or hurt or

heartbreak on this temporary, broken world? Of course not. The Lord, for sovereign purposes of His own, sometimes allows His deeply loved sons and daughters to suffer. The apostle James was beheaded with a sword while surrounded by angels (Acts 12:2). The apostle Paul was stoned by a vicious mob and left for dead while an angelic security team kept watch (Acts 14:19). Jesus Himself was abused, beaten, and crucified while more than twelve legions of powerful angel warriors stood by (Matthew 26:53). And I believe angels were on duty in 1967, when I dove off a raft into shallow water in the Chesapeake Bay and broke my neck.

Jesus told us very clearly that "in the world you will have tribulation" (John 16:33 NKJV). No one escapes that. But who can begin to calculate all of the trouble, hurt, missteps, folly, danger, darkness, and mortar attacks from hell that God's angels have kept from our door during our years on this planet? And when our time comes, Jesus indicates that angels will personally and tenderly carry us into the presence of our Father (Luke 16:22).

Throughout our lives, angels help to carry out God's will in and through us. But before we make too big a fuss over the angelic host hovering around us, remember this: Those angels don't give you high standing. You already have the Creator of the universe as your Father. You already have the Lord of the universe as your Elder Brother. You already have God's own Spirit as your Counselor, Helper, and Friend. And even the most highly decorated, top-echelon angels can't match that. Having even a legion of such high-ranking angels serving you doesn't increase your standing in the heavenly realms.

You are already a child of the King.

And that's as good as it gets.

FIND YOUR TRAIL

1. Read Hebrews 13:1–2. What does this passage say (or imply) about possible encounters with angels during the course of our lives?
2. In Luke 22:43, we read about an angel who came to encourage and strengthen Jesus before He went to the cross, and yet didn't deliver Him from that situation. What does this say about God's comfort in times of great trials?

A HIKER'S PRAYER

Thank You, Lord, for Your constant vigilance and care over my life. Thank You for Your promise that You will watch over my "coming and going both now and forevermore" (Psalm 121:8). I have never turned onto a road where You haven't turned first. I have never entered a room where You haven't gone before me. I have never encountered a situation where You haven't foreseen every detail and provided me with all that I need to get through. And when it comes time to let go of earth, You will guide me home with Your angels, and leave heaven's porch light on for my arrival.

PART TWO

Will Heaven Be Home?

> "I have come home at last! This is my real country! I belong here. This is the land I have been looking for all my life, though I never knew it till now . . . Come further up, come further in!"
>
> C. S. LEWIS, *THE LAST BATTLE*

In prison, chained to a Roman guard, the apostle Paul thought about departing for heaven—and liked that thought so much he had to remind himself about unfinished duties on earth (Philippians 1:20–26). Exiled on the desolate island of Patmos, a barren, unhospitable chunk of rock in the Aegean Sea, the apostle John saw a door open into heaven and heard a voice say, "Come up here" (Revelation 4:1). And he gladly went.

Our circumstances in this life, even the difficulties, disappointments, heartbreaks, and lonely seasons, remind us that we don't quite "fit" in today's world. A whisper echoing in the back parts of our soul reminds us, *Yes, but you are moving toward a place where you will fit perfectly.* The next four chapters talk about the Home you've always dreamed of and never quite realized.

But you will.

Four

Why Don't We Fit
ON EARTH?

Hey, lady, your suitcase is over there!" a baggage handler yelled. "Get that cart out of the way, would ya!"

"Taxi! Hey, stop—I said, 'Taxi!'" someone hollered outside.

It was mayhem. My friend was steering me in my wheelchair through thick crowds and piles of suitcases in the baggage claim area of Los Angeles International Airport. Angry passengers bemoaned lost luggage. A line of people jostled through a turnstile. Outside, taxis honked. Police officers hollered. It was a crazy ending to an even crazier day of bad weather and a late arrival. We found our luggage carousel, and my friend parked my chair to go retrieve our things.

While I waited in the midst of pandemonium, I did what I always do. I waited and sat still. Very still.

It's a fact of life. Because I'm paralyzed from the shoulders down, a large part of me never moves. I have instant stillness. I don't run; I sit. I don't race; I wait. Even when rushing, I stay put in my wheelchair. I could be scurrying through a jam-packed schedule, doing this and that, but a big part of me—due to my paralysis—is always quiet.

That's why, if you had seen me in that busy airport, you would have noticed a satisfied smile. Perhaps in an earlier time I would have felt trapped, useless, and resentful that I could not grab my own suitcase, elbow the guy who butted in line, or hail my own taxi. But faith, honed and sharpened from years in my wheelchair, has changed that. And so, I sat there thanking God for built-in quiet and stillness before Him.

I also thought about heaven. With eyes of faith I looked beyond the sight of bumper-to-bumper traffic; the smell of sweat, cigarettes, and exhaust fumes; and the sounds of my harried co-travelers and began humming quietly.

> *This world is not my home, I'm just a passing thru.*
> *My treasures are laid up somewhere beyond*
>   *the blue;*
> *The angels beckon me from heaven's open door,*
> *And I can't feel at home in this world anymore.*[1]

For me, it was a moment of faith. Faith merely the size of a grain of mustard seed. Remember, that's all it takes to be sure of things hoped for—future divine fulfillments—and certain of things we do not see, that is, unseen divine realities.

Of what was I so sure and certain? Here, let me sing it again: "The angels beckon me from heaven's open door, / And I can't feel at home in this world anymore."

I hum that haunting tune in other places besides the Los Angeles airport. Sometimes I get that "can't feel at home" sensation ambling down the aisles of Kmart, watching women grab for the Bluelight Specials. Sometimes it happens sitting with Ken and watching Monday Night Football's fourth instant replay of a team's third-down conversion. And I definitely feel "this world is not my home" as I sit on the Ventura Freeway–turned–parking lot.

Don't think I'm strange. Christians have felt the same for centuries. Malcolm Muggeridge, a British journalist who spent most of his years battling Christianity, finally succumbed to Christ in his seventies. The intellectual world had always been home to him, but now, in the hallowed halls of university life, he found himself saying this:

> I had a sense, sometimes enormously vivid, that I was a stranger in a strange land; a visitor, not a native . . . a displaced person . . . The feeling, I was surprised to find, gave me a great sense of satisfaction, almost of ecstasy . . . Days or weeks or months might pass. Would it never return—the lostness? I strain my ears to hear it, like distant music; my eyes to see it, a very bright light very far away. Has it gone for ever? And then—ah! the relief. Like slipping away from a sleeping embrace, silently shutting a door behind one, tiptoeing off in the grey light of dawn—a stranger again. The only ultimate disaster that can befall us, I have come to realize, is to feel ourselves to be at home here on earth. As long as we are aliens we cannot forget our true homeland.[2]

His words could have been mine as I wheeled through the Thousand Oaks Mall yesterday. I was a stranger in a strange land between the video game arcade on the second floor and the first-floor movie complex running the latest *Star Wars* movie. Actually, I felt like a blessed stranger. A displaced, but satisfied person. Everyone seemed absorbed by the fashion show going on in the center courtyard, but I found myself thinking, *Does anyone else here realize that there's more to life than the new fall designs?*

That's what blessed strangers and satisfied displaced persons feel. They see that heaven is *home*. It's where we belong. "We have a homing instinct, a 'home detector,' and it doesn't ring for earth," writes Peter Kreeft.[3]

I did not feel at home in that mall. I did not belong. I saw its world as trite and commonplace. Mind you, I didn't view the people as banal or boring; if anything, my heart went out to the kids hanging around the arcade and the women watching the fashion show. The troubling part was the "world" in which they were engrossed: The lure of shoe store posters on which grungy-looking kids scream, "Demand What You Deserve!" The morbid attraction of noisy video games that decapitate the heads and sever the arms of cartoon losers, and everywhere, huge discounts if you open up a credit account and purchase three pairs of anything. My heart especially went out to a teen girl in jeans and plaid shirt staring enviously at the gaunt figure of a female mannequin that stared back at her through lifeless eyes. That said it all.

I couldn't help but see something past this world; it was not unlike the moment of faith I experienced in the LA airport. How so? Because faith is double-sided. It not only verifies heaven as real, giving hard and fast reality to that which we do not see, but it also makes us look differently at visible things on earth. Through faith's eyes, heaven becomes a rock-solid home, and the concrete world in which we live becomes drained of substance and importance. When we look at life through eyes of faith, things around us no longer possess the glow of excitement. Everything from Rolex watches to the latest episode of *This Is Us*, from the newest Chanel fashions to the latest debates in Congress.

Because faith makes invisible things real, and visible things unreal, earthly dissatisfaction becomes the road to heavenly satisfaction. One place, heaven, supplants the other, earth, as home.

FOREIGNERS, EXILES, *and* MISFITS

Faith does another thing. The more homelike that heaven becomes, the more you feel like a foreigner and exile on earth (1 Peter 2:11). Maybe some people shop for top-of-the-line Porsches, but that only reveals that "their mind is set on earthly things. But our citizenship is in heaven" (Philippians 3:19–20). I'm not talking spiritual snobbery here, and I have no beef against Mercedes-Benz cars or St. John knits. It's simply a matter of focus: "For where your treasure is, there your heart will be also" (Matthew 6:21).

Please don't think I drive a clunker, wear my sister's hand-me-downs, hate the mall, and never turn on a television. I like nice stuff. Don't forget, I spent the first chapter describing all the present moments and past memories that make earth so rich for me. I'm the one who enjoys earth's good things, like prime rib rare with Yorkshire pudding, a night of romance with my husband at Bridalveil Fall at Yosemite, and the feel of raw silk on my face. There's nothing trite, banal, or boring about these pleasures. What's more, if I could be entrusted, I'm sure my conscience would be thrilled to permit me to don a beautiful Jones New York suit. (It would probably go to my head, which is why some of my Christian friends can wear this garb with grace while I can't.)

This feeling of being a foreigner or exile on earth has more to do with the song I told you about. The haunting echo. The longing and yearning I felt that hot afternoon by the Kansas wheat field, and many times since. The writer of Hebrews 11:14–16 definitely had me in mind when he wrote, "People who say such things show that they are looking for a country of their own. If they had been thinking of the country they had left, they would have had opportunity to return. Instead, they were longing for a better country—a heavenly one."

I'm a little like a refugee who is longing for my better country called heaven. My heart is in quasi-exile. In fact, 1 Kings 11:14–22 is just a brief story, but it's "me" all over. It seems that Hadad, an adversary of Solomon, had fled for safety to Egypt with some of his father's family. There he found great favor with Pharaoh, married into the king's family, and reared his son in the royal palace. Then things changed:

While he was in Egypt, Hadad heard that David rested with his ancestors and that Joab the commander of the army was also dead. Then Hadad said to Pharaoh, "Let me go, that I may return to my own country."

"What have you lacked here that you want to go back to your own country?" Pharaoh asked.

"Nothing," Hadad replied, "but do let me go!"

That's the part I identify with. Earth may be rich with past memories and present moments, as it was with Hadad, but I'm hot on his heels: "Let me go, that I may return to my own country." It is always the exiles who remember home. The Israelites, captive in a foreign land, remembered their true country when they mourned in Psalm 137:1: "By the rivers of Babylon we sat and wept when we remembered Zion." Like Hadad, like the Israelites, I carry in my exiled heart a hunger for my heavenly country, my soul's true home.

A person who feels at home "fits" with his environment, like a fish in the water, a bird in the sky, or a worm in the dirt. But we don't "fit" here. It's not our environment. There is no harmony, no "rightness," with our surroundings. Remember my experiences in the Los Angeles airport and the Thousand Oaks Mall? It wasn't as though the hustle and bustle of that world offended me; it's just that it didn't jibe; it didn't resonate with the peace and stillness in my heart, a peace that echoed, "You don't belong here."[4]

Feeling like an exile is simply feeling a fact.

> O LORD,
> I live here as a fish in a vessel of water,
>   only enough to keep me alive,
>   but in heaven I shall swim in the ocean.
> Here I have a little air in me to keep me breathing,
>   but there I shall have sweet and fresh gales;

Here I have a beam of sun to lighten my darkness,
a warm ray to keep me from freezing;
yonder I shall live in light and warmth for ever.

A PURITAN PRAYER[5]

WHY DON'T WE FIT?

As Christians, you and I are not made for this world.

Well, in one sense we are. Our hands, feet, eyes, and ears equip us for physical experiences on this planet made of water and dirt. Our ears process noise; our eyes register sights; our noses detect odors; and our stomachs digest food. But we are also spirit. This makes for incredible tension. One of my friends once told me that through faith we understand we are not physical beings having a spiritual experience but spiritual beings having a physical experience. Peter Kreeft writes about this tension, and I borrow some of his ideas in the next few paragraphs.

As spiritual beings, you and I are not made for this world because the earth is temporal. There is something in us that is definitely *not* temporal. That's why we squirm and groan against the confines of time. The clock, for us, is an adversary. Every heavenly moment—whether it be gazing into the soft eyes and gentle smile of the one we love or relishing the ecstasy of some glorious pleasure—we embrace so we might keep time at bay. But we can't. We would like to call these moments timeless, but they're not. Time snatches them from our grasp.

This is where the tension *really* kicks in. For in one sense, as Sheldon Vanauken writes, "We wished to know, to savour, to sink in—into the heart of the experience—to possess it wholly. But there was never enough time . . . Time is our natural environment. We live in time as we live in the air we breathe. And we love the air . . . How strange that we cannot love time. It spoils our loveliest moments."[6] I can't explain the tension any better than that. Time is our natural environment, yet time is *not* our natural environment.

It's not just Christians who kick against the traces of time. People who don't believe in God consider time an adversary. For them, the ticking of the second hand sounds like the stalking of an enemy. Each minute moves them toward death. And everyone, whether rich or poor, tries to grab the hour hand to shove it backward. "Slow down and live" is a slogan on everything from highway signs to health books. But we can't slow down time. Wrinkle cream won't do it. Pumping your brain and brawn with Vitamins E and A won't do it. And freezing your body in an iced hydrogen chamber won't stop time either. It's the honest person who would agree with C. S. Lewis when he writes, "Time itself is one more name for death."[7]

All of humanity senses this, for God "has also set eternity in the human heart; yet no one can fathom what God has done from beginning to end" (Ecclesiastes 3:11). Yes, people in general just can't fathom God, let alone this thing about a timeless eternity. They don't know what to do with it, except to buy the latest New Age bestseller or apply more Oil of Olay. Their only real recourse against the onslaught of time is their memories. "Memory is our only dike against the waves of time in this world," writes Peter Kreeft.[8]

LONGING *for* ANOTHER TIME

I know what it's like to grab hold of memories like bricks and build a dike against time. When I was first paralyzed in 1967— and still new to this eternity thing as a young Christian—heaven was in no way my home. I was less interested in looking forward to a glorified body and more interested in turning back the clock to days when my body worked. Time was also an enemy in that it kept putting more distance between the past on my feet and the present in my wheelchair. The only way I could slow down the weeks and months was to dive into my memories.

I couldn't do much but listen to the radio or to records. I lay on the Stryker frame in the intensive care unit and tuned in to Diana Ross moaning about a lost love or Glen Campbell crooning about an old flame wandering on the backroads of his memory. The Beatles were also popular then. I would fight back the tears when they'd sing of a yesterday when troubles seemed so far away.

Then there was Joni Mitchell. Folk music still lingered in the late 1960s, and I found refuge in her restless songs about the past. Her music evoked a more powerful and fundamental nostalgia than pining for a lost love or a trouble-free yesterday. You can hear it in the sixties anthem she penned for a lost and searching generation. It was a generation that came in droves to find itself on the hot, rainy hillsides of a farm in New York. Listen to the ache and the haunting longing in her song called "Woodstock":

> *Then can I walk beside you?*
> *I have come here to lose the smog,*
> *And I feel to be a cog in something turning.*
> *Well maybe it is just the time of year*
> *Or maybe it's the time of man.*
> *I don't know who I am,*
> *But you know life is for learning.*
>
> *We are stardust,*
> *We are golden,*
> *And we've got to get ourselves*
> *Back to the garden.*[9]

Joni Mitchell and thousands like her are looking for something incalculably precious that they've lost, something they've got to get back to. They may mistake it for the nostalgia of the fifties or the sixties; they may mistake it for a childhood memory, a lost love, or a yesterday when one's troubles seemed so far away, but it's much more than that. It's a nostalgia not for the innocence of youth, but for the innocence of humanity. "We've got to get ourselves back to the garden," a lost world groans, because it's Eden where we lost not just our youth but our identity.

We may not realize it, but the whole of humanity is exiled from the bliss of the intimate presence of God, "walking in the garden in the cool of the day" (Genesis 3:8). But being "dead in [our] transgressions and sins" (Ephesians 2:1), humanity doesn't realize this is what it longs for. Most people don't understand that to walk with God is to feel at home.

What's funny is that I'm convinced even if people could reach back into the garden, if Joni Mitchell could go back to the moment of the creation of the world, it wouldn't be enough. She'd stand there in the middle of a perfect environment and feel perfectly ill at ease, not realizing that satisfaction can only be found by taking one more step off the edge of time itself and into the mind of God. For our nostalgia for Eden is not just for another time, but for another *kind* of time. Those who do not believe still feel the tug. Even those who do not hope for heaven still wrestle with this vexing enigma of "eternity" set in their hearts.

Most people have it backward.

Unlike those who don't believe in God, our road is not back to the Garden of Eden, but forward. One should never look over one's shoulder on the road of hope. In Genesis, God sent the cherubim with the flaming sword to bar Adam and Eve from returning to Eden once they had fallen. As Peter Kreeft writes, "Their road to God is now ahead, 'east of Eden,' through the world of time and history and struggle and suffering and death. Ejected from Eden's eastern gate, we travel through and around the world, from west to east, forever seeking the rising sun (the

Rising Son!) and find Him standing at the western gate of Eden, saying, 'I am the door.'"[10]

OUR TRUE IDENTITY

Our lost youth and lost identity are not to be recovered in the innocence of Eden. God conceived of us before Eden, "before the creation of the world" (Ephesians 1:4). Only in heaven—the birthplace of our identity—will we find out who we truly are. Actually, we won't find it so much as receive it. This is beautifully symbolized in Revelation 2:17: "To the one who is victorious, I will give some of the hidden manna. I will also give that person a white stone with a new name written on it, known only to the one who receives it."

Did you get that part about our new name? George Mac-Donald explains the connection between our new name and our true identity this way: "God's name for a man must then be the expression in a mystical word—a word of that language which all who have overcome understand—of his own idea of the man, that being whom he had in his thought when he began to make the child, and whom he kept in his thought through the long process of creation that went to realize the idea. To tell the name is to seal the success."[11]

Our true identity will unfold in the new name that God will give us. And the name is a secret between God and you. Think about that, friend! In heaven, you will not only find what was irretrievably lost, but when you receive it—your new name, your true identity—you will be a thousand times more yourself than the sum total of all those nuances, gestures, and inside subtleties that defined the earthbound "you." On earth you may think you fully blossomed, but heaven will reveal that you barely budded.

What's more, you will be like none other in heaven. The fact that no one else has your name shows how utterly unique you are to God. You touch His heart in a way no one else can. You please Him like none other. It is a royal seal of His individual love on you.

This shouldn't surprise us. God hasn't carved out a gigantic celestial ballpark called heaven into which His entire family fits. Paradise is not a general commune for a lump sum of saints. God has chosen to save certain individuals, and you have a specific place niched in heaven—in God's heart—that fits you and you alone. In heaven you will reflect Him like a facet of a diamond, and people will say to you, "I *love* seeing that part of God in you. In fact, you show off that trait of His better than anybody up here!"

Everyone else will receive their true identity too. They also will reflect God in unique and complete ways, so you will probably say to that friend, "Well, I *love* the way you reflect Him this way!" And together the two of you, as well as all the other saints, will praise God that "Christ is all, and is in all" (Colossians 3:11) with such variety and beauty.

C. H. Spurgeon suggested this is why redeemed people will number more than the grains of sand on the beach or the drops of dew on the ground.[12] An endless number of saints will be required to fully reflect the infinite facets of God's love. Everyone is necessary in heaven. Could it be that without you, some wonderful nuance of God's love, dare I say, might not get reflected were you not in heaven?

United in perfect praise and love, we will finally and fully discover who we are, where we belong, and what God destined us to do—and we will have all of eternity to be and do that very thing. For centuries, theologians have attempted to describe this scene; I think Jonathan Edwards does a good job when he writes, "Thus they shall eat and drink abundantly, and swim in the ocean of love, and be eternally swallowed up in the infinitely bright, and infinitely mild and sweet beams of divine love; eternally receiving that light, eternally full of it, and eternally compassed round with it, and everlastingly reflecting it back again to the fountain of it."[13]

You will *recognize* the ones you love. On earth you only half-recognized them. But in heaven, you will discover rich, wonderful things about the true identity of your husband, wife, daughter, son, brother, sister, or special friends—things that were only hinted at on earth. What's more, you will *know* them like you never knew them on earth. After all, we won't be less smart in heaven; we will be *more* smart. My husband, Ken, will be a thousand times more "Ken" than he ever was in flesh and blood. You will exclaim to your loved one, "Wow, so *this* is what I loved in you for so long!" for you will see him or her as God intended all along.

Until we are there, doing what God purposed for us from the beginning, we will be the caterpillar writhing to be free of the cocoon, to breathe the celestial air. We will feel very much like Moses cocooned away on the back side of a desert, who cried out, "I have become a foreigner in a foreign land" (Exodus 2:22). And just as Moses was becoming in the desert the leader he would eventually be, we are pilgrims becoming in the here and now who we shall be in the hereafter.

So onward we pilgrims tread through this world of time and death, forever seeking the Son. We don't go backward, but "forgetting what is behind and straining toward what is ahead, [we] press on toward the goal to win the prize for which God has called [us] heavenward in Christ Jesus" (Philippians 3:13–14).

Humanity refuses to go in this direction. In an anxious search to fit, people take the world's sextant and try to locate their present position, using all the wrong coordinates: memories of childhood, an old romance, carefree days, songs, power, religion, wealth, or Woodstock. But humanity keeps failing to recognize that it is made in the image of God. Only believers who understand that the coordinates converge in eternity can sing, "This world is not my home."

OUR PLACE *in* TIME

Joni Mitchell won't make it back to the garden. She would do better to sing of God's Son in her quest for not only identity, but for another time. Jesus is the only One who was ever comfortable with His identity, as well as comfortable in or out of time.

One second Jesus was talking with friends on the road to Emmaus; the next He was bypassing the hours required to travel to Jerusalem and appearing there in no time flat. He could materialize one morning on a beach and start a fire and whip up breakfast for His friends. One minute He ate a fish; the next He passed through a wall. Stone walls and unopened doors in the upper room presented no barriers. Time, space, and therefore distance were a cinch for Him. This is *very* interesting, because His ability to move in and out of various dimensions clues us into where time fits in heaven. I don't think heaven will destroy time so much as swallow it up.

Let me explain by using a principle I learned in high school geometry. If we move a dot through time and space, it makes a line—the first dimension. Take that line and move it laterally through time and space, and it becomes a plane—the second dimension. Move a plane through time and space, and we get a cube or some other polyhedron—a cube is the third dimension, and it's comprised of a stack of planes.

And you and I, who are three-dimensional figures, move through time and space—we might consider that a fourth dimension. Each new dimension enfolds the previous ones, plus something more. This means eternity—we might think of it as a fifth dimension—will comprise all the interesting elements of the other dimensions, including time.

Hey, if you get that, you get an A in geometry. You also get the fact that time won't stop in heaven but will be swallowed up. Time will be folded into eternity and lose its distinction, much like egg whites do when they are folded into cream. Or more to the point, like folding one egg white into an ocean of cream. That's how all-encompassing eternity is.

Why is this thing about time so important? Peter Kreeft explains: "God fell in love with us creatures of time, us passing gusts of wind, us passing guests, and invited us into the inner sanctum of the Master of the House forever—all of us, lock, stock, and barrel full of time. How dare we deny Him His heart's desire? It is our heart's desire too."[14] He's right. There's something inside me that time helps define, and I'm not so sure I want to deny it as much as discover all its hidden treasure.

Jesus, having both a divine and human nature, presented a kind of formula for our nature and destiny. The way our resurrected Lord was able to move through time and space is a prescription for our future heavenly experience. Jesus perfectly embodies physical things caught in time, yet spiritual things that exist outside of time. We gusts of wind will one day feel as comfortable as Jesus when it comes to living with a physical *and* spiritual nature.

Bear with me on one more item regarding time, geometry, and dimensions, and we both may get an A+. All this stuff about third, fourth, and fifth dimensions proves just how *interesting* heaven will be.

Let me show you by asking a question: How long would staring at a dot on a piece of paper hold your interest? If you can say five seconds, I'm impressed. But what if you placed a pen on that dot and drew a line to create a two-dimensional stick figure? That's a bit more interesting, but certainly not as provocative as observing a three-dimensional sculpture of that figure, right? If it's a good sculpture, it might hold your attention for a long time.

Now, take it a step further. Because a sculpture is a far cry from being as fascinating as a real-live human being who moves through time and space in the fourth dimension. In fact, you could spend a lifetime getting to know this captivating person. It's a fact that each dimension is more interesting than the previous.

Now carry this little formula through to the fifth dimension, namely, to heaven. All the wondrous things about the previous dimensions will be in heaven, plus a whole lot more. This means heaven will be *extremely* interesting. It will be irresistible, ravishing, intriguing, and at least ten more columns of adjectives. We think *earth* is enthralling with all of its color, glory, and grandeur! The exotic peacock, the perfect hexagons in beehives, the aquamarine of a tropical lagoon, the orangutan that makes us giggle, and the inspiring snowcapped peaks of the Alps are all part of the fourth dimension. And—ta-da—the fifth one is about to be revealed! Our little lesson about dimensions proves that heaven will be far beyond all the beauty of earth combined. Can you now see why Paul says, "No eye has seen, no ear has heard, and no mind has imagined what God has prepared for those who love him" (1 Corinthians 2:9 NLT)?

Who knows what wonders the fifth dimension, and probably many other dimensions, will contain. In eternity everything is just a beginning. No borders. No limits. A. W. Tozer wrote, "How completely satisfying to turn from our limitations to a God who has none. Eternal years lie in his heart. For Him, time does not pass, it remains; and those who are in Christ share with Him all the riches of limitless time and endless years."[15]

Our pilgrimage to heaven is a journey not toward the end of time, but to another kind of time. And time travelers we shall be until we arrive . . . at the beginning.

DISCOVERING UNSEEN REALITIES

This dusty little planet keeps spinning through time and deep, dark space, not realizing that all the while, it is swimming in the ocean of eternity and surrounded by a host of unseen divine realities and divine fulfillments. But we realize it, because as pilgrims "we live by faith, not by sight" (2 Corinthians 5:7). By faith we live on a different plane, in another dimension, at a higher level than the earthly one. By faith the rock-solid world becomes drained of substance and importance, and we see a heavenly meaning behind *everything.*

People who lack faith look at the front range of the Rocky Mountains and assume, in a mechanistic way, that a tectonic plate pushed this way and that, causing a quake and a shifting in the earth's crust, and then—voilà—there appeared Pikes Peak. But pilgrims heading for heaven realize that "in [Christ] all things were created: things in heaven and on earth, visible and invisible, whether thrones or powers or rulers or authorities; all things have been created through him and for him" (Colossians 1:16). He has created invisible things that are just as real—no, *more* real—than the Rocky Mountains. No wonder we praise our Creator!

People who lack faith look at a beautiful cherry tree, shrug their shoulders, and suppose that a seed fell, rain poured, roots sprouted, and a sapling grew, and soon it will be someone's firewood. God, they think, just wound nature up like a clock to let it ticktock on its way. People with heaven-inspired faith, look at the same tree and marvel that literally "in [Christ] all things hold together" (Colossians 1:17). That means *all* things. Right now. This instant. Even buds, bark, and branches. Elizabeth Barrett Browning once wrote:

> *Earth's crammed with heaven,*
> *And every common bush afire with God;*
> *But only he who sees, takes off his shoes,*
> *The rest sit round it and pluck blackberries.*[16]

Those with an earthly perspective assume that the waves of the sea are made up of plain old H_2O, but those with a heavenly point of view believe that every proton on the periodic table of the elements is held together by God, for He is "sustaining all things by his powerful word" (Hebrews 1:3). Let that fact sink in. If God were to withdraw His command, the mountains, oceans, and trees wouldn't collapse into chaos; they would go poof and disappear! God's creation isn't static and inert; it's dynamic and actually in the process of being sustained this instant by His powerful word.

And when it comes to the marvel of the human body, those who have no faith claim we've risen out of slime to the status of *homo erectus*, and they assume that humans draw breath under their own power. But pilgrims with a heart for heaven know differently, "for in him we live and move and have our being" (Acts 17:28). In heaven we will be more human than what our species only hinted of here. We will be more the man or the woman than what our gender only whispered of.

The faith of which I've been speaking imparts heavenly purpose to everything—absolutely everything—around us. This happens to me every Tuesday, Wednesday, and Thursday morning when my artist friend, Patti, helps get me out of bed. Before I get in the van and she sends me off to work, we pause at the opened garage door and take a few moments to observe the day. We look at Mr. Arquilevich's white pine trees across the street—there's usually a cranky crow sitting in the branches. We enjoy the way the spiky tips of the cedar trees lining my side wall have such sharp points—each tip is a perfect vertical aiming above. We admire the way Mrs. Hollander's shrubs are starting to turn color from a silvery green to gold.

The other day Patti commented on a hibiscus bloom, reminding us, "God dreamed up that color! Perhaps just for the sheer fun of it." Pilgrims see His delight in giving us pleasure. Heavenly sojourners see God in everything; they see that every bush they pass on earth's wilderness is a burning bush, afire with God. And with such faith it is truly possible to please Him (Hebrews 11:6).

Heav'n above is softer blue,
Earth around is sweeter green;
Something lives in every hue
Christless eyes have never seen:
Birds with gladder songs o'erflow,
Flow'rs with deeper beauties shine,
Since I know, as now I know,
I am His, and He is mine.[17]

Madame Guyon, a seventeenth-century Christian noble-woman, wrote the following words from a French dungeon, having no hibiscus, cedar tree, sweet green earth, or soft blue heaven to cheer her on:

[The heaven-minded Christian] walks by a simple and pure faith . . . And when this sojourner looks out of his own eyes, he sees things as though he were looking through the eyes of God. He sees his own life, he sees his surrounding circumstances, he sees other believers, he sees friends and enemies, he sees principalities and powers, he sees the whole course of the pageantry of history itself through the eyes of God . . . and is content.[18]

Too Heavenly-Minded?

Don't think such heavenly-mindedness makes us pilgrims no earthly good. Don't pooh-pooh it as if it's looking at the world through pie-in-the-sky, rose-colored glasses. Sojourners who think the most of the next world are usually those who are doing the highest good in this one. It is the person whose mind is only on earthly things who, when it comes to earth, does little good. C. S. Lewis expands on this: "Aim at Heaven and you will get earth 'thrown in': aim at earth and you will get neither."[19]

When Christians realize that their citizenship is in heaven, they begin acting as responsible citizens of earth. They invest wisely in relationships because they know they're eternal. Their conversations, goals, and motives become pure and honest because they realize these will have a bearing on everlasting reward. They give generously of time, money, and talent because they are laying up treasures for eternity. They spread the good news of Christ because they long to fill heaven's ranks with their friends and neighbors. All this serves the pilgrims well, not only in heaven, but on earth, for it serves everyone around them.

A few weeks ago, I went to the Hair and Nail Shoppe to get a haircut. My secretary, Francie, met me at the salon to help me get out of the van and get settled in front of the mirror at the hairdresser's station. As the stylist whipped the plastic cape over me, I glanced around at the other women. Some were sitting under hair dryers and absorbed in *Vogue* magazines. A few women gabbed with their manicurists about the latest shades of red nail polish. Blow dryers whined over the sounds of Neil Diamond on the radio. I looked on either side of me: a redhead in jeans was cracking gum and cutting the locks of the woman to my right, while a short Asian woman with long black hair worked to the left.

What does a pilgrim do in an average, ordinary place like this? (At least average and ordinary for Southern California.) Sojourners look for the unseen divine realities around them. I tried to put myself in the shoes of these women, looking for their "realities"—divorce, dieting, raising children, running for the school board, fighting off alcoholism, and planning the next party. A few professional types in their power suits in for a quick repair on a fingernail were dealing with different "realities"— promotions, payoffs, and executive stress.

Because faith helped me see each woman as precious in God's sight, I knew God had His own divine realities in mind for each woman. I could pray, "Thy kingdom come, Thy will be done, in the Hair and Nail Shoppe as it is in heaven."

So as I sat with my hair all wet, I interceded off and on for each person, setting in motion God's powerful workings in their lives. All because of faith. This is the way ordinary pilgrims make themselves of some earthly good.

And not only through prayer. As I wheeled from the station to wait for my hair to set, I noticed a little girl who was sitting two chairs down, swinging her legs and flipping through a tattered magazine. I asked her what she was reading and learned she was the ten-year-old daughter of the Asian woman. Within minutes, we were engrossed in conversation, me telling her a Bible story, and her explaining the games she enjoyed playing with her best friend. I told the little girl I liked her smile, her friendly manner, and the way she looked past my wheelchair and into my eyes. I also told her about Jesus. For those twenty minutes, I knew I was one heavenly-minded person doing this child real and lasting earthly good.

My husband, Ken, lives like this. He's been fostering a relationship with two young men from Iran who work at the Shell station down the road. Most people are in and out for a quick fill-up, but Ken keeps his eyes open for the unseen divine realities at work in the lives of these two men. We're convinced that time, prayer, friendship, and a Bible in the Farsi language will make a difference. He's one heavenly-minded person looking for ways to do earth some good.

Besides this, pilgrims do battle. The spiritual war raged hot and heavy one year when Ken and I helped chaperone the prom of the public high school where he taught. The early hours of the prom were a great time to connect with students, admire their tuxedos, and wish them well at college. After dinner, though, the lights went out, the music went up, and the ballroom reverted into a wild disco. Ken had to head over to check on the bathrooms;

I tried talking to my dinner partner, but we got tired of screaming at each other. Through the dark and deafening noise, I spotted a senior girl in a skimpy white-sequined dress sitting on her boyfriend's knee. I decided to pray for her. As I stared at her, silently mouthing my prayer, it struck me that although the ballroom was shaking, my prayer was more powerful than the 600-watt Bose speakers angled over the dance floor. A simple intercession was shaking and sending repercussions across heaven, as well as scattering a few demons.

This is how heaven's citizens live while temporarily residing on earth. Heaven tells us that every person, place, and thing has a purpose. This is why "we do not lose heart . . . So we fix our eyes not on what is seen, but on what is unseen, since what is seen is temporary, but what is unseen is eternal" (2 Corinthians 4:16, 18).

HOMESICK *for* HEAVEN

We pilgrims walk the tightrope between earth and heaven, feeling trapped in time, yet with eternity beating in our hearts. Our unsatisfied sense of exile is not to be solved or fixed while here on earth. Our pain and longings make sure we will never be content, but that's good: it is to our benefit that we do not grow comfortable in a world destined for decay.

And so we squirm and writhe, knowing we don't quite fit; "we groan . . . because we do not wish to be unclothed, but to be clothed instead with our heavenly dwelling" (2 Corinthians 5:4). But, oh, what a blessing are those groans! What a sweetness to feel homesick for heaven! What a glorious longing fills my heart to overflowing!

Perhaps you're thinking, *Wait a minute, Joni. I'm not homesick for heaven. I rarely groan and long to be there. I want to, but I don't know where to begin. It's not like I'm absorbed by the things of earth; it's just that heaven doesn't feel like my home yet. Besides that, I don't have a real prayer burden for women at hair salons, girls at proms, or guys at gas stations.*

If this is you, don't panic. If for you heaven is still a glass house on some golden street rather than a warm and loving home, then hang in there. If you find it difficult to muster up a longing for celestial mansions, if you aren't into this pilgrim thing, then perhaps you need to take the focus off heaven as a place.

It's more than that . . . much, much more.

CLIMBING HIGHER

Not far from the farm where I grew up was a stone quarry called Sylvan Dell.

Riding our horses on the bridle path near the quarry, we were careful to stay on the trail. That's because the ground—not twenty feet from the path—dropped into a sheer cliff plunging to the bottom of a deep pit.

Sylvan Dell was a busy, almost frenetic place, filled with noise, hammering, and clouds of dust. Steam shovels and trucks belching diesel exhaust hoisted and hauled huge rocks that became flagstone for the new housing developments springing up near the farm. The quarry was a beehive of motion and clamor, churning out not only flagstone but exquisite quartz crystal as well.

As we rode our horses along the bridle path, we could see sparkling bits of quartz scattered all around. If we rode in the evening, the tiny stones would flash and sparkle in the setting sun. When I was little, I imagined we were riding on diamonds. To my eyes it looked like thousands of gemstones scattered carelessly in the dust.

Now that I'm grown and married, I have a real diamond in my wedding band. And when I take it off to clean it, I occasionally think of those glittery pebbles along our old quarry path. But my diamond is neither dusty nor neglected. In fact, I regularly care for that little stone, scrubbing and scouring it with toothpaste to keep it clean.

Why do I treat it so faithfully? Because I want it to sparkle. I don't want the multicolored fire in the heart of that carefully faceted stone to be quenched or diminished by dirt and dust.

Diamonds, hard as they are, can handle any amount of scouring. And the truth is, so can we. We are jewels that God thinks can take a good scrubbing. He says in Zechariah 13:9, "I will refine them like silver and test them like gold."

God uses our suffering, of course, as part of that shaping, cleaning, refining process in this life. I'm not glorifying the hardships or pain it takes to be a jewel in God's crown, but I am glorifying the God who is reflected on the surface of any smile that's hard fought for through pain and problems.

And what happens as we fit ourselves for heaven's crown, trusting and obeying God in our seasons of loss, disappointment, and pain? What do you know—we become shining jewels in spite of ourselves! All because we choose to trust the Master Jeweler. With precision tools, He scours away any dirt—any cranky, sour, peevish attitude or resentment—and He continues to chip away at us and refine us as we "arise, shine, for . . . the glory of the LORD rises upon [us]" (Isaiah 60:1).

You don't have to endure a half century of pain and paralysis like me. You have your own set of temptations, attitudes, and unyielding habits of the flesh to deal with. And Craftsman that He is, God knows the precise tools to use in your life to cut, cleanse, and refine the diamond that is your eternal soul. Quite frankly, the hurting and hammering won't end until we, like a diamond, reflect the most beautiful light this world will ever see. The apostle Paul called it, "Christ in you, the hope of glory" (Colossians 1:27).

The old quarry is now a lake, flooded from an underground

spring, and our old bridle path is overgrown with brush and foliage. It's a peaceful place these days. Birds flit through the branches of the oaks and hickories, and wind whispers in the leaves. When Ken and I visited a few years ago, it was like a slice of heaven to me, just to feel the serenity. It reminded me of 1 Kings 6:7: "In building the temple, only blocks dressed at the quarry were used, and no hammer, chisel or any other iron tool was heard at the temple site while it was being built." When Solomon was building the temple, God wanted it to be a picture of heaven. So He told Solomon that all the stones for the temple should be dressed at the quarry. All the chiseling and hammering was done at the worksite, not at the temple site.

This world is God's worksite. Earth is His quarry, and it isn't always peaceful and pleasant. We are being mined and refined out of the stone pit of this planet, a place of noise, dust, hammering, sweat, tears, chiseling, and pain. Let's be honest: it *hurts* to be quarried. But God is dressing and fitting *you* for heaven. You are a living stone being built into a holy temple, a "spiritual house," just like it says in 1 Peter 2:5.

Friend, you aren't an ordinary pebble with no purpose. *You* are a living stone in the kingdom building. And Zechariah 9:16 reads, "The LORD their God will save his people on that day . . . They will sparkle in his land like jewels in a crown."

Soon the dust, dirt, and noise will be behind us. God will close the curtain, and something so grand and glorious will happen in the world's finale that it will suffice for all of our hurts.

So bear a bit longer with the hammering, hurt, and disappointment. Yield to the chisel.

And get ready to shine.

"Men and women who have lived wisely and well will shine brilliantly, like the cloudless, star-strewn night skies. And those who put others on the right path to life will glow like stars forever" (Daniel 12:3 MSG).

FIND YOUR TRAIL

1. Ephesians 2:10 reads, "For we are God's handiwork, created in Christ Jesus to do good works." Another translation (NLT) says that we are His "masterpiece." What might that imply about the squeezing, pulling, pushing, and pressure of the circumstances in which you find yourself?

2. In 2 Corinthians 4:7, Paul says that we are clay jars containing radiant, priceless treasure—Jesus Himself! What comfort should that give us when we feel common, ordinary, or even broken?

A HIKER'S PRAYER

Lord Jesus, I need gentle persuasion today. Please reassure me—by Your Spirit who dwells within me—that my worst earthly pains will one day seem like a mere nuisance. I want to picture myself on celestial sod, utterly amazed at the mountain of joy and the forever pleasures accrued by my trustful response to earthly suffering. I want to have no regrets, lamenting, "Why, oh why didn't I trust God more?" Sway my soul, coax my heart, and utterly convince my spirit that trusting You through these trials is worth it.

Five

Heaven Has Our
HEART'S DESIRE

Let your imagination run wild for a moment. Jesus has gone on to prepare a place for us, and each of us is to have a big mansion—no down payment or mortgage to worry about, thankfully—on a golden avenue overlooking acres of fields and flowers. Wow!

Or for you, not "wow."

Perhaps, "Well—that's nice."

When it comes to a glass house on a golden street, you may be tempted to throw a stone through the glass—out of sheer gumption—to see if celestial plate glass cracks. Or maybe you're simply feeling awkward and uncomfortable in God's glittering, golden throne room. For that matter, you're still hung up in this tangle of earthly imagery whenever you picture heaven. You see yourself seated at the wedding feast of the Lamb where, presumably, there's no need for air-conditioning or central heating in the banquet hall. But where do you draw the line in dispensing with the paraphernalia of earth when picturing heaven? If the banquet is to be eaten decently, surely we will need knives and forks. Pots and pans to cook stuff in. Mixers must be somewhere in the background. And who does the dishes? People in hell?[1]

I can understand if these images don't make you yearn for your heavenly dwelling. It's not that you're absorbed by the things of earth; it's just that heaven doesn't *feel* like home. Yet the images painted in the Bible represent something designed to grip our hearts, possess our souls, and call forth a powerful homesickness that makes us want to hurry up and unlock the front door of that mansion of ours.

Wouldn't it be nice to feel nostalgic for heaven that way?

Take a minute to consider a time when you were actually homesick. Not for heaven, but for your earthly home. Remember the aching? The sense of feeling like a stranger in your surroundings?

Boy, I remember it well. I felt like my guts were being ripped out. I bawled when I was a little girl and had to stay at Aunt Dorothy's while my mother had a gallbladder operation. Then there was church camp. I was miserable. And that Thanksgiving when I first moved to California (of course, everyone first feels like a misfit in California).

One of my bouts with homesickness was in Bucharest, Romania. It was the middle of the night, and I knew I was a foreigner as soon as I wheeled into the musty hotel lobby. A single dangling lightbulb cast long shadows over dusty sofas and lamps left over from the fifties. Prostitutes puffing cigarettes hid in the dark corners. From somewhere behind the desk, a radio featured Elvis Presley wailing, "I wanna be your teddy bear." There were bullet holes in the concrete walls. Moths and exhaust fumes filtered in through the open door, and somebody was screaming at a neighbor down the street.

I was tired, hungry, and dirty. There were no ramps for my wheelchair. I didn't fit in the bathroom. I didn't feel at home in the restaurant, where they served tough meat swimming in oil and garlic. Everything about the place—the language, the culture, and especially the pillow on my mattress—made me long for Calabasas, California. It was awful. I know you've felt the same.

Why did Calabasas grip my heart? Was it the sidewalk ramps and curb cuts? Radio stations playing better tunes than Elvis hits? Superior restaurants? Why do I feel I fit in California and not in Romania?

Because home is where your heart is.

This powerful truth needs to be elevated for a moment above the cross-stitched plaques on which we usually read it. Because if "home is where the heart is," then home must be more than the street address where you live. When you get homesick, your heart may tug for your own mattress and pillow, but this doesn't account for that gut-wrenching ache. What makes home is not a place, but who lives there. You feel at home when your heart is nestled near the one you love.

But sometimes, when you least expect it, even the people who make up home aren't enough. Sometimes when you're all tucked in with your own pillow and blanket, with the voice of the one you love close by, another kind of homesickness—a deeper kind—sneaks up on you.

STILL NOT SATISFIED

Fragrant pine branches and the softness of falling snow. Cinnamon-spiced tea and vanilla candles. It was home at its 1957 best. Especially with a Christmas Eve visit from Uncle George and Aunt Kitty, who, when she leaned down to give me a big hug, let me bury my nose in her fox stole scented with Evening in Paris perfume. Together with the rest of the family in the candlelit living room, we sat on the couch and listened to Bing Crosby Christmas music on the radio. It was a quiet time. It was home.

Suddenly, out of nowhere, I was broadsided with homesickness. Good grief, there I was in the coziest of houses, snug on a couch between people I loved, yet mantled with homesickness—a nostalgia for a bigger kind of home. I didn't catch on at first, but I was in the middle of another one of those heavenly longings. It may have been winter and far away from that Kansas wheat field we visited the summer before, but it was the same.

The next morning, that sensitive longing retired in the presence of mundane things, and I became my ordinary self. It was Christmas Day. I shelved my fascination with the strange longing and rushed headlong into my pile of presents. I ripped open the wrapping paper of one gift and asked, "Is there more?" And then another gift, asking, "How many left?" and then after the final present, I whined, "Is that all there is?" What was I looking for? Why wasn't I satisfied?

Throughout the day, I knew I was free to play with my toys, but occasionally I would leave my gifts, go upstairs to my room, and lean on the windowsill to gaze outside. What was I pining after? What did I want?

WHAT DO WE WANT?

When it comes to heaven, we are all children opening a thousand beautiful Christmas presents and asking after each one, "Is that all there is?"

In fact, when it comes to heaven, why don't you make a Christmas list—all the best joys, gifts, and presents that you imagine heaven will offer. Ask your heart the question, "What do you want?" There are no restrictions on the list. The sky's the limit. Would it be beauty or wealth? Fame? Driving a Ferrari?

Now imagine getting it all. How soon do you think you would grow restless? How soon before you would say, "Is that all there is?"

Try another list, a deeper one. Endless talks with Beethoven about scoring music or long chats with Mary Cassatt discussing French Impressionism. Strategizing football plays with Bill Belichick. How about a fit, healthy body for all of you who have disabilities? Running? Dancing? Cooking with Julia Child? Playing the guitar with Eric Clapton? A good conscience, freedom, peace of mind? It might be a few more thousand years before these would bore you, but eventually even they would become ho-hum.

Peggy Lee was on to something back in the seventies when she serenaded us, asking, "Is that all there is, is that all there is? If that's all there is, my friends, then let's keep dancing, let's break out the booze and have a ball, if that's all there is."[2] The song scared me then, and it scares me now. Is there *nothing* that will ultimately satisfy our hearts? Peter Kreeft suggests:

> Can you imagine any heaven that would not eventually be a bore? If not, does that mean that every good thing must come to an end, even heaven? After eighty or ninety years most people are ready to die; will we feel the same after eighty or ninety centuries of heaven? . . . But if . . . we don't want boredom in heaven, what do we want? If heaven is real, what real desire does it satisfy? . . . We want a heaven without death and without boredom. But we cannot imagine such a heaven. How can we desire something we cannot imagine?[3]

We cannot conjure up heaven in our minds because our desires go deeper than what our minds can imagine.

Thankfully, our hearts are always a beat ahead of our minds and bodies. Proverbs 4:23 is not off-base when it says that the heart goes deeper than the mind: "Above all else, guard your heart, for everything you do flows from it." True, the Bible also says the heart is desperately wicked, but that still demonstrates it is the seat of deep passions. Important things happen in the heart. Out of it flow "the issues of life" (Proverbs 4:23 KJV). We may have one foot here and the other in the hereafter, but our heart is often that part of us that tugs at that one foot stuck in the mud of earth, saying, "Get off of the earthly images, would you? Look, here's your other foot anyway. Up here is what you're longing for."

Really? Does our heart have the answer?

Does our heart have something to say in response to this haunting echo?

Can we trust our heart to *really* know what it wants?

When people approached Jesus with a need, it's curious that He often responded, "What do you want?" I've always thought this was an odd thing to say since, first, He could read their minds, and second, their need was often obvious—like Bartimaeus, the blind beggar, for one. But Jesus has His reasons for asking. He urges us to explore our heart's list of wants because He knows we desire something deeper than getting a few surface needs satisfied.

And when it comes to heaven, He knows we desire something more fundamental than pleasure, prosperity, or power. Our heart thinks it's desperate to get back to the garden, or, if not there, then someplace where our innocence and identity are sequestered. Writes C. S. Lewis:

> Our lifelong nostalgia, our longing to be reunited with something in the universe from which we now feel cut off, to be on the inside of some door which we have always seen from the outside, is no mere neurotic fancy, but the truest index of our real situation. And to be at last summoned inside would be both glory and honour and also the healing of that old ache.[4]

HEALING THAT OLD ACHE

When it comes to attempting to heal that old ache, the human heart has had lots of experience. It is restless and raging, trying this and dabbling in that, hoping to find fulfillment, to possess something that will give us innocence, identity, and . . . heaven. Our poor bruised heart, though, does not really want to possess heaven so much as to be possessed by it. It desires not so much pleasure, for pleasure can be exhausted. After we experience it, it's over. Our heart wants something glorious that lasts. For forever? Yes, if it were possible.

What the heart desires is ecstasy.

Ecstasy is that marvelous euphoria in which we totally forget ourselves and yet find ourselves. The dictionary describes it as a state of "overpowering emotion or exaltation," and a sidebar explains that in Greek, *ecstasy* means "to stand outside oneself." But a powerful experience like this can't be defined by a dictionary. To appreciate its meaning, ecstasy has to be experienced.

It is rapturous delight. Intense joy. Pure passion. When it comes to heaven, we want to be overpowered and caught up in something grand and wonderful outside ourselves. We want to be swept up and wrapped up in a joy that weaves itself through every nerve and fiber. A joy that makes time stand still. We want to lose all sense of time and therefore disappointment. Like Elijah in his chariot, we want to be captured and carried away.

This is what our heart wants. This would be heaven without boredom.

I'm convinced that the ecstasy of heaven is not to be found in the halls of a hallowed habitat tucked behind a galaxy where birds chirp and organs play with heavy vibrato and angels bounce from cloud to cloud. An earthly image like this falls flat. It's not even a biblical symbol; it's a syrupy, superficial image.

No, when I allow my Spirit-inspired heart to take over, I get a different picture. Last night I experienced a taste of heaven when I wheeled out to my backyard to look at the full moon. It shone perfectly round and pale white through a sheer curtain of high, thin clouds. A sprinkle of blue stars peeked through the haze, and someone down the street was playing a Chopin melody on a piano.

A warm breeze touched me. A half-forgotten poem came to mind as I strained to see the stars: "They were tiny peepholes in a great black wall with the party lights of heaven streaming through."

For a split second I was in ecstasy. My heart broke for joy, and then . . . it was gone. Whenever we stumble upon ecstasy, our heart knows beyond a doubt that this is *it*. It's a glorious healing of that old ache, even if but for a short moment. Lovers who speak of being "in love" feel it most often. They stumble into love, lose themselves, and then find themselves overwhelmed by something gloriously larger that possesses them. And it's ecstatic.

You know what it's like. You know how it feels. Your heart grows faint and your breathing grows short just picturing the soft eyes and tender smile of the one you adore. Just being in the same room together is a thrill. You ply him with questions just to hear the sound of his voice. And the thought of a kiss? An embrace? You all but melt.

This kind of love, romantic love, is as close as many people get to the healing of that ache. The trouble is, most people forget that romantic love (*eros*), like all the other loves—*storge*, *phileo*, or *agape*—is meant to point us to a greater, more fulfilling joy that enraptures. People cherish the glory they see in their lover, and they forget that the glory is not *in* the one they love so much as it is shining *through* him or her. Most people are blind when it comes to this. They don't realize that all the glory comes from beyond the one being cherished, like a light reflecting in a mirror. They make the mistake of idolizing the one by whom they are smitten rather than reading the cues that keep whispering, "It's not me; it's not in my eyes. I'm only a reminder of something else, Someone else. Quick, who do I remind you of? Here's a hint: I'm made in the image of God."

Most people never take this broad and glorious hint. They forget that the human soul was made to enjoy some object never given but only alluded to. They forget, and so they place in the hands of the one they love the incredible burden of keeping the cup of joy overflowing. They heap on the lover's shoulders the weight of sustaining the ecstasy that only God can carry. The result? They are bitterly crushed when romance fades and the one they adore fails to be God, falling short of keeping them enraptured. And so it's on to the next lover. And the next god. And the next.[5]

With Christians it is different. We are rightfully urged in 1 Peter and elsewhere to "love one another deeply, from the heart" (1 Peter 1:22; see also 4:8). And for good reasons. In the first place, Christians get the hint, recognize the cues, and understand that the person we love is stamped with the image of God. We have the "homing detector," the flight instruments, to help us see that the converging points in eternity *do not* meet in the face of the one we love, but pass through to meet in the face of God. To love one another deeply is to acknowledge that the divine glory that we see in the eyes of another *is* a reflection from beyond. This makes Christian love all the sweeter, and each friend is an open invitation to see Jesus in him or her. As the old song goes, "I see Jesus in your eyes, and it makes me love Him. I feel Jesus in your touch, and I know He cares. I hear Jesus in your voice, and it makes me listen."[6]

What's more, the love that Christians share lasts much longer than any old romance. It lasts longer than a lifetime.

Second, we have a built-in warning system that sounds an alarm if we start to idolize the one we love. It blares, "Wrong coordinates! The points converge not in this face but in God's. Get back on track!" God wants us to learn that human love is a signpost pointing to divine love. We are to learn where love's focus should be, and not act like a puppy dog that wags his tail and sniffs your finger when you're trying to point him to his food. Christians can and should properly read the signs. The one we love is a gift from God and, as a gift, points us to the Giver who is the only One who can provide an overflowing cup of joy, if not occasional ecstasy.

This warning system keeps love—whether it's for our husband, wife, or friend—rightly focused and constantly refreshed.

Third, and most important, when we Christians love each other deeply, we catch a glimpse of that particular facet of God's love that is being cut, honed, and shaped in the life of the one we deeply love. We savor a foretaste of their true identity reserved in heaven; we inhale the fragrance of the heavenly person they are becoming. We see a particular aspect of heaven in them, and we rejoice. And God receives glory—the mirror reflects His image back to Himself, and, we are once again reminded that one day in eternity He will indeed be all, and will be in all (Colossians 3:11).

C. S. Lewis was intimately acquainted with the way humans mirror a higher, more heavenly glory when he wrote, "It is a serious thing to . . . remember that the dullest and most uninteresting person you can talk to may one day be a creature which, if you saw it now, you would be strongly tempted to worship."[7]

For me, this is one of those unseen divine realities. When I look into the eyes of a brother in Christ whom I love or a sister whom I cherish, I can almost see the spiritual being they are right behind their pupils. I also can't help but see their future divine fulfillment: "Christ in you, the hope of glory" (Colossians 1:27). So you know what I do? In my mind, I get out my brush and mix some flesh tones, and then I paint their face. I choose a certain color for the eyes, or I angle my brush for the slant of the cheek. Often I get so engrossed in the face that I forget what's being said. It's interesting that I don't pick the hands or the body. The face is where matter is subdued by the mind; it is where the eyes unveil the lamp that's lit in the soul. And, my, is that person beautiful! I just have to paint them! I hear the heavenly echo in their voice, the haunting in their eyes, and I just have to portray it. As I said in the introduction, it is painters who most often try to capture the echo of heavenly music. And when I see that timeless look in someone's eyes, I head for that art easel in my imagination.

Within our hearts we find a shadow of heaven, especially as we "love one another deeply," for love is an unconscious desire for heaven. We now know what we want. We know the answer to our heart's longing.

IN *the* HEART *of* GOD

What you do find in your heart and what you see reflected in the ones you love is God. He and He alone provides the healing of that old ache. That's why heaven has to be more than a place.

Much, much more.

It must be a Person.

If you need a bit more convincing, then take this test that Saint Augustine gave his students centuries ago. Imagine that God appeared to you and said, "You want heaven? I'll make a deal with you. I'll give you anything and everything you ask. Nothing will be a sin; nothing will be forbidden; and nothing will be impossible for you. You will never be bored, and you will never die. Only . . . you shall never see my face."[8]

Brrrr! Do you feel that chill in your soul? Your heart and mind recoil in unison on this one. Your primordial desire is that you want God more than anything else in the world. As Augustine said, "Thou hast formed us for Thyself, and our hearts are restless till they find rest in Thee."[9]

Yes, your heart's home is in the heart of God. He has placed within you a yearning for Himself, a desire to know Him and understand what He is like. Every soul feels the void and the emptiness until it connects with its Maker.

Like tides on a crescent sea-beach,
When the moon is new and thin,
Into our hearts high yearnings
Come welling and surging in—

Come from the mystic ocean,
Whose rim no foot has trod—
Some of us call it Longing,
And others call it God.[10]

Pleasures and treasures on earth may be sought and not found, but only God comes with the guarantee that He *will* be found: "'You will seek me and find me when you seek me with all your heart. I will be found by you,' declares the LORD, 'and will bring you back from captivity'" (Jeremiah 29:13–14). Hurrah, no more exile! No more strangers in a strange land! God assures us, "I will be found by you."

More specifically, He will be found in Jesus Christ. God illumines our hearts and minds when we sincerely search for the Truth, and He reveals Jesus, the photo image of the Father, who dwells in unapproachable light. Jesus is the source of the haunting echo and the heavenly song. Jesus is God wearing a human face. He is real and not abstract. He invites us to do what we cannot do with the Incomprehensible: He invites us to drink and eat of Him, and "taste and see that the LORD is good" (Psalm 34:8).

All my life long I had a longing
For a drink, from some clear spring,
That I hoped would quench the burning
Of the thirst I felt within.

Hallelujah! I have found Him
Whom my soul so long has craved!
Jesus satisfies my longings,
Through His blood I now am saved.[11]

A. W. Tozer wrote, "That God can be known by the soul in tender personal experience while remaining infinitely aloof from the curious eyes of reason constitutes a paradox best described as 'darkness to the intellect but sunshine to the heart.'"[12] Jesus is sunshine to our hearts. Not just to our logic, but to our hearts. Praise God, we *know* the answer to our hearts' longing. It's Jesus!

The disciples of Jesus, at first, weren't so sure that this person in their midst would fulfill their deepest longings, so one of them— Philip—said, "Lord, show us the Father and that will be enough for us." Jesus responded with these words: "Don't you know me, Philip, even after I have been among you such a long time? Anyone who has seen me has seen the Father" (John 14:8–9).

Our longings are satisfied in Him for "the Son is the radiance of God's glory and the exact representation of his being" (Hebrews 1:3). We can know God—our Father in heaven—if we know Jesus. And knowing Him, as we would desire to know a Lover, is ecstasy. His invitation to "enter into the joy of your master" (Matthew 25:21 ESV) is like stepping into a raft and being carried helplessly along a surging current, spilling over and splashing with joy. Please note that the joy of the Lord does not enter into us, but we, into it. We are enveloped by something larger, something greater than ourselves, a heavenly "in loveness" in which we can do nothing but laugh and enjoy the ride. Jesus smiles, stretches out His hand, and welcomes us into His raft with the invitation, "Whoever loses their life for my sake will find it" (Matthew 10:39).

When we enter into the Lord's joy, ecstasy spills not only into laughter but also into song. A song, like poetry, is more the language of the heart than mere prose. This is why the old hymn writers who were ecstatic about God *always* sang about heaven. I bet Charles Wesley was enraptured when he wrote the fourth stanza to "Love Divine, All Loves Excelling":

> *Finish then Thy new creation,*
> *Pure and spotless let us be;*
> *Let us see Thy great salvation*

Perfectly restored in Thee!
Changed from glory into glory,
Till in heav'n we take our place,
Till we cast our crowns before Thee,
Lost in wonder, love, and praise.[13]

Tears have streamed down my cheeks in church when I've sung that last line. Heaven is a place and also a Person in whom I am lost in wonder, love, and praise. My heart insists that I sing when heaven courses through my veins.

FACE-TO-FACE

Remember when I shared that lovers always focus on the face of the one they adore? And in that face, they find ecstasy, albeit fleeting? Here's a pop quiz for all you romantics: *In whose face do we find ecstasy lasting?* Take a broad and glorious hint from Psalm 27:4, 8:

> "One thing I ask from the LORD,
>   this only do I seek:
> that I may dwell in the house of the LORD
>   all the days of my life,
> to gaze on the beauty of the LORD . . .
>
> My heart says of you, 'Seek his face!'
>   Your face, LORD, I will seek."

And if you need another reminder, listen to Psalm 105:4: "Look to the LORD and his strength; seek his face always." The points of eternity converge in the face of our Savior. Little wonder that I want to paint in my mind, not only the faces of friends I love, but also the face of Jesus.

Since you got the answer to that question, this next one is easy: *What are the correct coordinates for focusing our faith?* The faith of which I have been speaking up until now is only the lens, the spectacles through which "the eyes of your heart may be enlightened" (Ephesians 1:18). The faith I've been describing is only a way of seeing and therefore believing something. But this isn't the whole story.

The correct coordinates on which to focus the eyes of the heart are Hebrews 12:1–2: "Let us run with perseverance the race marked out for us, fixing our eyes on Jesus, the pioneer and perfecter of faith." Jesus is the *unseen divine reality*. Everything will find its future divine fulfillment in Him. "For no matter how many promises God has made, they are 'Yes' in Christ," reads 2 Corinthians 1:20. This means *every* promise. The Pioneer and Perfecter has conceived every unseen divine purpose and has planned its fulfillment to be a part of the wonder of heaven, "so that in everything he might have the supremacy" (Colossians 1:18).

Everything from Pikes Peak to my backyard awash in the glow of a full moon—every bit of beauty here is but a shadow of something far more beautiful there, and "we know that the whole creation has been groaning as in the pains of childbirth right up to the present time" (Romans 8:22). The creation is groaning, longing to be clothed with the beauty its Designer originally intended.

Not only will this dusty little planet find fulfillment, but, God willing, so will the teen in the white-sequined dress too. The Iranian gas station guys. And the little Asian girl in the Hair and Nail Shoppe, for "we ourselves, who have the firstfruits of the Spirit, groan inwardly as we wait eagerly for our adoption to sonship" (Romans 8:23). God will give us much more than the innocence we were groping for back in the garden; He has imputed to us His righteousness. Our future divine fulfillment is alluded to in 1 John 3:2, for one day "we shall be like him, for we shall see him as he is." Completely.

To pursue heaven is to pursue Him. To pursue Him is to find heaven.

It's that simple. If you wholeheartedly pursue Jesus, you can't help but be heavenly-minded and sigh with Psalm 73:25: "Whom have I in heaven but you? And earth has nothing I desire besides you."

Some will say, though, "Wait a minute, there are a lot of other things on earth I desire. Besides, I already know Jesus. I'm saved—have been for fifteen years—but I'm still not gripped by heavenly glories above. I'm still not homesick for heaven."

SET YOUR HEARTS *on* THINGS ABOVE

There's a solution. It may take effort, and it will require commitment. But it can be solved: "Since, then, you have been raised with Christ, set your hearts on things above, where Christ is, seated at the right hand of God" (Colossians 3:1).

This verse is a command. We may think this command isn't as necessary as other mandates in Scripture, but it is. When we consider that the first and greatest commandment is to love the Lord with all our *heart, soul, and mind* (Matthew 22:37), it follows that we should set our *entire being* (that's what "with all your heart and with all your soul and with all your mind" means) on things above.

My heart is the seat of all kinds of appetites and affections. Isn't yours? Our hearts are hungry, not for food, but for a whole range of wrong coordinates. Sometimes the hunger in our hearts gets us into trouble, and we wish we could curb the appetites. You'll be surprised, though, to learn who gives us these desires:

Remember how the LORD your God led you all the way in the wilderness these forty years, to humble and test you in

order to know what was in your heart, whether or not you
would keep his commands. He humbled you, *causing you
to hunger* and then feeding you with manna, which neither
you nor your ancestors had known, to teach you that man
does not live on bread alone but on every word that comes
from the mouth of the LORD.

DEUTERONOMY 8:2--3, emphasis added

The Lord is the one who causes us to hunger. He is the one
who has put within our hearts those yearnings. At first, this seems
odd. Doesn't God know the "hungries" often get us into trouble?

God has good reasons for placing within us a heart that has
such burgeoning appetites. He does so in order to test us and
humble us, to see what is in our innermost being, to see whether
or not we will follow Him. According to Deuteronomy, He places
in our sight a whole range of things that *could* get us off track, but
His purpose is never to tempt, only to test to see if we will zero in
on the right coordinates. Will you succumb to the handsome face
of your best friend's husband, or will you choose heaven? Will
you covet that third Penn International II 50VSW fishing reel, or
will you desire heaven? Will you max out four credit cards on new
countertops, carpet, and furnishings, or will you invest in heaven?

To hunger is to be human, but to satiate yourself on God is
to send your heart ahead to heaven. Feed on Him in your heart,
and you will be yanking that foot out of the mud of earth and
stepping closer to eternity.

I admit it's a constant struggle to set our hearts on things
above. Always and always we want more. And where we place our
citizenship, whether in heaven or on earth, is revealed by those
things we passionately desire. If we desire dull, sensual things of
earth, our souls reflect that dullness; if our desires rise to find
fulfillment in the exalted, in the noble, pure, and praiseworthy,
then and only then do we find satisfaction, rich and pleasurable.

The great in the kingdom of heaven will simply be those who set their hearts on Christ and loved Him more. The great will be those who, having received a "you're off course!" warning from the heart's homing detector, simply got back on track.

That's the way I want to live. When I read, "Take delight in the LORD, and he will give you the desires of your heart" (Psalm 37:4), I want to focus on Jesus, not on my heart's list of desires. Yes, I realize that curbing the appetites of my heart will heighten my loneliness on earth, but I'm convinced I am destined for unlimited pleasure at the deepest level in heaven. I also know that nothing now quite meets the standards of my yearning heart, and this quiet but throbbing ache drives me to anticipate heavenly glories above.

For me, true contentment on earth means asking less of this life, because more is coming in the next.

Godly contentment is great gain. Heavenly gain. Because God has created the appetites in your heart, it stands to reason that He must be the consummation of that hunger. Yes, heaven will galvanize your heart if you focus your faith, not on a place of glittery mansions, but on a Person, Jesus, who makes heaven a home.

SET YOUR MINDS *on* THINGS ABOVE

Colossians 3:1–2 is really a double command. We are not only to set our *hearts* on things above, where Christ is seated, but to "set [our] minds on things above" as well. That's hard. Our hearts hold a shadow of heaven, but not our minds. I can prove it.

Take last week. After Bible study, a few of the women hung around and talked as we sipped coffee. You'd think we would have discussed the apostle's encouragement to set our hearts and minds on things above, right? Wrong. Instead, we discussed the advantages of the new Clean & Easy, Stand-Up toothpaste tube with the convenient cap that flips up or unscrews for ease of use and cleaning. We discussed the sale at the May Company department store, whether or not Excedrin PM is just a marketing ploy to get more people on sleeping pills, and the latest reports of what the First Lady has been up to.

There's nothing wrong or immoral with these thoughts, but it's no surprise that God revealed to Isaiah, "For my thoughts are not your thoughts, neither are your ways my ways . . . As the heavens are higher than the earth, so are my ways higher than your ways and my thoughts than your thoughts" (Isaiah 55:8–9). Somehow, I don't think God stays up at night wondering why they don't standardize electric plugs worldwide.

God's thoughts are higher than ours. And the gap needs to be bridged. My thoughts need to rise to the heavenlies, where Christ is seated. This means more than just thinking nice Girl Scout thoughts that are clean and reverent. "Set your minds on things above" means just that: thinking about things above.

This struck me not long ago when, during a visit to Italy, we explored Rome's St. Peter's Basilica. At the front of the cavernous cathedral, resplendent in Italian marble, mosaics, and statuary, was not the altar I expected to see. Instead, there was a large throne. It was fashioned from dark gold wood and surrounded by gilded clouds and bolts of lightning. Sun streamed through the windows above, washing the entire area in warm and beautiful tones. It sounds gaudy, but actually it was rather inspiring. It was a pleasant surprise, albeit a feeble representation of the real throne of glory in heaven.

After I returned home, I thought about the throne in the Basilica as I laid in bed one night. It was nothing like the throne depicted in Daniel 7:9–10: "The Ancient of Days took his seat . . . His throne was flaming with fire, and . . . thousands upon thousands attended him." I tried to picture the real thing, and it became a wonderful exercise in setting my mind on things above. The earthly imagery of a throne engulfed in flames, to my mind, sounded a bit like *Star Wars*, so I focused on Psalm 22:3 (ESV): "Yet you are holy, enthroned on the praises of Israel." God sits on the throne of our praises.

I decided to *think* about just that: A throne made up of people's praises. Each joint and leg represents "You art worthy" or "You are holy" or "Your name is wonderful" and many more such accolades. I pictured God's delight in reclining on such praises. Not your garden-variety delight, but joy-filled laughter, for "the One enthroned in heaven *laughs*" (Psalm 2:4, emphasis added). Before long, I found myself laughing too, lighthearted and raised with Christ in the heavenly places; then, falling prostrate and praising Him for granting me access to the inner sanctum as well as for the honor of building Him a throne of praise.

Is this all too heavenly-minded? No way! When my mind chews on Scripture, as well as on its symbols of heaven, faith has something to grow on. That time of contemplation helped yank my foot further out of the mud of earth, making my heart airier and my mind purer.

To set our minds on Christ involves not only the contemplation of the divine in heaven, but of the divine on earth. Think about Jesus and Him alone. Contemplate Philippians 4:8, and think about "whatever is true, whatever is noble, whatever is right, whatever is pure, whatever is lovely, whatever is admirable" about Christ. Picture Jesus blessing the little children, and remark to Him in prayer how gracious or kind you think He is, how tender of Him to take a baby out of the arms of his mother, rock him gently, and kiss his cheek. Think about Him tousling the hair of a little boy or taking in His hands the face of a child and blessing her. How noble, how lovely, of Jesus. Think about Him reaching out to heal the bleeding hurt of a woman with a hemorrhage. How tender, how compassionate, of Jesus. Think about Him turning a face of steel toward religious phonies and squaring off against sin. How holy and awesome of Jesus. And how changed you are after thinking such thoughts.

This is where love really builds between you and God. Because remember, He is also thinking about you. Psalm 139:17–18 reads, "How precious to me are your thoughts, God! How vast is the sum of them! Were I to count them, they would outnumber the grains of sand." The Son makes the Father's thoughts available by stooping to make Himself comprehensible to our pea-sized brains. In the Bible, Jesus has given us His thoughts, and we have "the mind of Christ" (1 Corinthians 2:16) when we lay hold of Him and His ideas. Then and only then can we be drawn up to heaven.

HEAVEN *and* GOD . . . GOD *and* HEAVEN

To think about heaven is to think about Jesus. To pursue heaven with your heart is to pursue Him.

I'm not taking literary license. I'm not being lazy with Bible interpretations. Heaven and God are intimately entwined, and the pursuit of one is the pursuit of the other. Matthew 23:22 reads, "Anyone who swears by heaven swears by God's throne and by the one who sits on it." If you swear by heaven, you are swearing by God. Heaven is the place where *God so much is* that you can refer to one or the other and virtually mean both.

Whenever Scripture refers to the kingdom of heaven, it means the kingdom of God. John MacArthur explains:

> It's just another way to express God. In the period between the Old and New Testaments, the Jews never used the name of God . . . because they thought it was too holy to come through their lips. One of the things they substituted for the name of God was heaven. Instead of saying,

"I worship God," they would say, "I worship heaven."
Instead of saying, "Call upon the name of God," they would
say, "Call upon the name of heaven." To enter the kingdom
of heaven is to enter the kingdom of God.[14]

The King of heaven wants us to see this tight connection
between the Place and the Person. When our hearts melt into God's
and when our minds think on Him, Place and Person no longer
seem separated. "God raised us up with Christ and seated us with
him in the heavenly realms in Christ Jesus" (Ephesians 2:6). Amazing! When we understand our position in Christ, we begin to grasp
our position in the heavenly realms. We are *already seated* with
Christ in the heavenly realms. I'm not talking about astral projec-
tion or anything spooky. We're not actually in heaven, the place,
yet. But we *are* in the heavenly realms in that it's a sphere in which
we live under God's rule and His Spirit's blessing. We are under the
dominion of the King of heaven, and that places us in His realm.
The King has come, and His kingdom has as well. The King is in
our midst, and His kingdom is within us. All signs point to there
and here. All signs lead to Him because all signs come from Him.

Use your eyes of faith here. This is another one of those
unseen divine realities. "You have come to Mount Zion, to the
city of the living God, the heavenly Jerusalem. You have come
to thousands upon thousands of angels in joyful assembly, to
the church of the firstborn, whose names are written in heaven"
(Hebrews 12:22–23). Why are all the verbs in the present tense?
Well, as I said in an earlier chapter, it *may* have something to do
with the different kind of time in which heaven exists, or the next
and new dimension of mansions and golden streets. More likely,
God simply wants to get our minds racing and hearts beating with
a present-tense excitement, a right-around-the-corner anticipation
of heaven. Isn't that the way strangers on foreign soil are supposed
to feel about their homeland?

Live in the present tense of heaven, and you will smell the heavenly fragrance of the person you will become. Your life will have intensity and depth. You will sit close to self-scrutiny, understanding that by your words and actions you are doing earth a world of good. Your heaven-inspired faith will give you joy and peace, without parade or noise.

Most of all, you will begin to feel at home. You will begin to see "our Father in heaven" not as the Incomprehensible, but as Jesus sees Him: *Abba*, Father. Daddy.

Home is where Daddy is.

LET'S GO HOME

I like earth. But my heart pumps for heaven.

Calabasas, California, is nice, but it pales in the light of the heavenly realms. Home is pretty good here, but my homing instincts often have me pulling up a chair on the front porch of my mansion to shade my eyes and scan "a land that stretches afar" (Isaiah 33:17). I have a glorious homesickness for heaven, a penetrating and piercing ache. I'm a foreigner in a foreign land, a displaced person with a fervent and passionate pain that is, oh, so satisfying. The groans are a blessing. What a sweetness to feel homesick for heaven, for "a longing fulfilled is sweet to the soul" (Proverbs 13:19).

Never was this symbolized more clearly than at one of our recent Joni and Friends Family Retreats that I helped lead for families of persons with disabilities. After a week of wheelchair hikes, Bible studies, and arts and crafts, I listened as the microphone was passed from family to family, each tearfully sharing how wonderful the time had been. Some talked of meeting new friends. Others, of the games, music, and hikes. A few confessed that they wished the week would just go on and on.

Then little red-haired, freckle-faced Jeff raised his hand. He had Down syndrome and had won the hearts of many adults at the retreat. People had been captivated by his winsome smile and joyful spirit. Everyone leaned forward to hear his words. Jeff grabbed the mike and kept it short and sweet as he bellowed, "Let's go home!" He smiled, bowed, and handed back the microphone. All the families roared with laughter.

His mother told me later that, even though Jeff thoroughly immersed himself in the week's festivities, he missed his daddy back home.

I identify with Jeff. The good things in this world are pleasant enough, but would we *really* wish for it to go on as it is? I don't think so. The nice things in this life are merely omens, foreshadowings, of even greater, more glorious things yet to come. God would not have us mistake this world for a permanent dwelling. It was C. S. Lewis who wrote, "Our Father refreshes us on the journey with some pleasant inns, but will not encourage us to mistake them for home."[15] I'm with him, and I'm with Jeff. It's a good life, but I am looking forward to going home.

I miss my home.

I miss God.

CLIMBING HIGHER

The older I get, the more precious each moment feels. It's the same with friends. In these latter years, they add so much heaven-sent richness to my life. Like my friend Care Tuk. She's been volunteering with Joni and Friends, going full tilt, for many decades.

Just lately, however, she's had to slow down a bit.

Care has endured more than ninety surgeries. Cancer, broken bones, and a great deal of pain will do that to you. But you'd never know it to be around her. The fact is, I can't get enough of this remarkable woman's happy perspective. As she so often says, "It's okay to be *in* pain, but please don't *be* a pain!"

With all of Care's surgeries, she has quite a collection of plates, screws, and rods in her body that are holding things together. (You should see her X-rays!) In keeping with her bright, upbeat approach to life, however, she calls all that unseen hardware her "inner bling."

The most important fact about Care Tuk is that she is a strong believer who holds fast to the grace of Jesus Christ with all her heart, soul, and mind. Her motto? Just ask her, and she will be happy to tell you: "People who live for tomorrow die wishing. People who live for yesterday die discouraged. But people who live for today have no regrets, for they are living the very moment."

There's the heaven-sent richness. Valuing the moments!

We talk about special days or weeks or seasons in our lives. But when you think about it, our whole time on earth is really nothing more than a succession of moments—countless tiny snapshots that, run together, create a motion picture of our pilgrimage. Yes, God is with us through the days and years of our lives, and we're grateful for that. But He is also with us moment by moment. And moments with Him are meant to be savored.

I especially like Care Tuk's words about "no regrets." What does it mean to live with no regrets? In 2 Corinthians 7:10, Paul writes, "Godly sorrow brings repentance that leads to salvation and leaves no regret."

Here's my present take on that verse. To be saved means to realize your low estate before a holy God. You *are* nothing and *have* nothing apart from His mighty grace. That's what godly sorrow is all about. And when you realize how "low" you are, your worldly expectations can't help but be scaled back. Yes, you may endure hardship; yes, you may experience heartache and pain, just like my friend Care Tuk has had to endure. *But a lowly spirit will have you expecting and demanding less of this life.* Why? Because you know that more—so very much more—is coming in the next life. You understand and accept that this "threescore and ten," with all its glitz, glitter, and glamour, is not the only life there is.

For the humble who suffer, salvation leaves absolutely no regrets about this world. None! Z-E-R-O.

If I were to adopt Care Tuk's attitude (and I do), I would say it this way: "I would a million times rather be confined in this wheelchair knowing Jesus than free and on my feet without Him."

Looking back on fifty years of paralysis, fifty years in a wheelchair, I have no regrets, my friend. Absolutely none. *Everything* else, everything this world has to offer *pales*—fades to less than nothing—in comparison to daily companionship with the Son of God and the prospect of being Home with Him forever.

When you see yourself as among the least, the last, the littlest, and the lost, God becomes everything. When you let go of all your winnings, press clippings, and dime-store trophies in this world, you find yourself drawn nearer to the Lord Jesus by the smallest of enjoyments. In other words, you enjoy the moments, the precious moments, that the Lord of time drops like the choicest jewels.

An hour of listening to Bach reminds you of God's majesty.

Sitting in front of a cherrywood fire on a cold night reminds you of His fiery holiness and the warm embrace of His love.

Resting under a tree on a blustery autumn day, watching leaves fly in the wind, reminds you that your body may be falling apart, but that a new season of endless, indestructible life is on its way. You have no regrets about this world because all your hope is in the next, which, by the way, helps you live life better down here on earth.

Just ask my friend Care Tuk. Her life is richer, fuller, deeper, and more meaningful—yes, even after dozens and dozens of painful surgeries. First Corinthians 3:21–23 says it best: "All things are yours . . . the world or life or death or the present or the future—all are yours, and you are of Christ, and Christ is of God."

A sober attitude about this earth leads to repentance, which in turn leads to salvation.

And not a single regret.

Find Your Trail

1. Does feeling homesick for heaven mean you don't value or appreciate the life, family, and home God has given you on earth? Describe the balance the apostle Paul achieved in his statement in Philippians 1:19–26.
2. Read again the incomparable words of John 14:1–4. What does it mean to you that God's Son is right now preparing—providing, getting ready, putting the final loving touches on—a place especially for you?

A Hiker's Prayer

Lord God, You could have taken me immediately to heaven when I first believed, but You wisely chose for me to remain on this side of eternity, plowing deep and plodding ahead through my trials. I realize, dear Lord, that I only have this one chance to be made fit for all eternity. So help me to be Your faithful sower, scattering good seed, breaking up fallow ground, and speaking words of encouragement and salvation to all my family and friends . . . until You come or call for me, Your servant, Your daughter.

Six

Heaven:

THE HOME OF LOVE

When you're in love, waiting is hard.

It's as true now as it was about two thousand years ago. Just ask Judith, a young Jewish maid who lived in the hills beyond Jerusalem, and Nathaniel, who grew up in the city.

For Judith, the romance began long before her betrothal to Nathaniel. She was just a little girl drawing water at a well outside the city walls of Jerusalem when they met, and the smiles between them caught the eyes of their parents. The years passed and their friendship grew, and it wasn't long before the families of both Judith and Nathaniel were happily contemplating a wedding. The parents made the decision, while Judith and Nathaniel freely consented. That was the custom. That was the Jewish way.

The wedding bells started ringing for the two of them when Nathaniel took the first step. Leaving his home in Jerusalem one morning, he traveled to Judith's village to speak with her father about a betrothal. As he approached her home, Nathaniel got sweaty palms—Jewish tradition treated the betrothal as more important than the wedding itself!

He knew there were two things to discuss regarding the

establishment of a betrothal covenant. First, he would ask Judith's father for his daughter's hand in marriage. Then he would negotiate concerning the price to secure his bride, a dowry showing Judith's family that he, Nathaniel, had the means to be able to properly care for her. He loved Judith so much that he was ready and willing to commit a large sum—he and his dad had talked it over, and they both agreed that Judith was worth whatever it took.

That morning, Nathaniel was not disappointed. Judith's father was glad to give his daughter's hand in marriage, and a dowry was agreed on. Nathaniel happily purchased his new bride, and the betrothal contract was sealed. That afternoon, in a formal ceremony, the bride and groom confirmed their covenant by drinking together from a cup of wine. It was a beautiful symbol of their marriage covenant, and Judith's family spread hugs, kisses, and tears all around. Nathaniel and Judith at that point were officially married, a union that could not be dissolved except by divorce. However, it would be a long time before they would actually live together.

Nathaniel, full of happy anticipation, excused himself late that afternoon and traveled back to his father's house. As Judith watched her groom leave, she realized that both of them had a great deal of work to do to get ready. Nathaniel was returning to his father's house to prepare a place for them to live. She knew he would be constructing a nice, large addition onto the home where they would live under the same roof with Nathaniel's family. In all probability, it would be an entire year before her groom would return for Judith and take her into his own house. She could hardly wait!

Weeks and months dragged by for the bride-in-waiting, but Judith knew he'd be faithful to his promise. She busied herself by gathering items for her new house, learning all she could about being a good wife, and daydreaming with her bridesmaids about what married life would be like. In private moments, though, when she was alone in her room, she pined for Nathaniel. The separation between them seemed endless.

One morning, Judith woke up and realized a full year had almost passed. She knew Nathaniel could be coming for her at any time. She also knew he and his groomsmen would come for her at night. That was another custom. Which night? She had no idea and that made it all the more exhilarating. Judith spread word to her bridesmaids to be ready at any moment.

One evening after dinner, as she was leaning on the window-sill, Judith heard a faint voice in the distance. "The bridegroom is coming! He's coming!" This was it! She quickly jumped up and ran to her room to gather the things she had packed, hoping all the while that her girlfriends in the village also heard the shout. Meanwhile, Nathaniel was marching toward the village with his friends in a torchlight procession. As more bystanders recognized the wedding party, they took up the call of celebration and cried out the good news, passing the word from block to block. The bridegroom was on his way!

The bridesmaids caught wind of the warning and hurried to Judith's home to help her get dressed in her bridal garments. In a matter of moments, the torchlight processional halted outside her home. Judith peeked out her window. The oil lamps threw off flashes of light as they dangled at the end of their long wooden poles held aloft. Her bridesmaids heard laughter and singing in the street below and began singing a song of their own. She took one glance in the polished metal mirror before she and her family and friends rushed outside to meet Nathaniel and his groomsmen.

When the bride, dressed in her gown, stepped through the door and onto the street, the wedding party cheered. Amid singing and laughter, Nathaniel took Judith's hand, and together, with the party, they walked by torchlight back to the home of Nathaniel's father, where the wedding guests were already waiting.

When they arrived at the house, Judith and Nathaniel greeted the guests and welcomed everyone to the wedding banquet. The time had finally come for them to consummate their marriage, so after excusing themselves, they moved to the bridal chamber. While the groomsmen and bridesmaids waited outside, Nathaniel took the hand of his beloved, and they entered the chamber alone. In the privacy of the room, he took her into his arms, kissed her, and after a time, laid with her in their bed, fulfilling the covenant they had made the year before. For the two of them, it was ecstasy, and the long waiting period only made their lovemaking sweeter and more pleasurable.

After a while, Nathaniel left the bridal chamber and announced the consummation of his marriage to the other members of the waiting wedding party. Word spread like wildfire to the other guests at the banquet table, and the real feasting and celebration began—there was dancing, music, and laughter up and down the street where Nathaniel lived. During all this time, though, Judith remained hidden in the bridal chamber. This was a Jewish custom as well, known as "the days of hiding." But at the very end of the seventh day of the wedding feast, the groom brought his bride from the chamber with her veil removed. "Please greet the wife of the groom," Nathaniel's friends announced, and everyone wildly applauded the new couple.

The two of them had longed for this moment all their lives, and from that day on, Nathaniel and Judith lived happily ever after.[1]

BEHOLD *the* BRIDEGROOM!

I brushed off the dust from this story depicting the ancient Jewish custom of betrothal, not to give a history lesson, but a spiritual one. The romance between Judith and Nathaniel is jampacked with glorious symbols for you and me as we wait for heaven—symbols that explain why I long for and actually *miss* my Savior.

John 3:29 tells me that "the bride belongs to the bridegroom," and unlike the situation in modern marriages, I'm His possession. My life is hidden with Christ in God (Colossians 3:3), and who I will be won't appear until He appears (1 John 3:2). My life is wrapped up in the One who redeemed me. Redeemed me in *love*. So naturally, I'm going to pine for Him and feel homesick to be with Him, especially when I know where He is and what He's doing: "My Father's house has many rooms; if that were not so, would I have told you that I am going there to prepare a place for you? And if I go and prepare a place for you, I will come back and take you to be with me that you also may be where I am" (John 14:2–3).

These are the words of a Lover. The Lover of my soul. Maybe at one time the meaning in this verse eluded me, but when placed in the context of Him as Bridegroom and me as bride, it has me packing my trousseau and getting ready to go.

My love for heaven is energized because I know how He feels about me: "The LORD will take delight in you . . . As a bridegroom rejoices over his bride, so will your God rejoice over you" (Isaiah 62:4–5). Ponder that for a moment. He *rejoices* over you, and don't say that word like a plaster-of-Paris saint in a less than amazing tone of voice. It's a jump up and down, clench your fist, throw your head back, and yell out loud, "Rejoice!" Jesus is brimming with heartfelt love for you when He says in Song of Songs 2:14, "Show me your face, let me hear your voice; for your voice is sweet, and your face is lovely." This is a God in love.

It's not a matter of sweet words. No. He gave His life as His dowry, and the cross shows me that He and His Father agreed on an exorbitant price. Every time I drink from the Communion cup of wine, I remember the covenant between my Bridegroom and me. And I've promised Him that I will drink from that cup in remembrance of Him until He comes.

Until He comes. That's the hard part.

Waiting is so hard. It's even harder when you love someone.

Like Judith in our story, I sometimes find myself leaning on the edge of time's windowsill, wondering when, oh, when will He return? It makes me wonder about the rest of the marriage symbols between Judith and Nathaniel. Do the shouts in the city street represent the shout of the archangel heralding the coming of Christ, the Bridegroom (1 Thessalonians 4:16)? Does the sudden arrival of the wedding party mean that He will surprise us and come like a thief in the night (Matthew 24:42–44; 1 Thessalonians 5:2)? Jesus drops a hint in Revelation 16:15 when He says, "Look, I come like a thief! Blessed is the one who stays awake."

What about the bride and His groomsmen waiting in the street? Is this a symbol of the Lord rapturing us from our homes and meeting us in the clouds? For "the dead in Christ will rise first. After that, we who are still alive and are left will be caught up together with them in the clouds to meet the Lord in the air" (1 Thessalonians 4:16–17). There are some who say that the wedding feast of the Lamb will be celebrated during the seven years of tribulation, and that just as the groom brought out his bride after her seven "days of hiding," so, after the seven years of tribulation, Christ will return with His bride to crush His enemies and set up housekeeping on earth. Is this the meaning behind these symbols?

I don't know. And I don't need to know. My responsibility as the betrothed is to be prepared and to wait.

BE PREPARED . . . *the* PURE *and* SPOTLESS BRIDE

I want to see the face of my Savior.

You may not realize it, but you do too. We want to see. We find it hard to rest comfortably in a relationship—with God, with anyone—when we cannot see the face of the one we adore. This is why I paint in my head the faces of friends I care deeply about, especially when I'm away from them. The essence of who they are is held in the eyes, the mouth, the smile. The face is the focal point of personality.

When it comes to brides and bridegrooms, full intimacy comes between a man and a woman face-to-face. And when the Bible speaks of longing for God, it speaks in terms of wanting to see His face. The psalmist pleads with God to "make his face shine on us" (Psalm 67:1), and "do not hide your face from your servant" (Psalm 69:17). Ultimately, "I will be vindicated and will see your face; when I awake, I will be satisfied with seeing your likeness" (Psalm 17:15).

To hold the gaze of God is to find love, acceptance, and satisfaction.

Well, yes and no.

There is still a thick shield between God and us. We cannot see what our heart longs to, because as 1 Timothy 6:16 reads, God "lives in unapproachable light, whom no one has seen or can see." When Moses pressed hard on God to see His face, he would have been glad to use thick glass coated with a UV blocking layer and grab a quick peek at God through his fingers. But no. Moses was only permitted to glimpse the back side of God's glory, for the Lord warned, "My face must not be seen" (Exodus 33:23). God didn't say this because there was nothing for Moses to see; He said it because He knew that His light would kill. No one can see God and live. The Lord's glorious radiance would have snuffed Moses out in a nanosecond.

Even when Isaiah "saw" the Lord, high and exalted on a throne, he did not behold God's face. He only glimpsed the periphery of the radiance of God. The sight threw Isaiah so deeply into despair over his sin that he cried out, "Woe to me! . . . I am ruined! For I am a man of unclean lips" (Isaiah 6:5).

Sin is the problem. Sin is more than a thick shield between

God and us, and acknowledging our stockpile of iniquities won't make it go away. No amount of confessing our sin will help us see God. That's backward. We don't have a clue as to the heinous nature of our sin until first we glimpse God's radiance, and then the words come tumbling out, "Woe to me!" The closer the apostle Paul got to God, the more he cried out, "I am . . . the worst of sinners" (1 Timothy 1:15–16). I used to think this was a pompous, grandstanding thing for Paul to say, but not anymore. It's the cry of a saint sensitized to sin.

Our longing to see God is a longing, whether we know it or not, to see our sins exposed and to be cleansed by God Himself. Just as guilt will cause a child to hide in shame from her daddy's face, our deepest desire is to be clean, to be free, to be transparent before the Father. And it won't happen until we see His face.[2]

This is a living paradox. We desire to see the face of God, but we cringe at seeing the face of God. We are cleansed from our sin, but we're still unclean. We're justified before God, but we've got miles of sanctification to go before we sleep. We're in the household of God, but not home yet. Our eyes have been opened, but we can only see through a glass darkly. It's frustrating!

This is partly why it's so hard to muster strong feelings about heaven. You and I going to heaven for a wedding? Our wedding? "'His bride has made herself ready. Fine linen, bright and clean, was given to her to wear.' (Fine linen stands for the righteous acts of God's holy people.)" (Revelation 19:7–8). Righteous acts! We glance down and see stains and smudges all over our wedding gown, which, by the way, is tearing at the seams and missing a few pearls and fasteners. Little wonder we cower at seeing our Bridegroom.

It's one thing to have funny feelings about a heavenly wedding, but I actually felt this way at my earthly wedding.

On the morning of the big day, my girlfriends placed me on a couch in the church's bridal salon to dress me. They strained and grunted to shift my paralyzed body this way and that, fitting me into the huge, cumbersome wedding gown. When I got back into my chair, an usher brought word that the guests were seated, and it was time to line up. We reached the glass doors of the church, and as they swung open, the blast from the organ gave us goose bumps.

Just before the wedding march began, I glanced down at my gown. I had accidentally wheeled over the hem, leaving a greasy tire mark. My bouquet of daisies was off-center on my lap, since my paralyzed hand couldn't hold them. No amount of corseting and binding my body could have given me a perfect shape. The dress just didn't fit. It was draped over a thin wire mesh covering my wheels, but it still hung clumped and uneven. My chair was spiffed up as much as possible, but it was still the big, clunky gray thing with belts, gears, and ball bearings that it always was. I was not the picture-perfect bride you see in magazines.

My last bridesmaid began her walk up the aisle, and I inched my chair closer to the last pew to catch a glimpse of Ken at the front. I saw him waiting at attention, looking tall and stately in his formal attire. He was craning his neck to look down the aisle. He was looking for me. My face grew hot, and my heart began to pound. Suddenly, everything was different. I had seen my beloved. How I looked no longer mattered. All that mattered was getting up to the front of the church to be with him. I *could* have felt ugly and unworthy, except that the love in Ken's face washed it all away. I was the pure and perfect bride. That's what he saw, and that's what changed me.

Years later, somewhere around our tenth wedding anniversary, I asked him, "What were you thinking on our wedding day?"

His answer delighted me. He said, "I woke up so early that morning so excited that I would see you in your wedding gown. And even though I knew there would be hundreds of people in the church, I knew my eyes would be for you only. In fact, I'll never forget that wonderful feeling when I saw you wheeling up the aisle in your chair. You looked so beautiful."

"You mean you didn't think much about my wheelchair? My paralysis?"

He thought for a second and then shook his head. "No. Really, I just thought you were gorgeous."

Our entrance into heaven may be something like this. One look from God will change us. And earth is just the dress rehearsal.

True, we presently see stains and smudges all over us, and we cower, thinking, *He'll never see anything lovely in me.* But still we ache to see Him. And so, like Judith in the story, we live in hope. God *will* find us, and He will *not* always remain beyond our sight. Our Bridegroom desires that I long and look for Him "while we wait for the blessed hope" (Titus 2:13). And "all who have this hope in him purify themselves, just as he is pure" (1 John 3:3).

It's called "being prepared," all you saints in your torn bridal garments, and "it teaches us to say 'No' to ungodliness and worldly passions, and to live self-controlled, upright and godly lives in this present age, while we wait for the blessed hope—the appearing of the glory of our great God and Savior, Jesus Christ, who gave himself for us to redeem us from all wickedness and to purify for himself a people that are his very own, eager to do what is good" (Titus 2:12–14).

One day He will come for us and look into our eyes. We will hold His gaze. And all the stains and smears of sin will be purified out of us just by one searching of those eyes. It will be more than we dreamed of, more than we longed for.

> *Here, O my Lord, I see Thee face to face;*
> *Here would I touch and handle things unseen;*
> *Here grasp with firmer hand eternal grace,*
> *And all my weariness upon Thee lean.*[3]

Waiting *on* the Groom

We may be separated from our Savior, but that's no reason to sit around killing time until He comes. Jesus explains what brides ought to be doing while they're waiting for their groom:

> "At that time the kingdom of heaven will be like ten virgins who took their lamps and went out to meet the bridegroom. Five of them were foolish and five were wise. The foolish ones took their lamps but did not take any oil with them. The wise ones, however, took oil in jars along with their lamps. The bridegroom was a long time in coming, and they all became drowsy and fell asleep.
>
> "At midnight the cry rang out: 'Here's the bridegroom! Come out to meet him!'
>
> "Then all the virgins woke up and trimmed their lamps. The foolish ones said to the wise, 'Give us some of your oil; our lamps are going out.'
>
> "'No,' they replied, 'there may not be enough for both us and you. Instead, go to those who sell oil and buy some for yourselves.'
>
> "But while they were on their way to buy the oil, the bridegroom arrived. The virgins who were ready went in with him to the wedding banquet. And the door was shut.
>
> "Later the others also came. 'Lord, Lord,' they said. 'open the door for us!'
>
> "But he replied, 'Truly I tell you, I don't know you.'
>
> "Therefore keep watch, because you do not know the day or the hour."
>
> MATTHEW 25:1–13

Foolish virgins are those who think that the betrothal is just one big insurance policy guaranteeing them access to the wedding without lifting a finger. Wise virgins understand that the betrothal carries with it big responsibilities. They recognize that they are married, albeit separated from the groom, and so they act like they're married. They watch. They work. They stay awake. They see the kingdom of heaven as the "pearl of great price" (Matthew 13:46 KJV), as the treasure in the field that *quickly* must be purchased and plowed. They don't sit around on their hands. They pour their heart into the marriage covenant. In short, they act like they are loved and in love.

Before you rush to assume this means *doing* something, remember it means *being* someone. To wait is an occupation of the heart. To wait on the Lord is to love Him with spirited affection. With passionate delight. To wait on Him is to fix your eyes on those converging points in eternity—namely, Jesus.

The Bridegroom invites us to know Him this intimately. Jesus presses home the point about this intimacy more dramatically in John 6:53–57:

> "Very truly I tell you, unless you eat the flesh of the Son of Man and drink his blood, you have no life in you . . . For my flesh is real food and my blood is real drink. Whoever eats my flesh and drinks my blood remains in me, and I in them. Just as the living Father sent me and I live because of the Father, so the one who feeds on me will live because of me."

It's no wonder language like that sent the disciples scattering! But remember, He's talking about a spiritual intimacy.

Now, I'm not one to pipe up and call myself a wise virgin. But, thankfully, I've got some help with this thing called spiritual intimacy. My wheelchair. I get exhausted after a long day of sitting in my chair, and so most evenings, I have to lie down at around 7:30. Lying in bed paralyzed, I have all the time in the world to wait on Jesus, to focus the eyes of my heart on those heavenly coordinates. My bedroom is a quiet place and softly lit. No music. No TV. The clock ticks. If there's a breeze outside, the wind chimes tinkle. Our dog, Scrappy, may curl up at the edge of the bed and softly snore. It's a place where I cannot *do* anything; I can only *be*. And I choose to be the wise virgin who pours my love into the marriage contract.

I press my heart heavenward, maybe singing to the Lord a song just for His listening pleasure. Perhaps this one.

> *Loved with everlasting love,*
> *Led by grace that love to know;*
> *Gracious Spirit from above,*
> *Thou hast taught me it is so!*
> *Oh, this full and perfect peace!*
> *Oh, this transport all divine!*
> *In a love which cannot cease,*
> *I am His, and He is mine.*
>
> *Things that once were wild alarms*
> *Cannot now disturb my rest,*
> *Closed in everlasting arms,*
> *Pillowed on His loving breast.*
> *Oh, to lie forever here,*
> *Doubt and care and self resign,*
> *While He whispers in my ear*
> *I am His, and He is mine.*[4]

After an hour or so, Ken will amble in from the living room to check on me. Sometimes he gets concerned that I'm alone, or I should say, *choose* to be alone. But he doesn't need to worry. He finds me striving to "boast all the more gladly about my weaknesses," to "glory in my infirmities" (2 Corinthians 12:9 NIV, KJV), grateful that the paralysis affords me such a luxury. Many women I know are doing a second load of laundry at 7:30 p.m. or putting their third child to bed. Their healthy bodies are at work, while my paralyzed one is forced to rest. What else is there for me to do but wait?

Lying there looking at the ceiling, I squint my eyes of faith to focus on unseen divine realities and their future fulfillments. I set my heart and mind on heavenly glories above. And in the face-to-face intimacy I enjoy with my betrothed, I take Him at His word and "eat the flesh of the Son of Man and drink his blood" (John 6:53).

Feeding on Him? I "taste and see that the LORD is good" as I ingest favorite Scriptures (Psalm 34:8).

Drinking His blood? "[His] love is more delightful than wine" in praying and singing hymns (Song of Songs 1:2).

Within a short time, I'm in the heavenly realms, picturing myself kneeling on the throne room floor where Jesus is seated. Maybe one evening, I'll imagine I'm His handmaiden at the foot of His throne to serve. Another evening, His fellow intercessor kneeling next to Him by the rock in Gethsemane. On another night, His sister. Sometimes His child. If I'm under spiritual attack, I go to Him as the Captain of the heavenly hosts.

When I relate to Him as the Lover of my soul, I'll quote out loud to the Lord a few verses from Song of Songs. I'll tell Him He's the Rose of Sharon, the Lily of the Valleys, the Fairest of Ten Thousand. "Let my Beloved lead me to the banquet hall, and let His banner over me be love. May He strengthen and refresh me, for I am faint with love. His left arm is under my head, and his right arm embraces me" (Song of Songs 2:4–6, my paraphrase). And then maybe I'll sing another hymn of love.

> O Love that wilt not let me go,
> I rest my weary soul in Thee;
> I give Thee back the life I owe,

> *That in Thine ocean depths its flow*
> *May richer, fuller be.*
>
> *O Light that followest all my way,*
> *I yield my flickering torch to Thee;*
> *My heart restores its borrowed ray,*
> *That in Thy sunshine's blaze its day*
> *May brighter, fairer be.*[5]

This intimate spiritual union is a two-way street. Occasionally, I'll picture Jesus whispering something to me that the Father said to Him in Isaiah 42:1: "Here is my servant, whom I uphold, my chosen one in whom I delight." Earth is one big premarital session for heaven, and although Jesus wants us to love Him passionately and single-heartedly, He more than matches it with a love that is pure and fervent.

On some evenings, He's the Father running down the trail to embrace me, the prodigal, before I can speak a word of contrition. At other times, He is the crazy-generous Farmer showering on me a full day's wage when I've hardly worked. On other evenings, He is the Master forgiving me, the sinful woman, before I realize I've done anything wrong. He's the King lavishing on me a banquet when I'm not even aware I'm malnourished. This is a God whose love for us is so active and so strong that most would say He was mad.[6]

WHILE *the* GROOM IS ABSENT

It is "heaven" to know Jesus this way. And I mean that literally. Because "this is eternal life: that they know you, the only true God, and Jesus Christ, whom you have sent" (John 17:3). Eternal life *is* knowledge of God. When we deepen our relationship with Jesus, we get a head start on our eternal life here on earth. Heaven is already happening to us.

However, there are two kinds of knowledge. Just ask the wise and foolish virgins. If you asked a foolish virgin, "Do you know Jesus?" she would probably say, "Yes, I gave my heart to Him at a retreat in 1962, so I'm saved and going to heaven." She's reading a statement right off her insurance policy.

What would the wise virgin reply? "Yes, I know Jesus. I've given my life to Him, and I enjoy such wonderful intimacy with Him in prayer and studying His Word. Let me tell you about some of the experiences we've shared together . . . what kind of Person He is. Honestly, spending time with Him is the highlight of my day."

The apostle Paul knew Jesus and *knew* Jesus. He wrote in Philippians 3:8–9 of "the surpassing worth of *knowing* Christ Jesus my Lord, for whose sake I have lost all things. I consider them garbage, that I may gain Christ and be found in him, not having a righteousness of my own that comes from the law, but that which is through faith in Christ—the righteousness that comes from God on the basis of faith" (emphasis added). Here Paul is talking about his position with God. He's talking about God doing something for him on His ledger, pronouncing, "You are forgiven." It's wonderful to have this kind of right standing (that's what righteousness means), but there's more to knowing Christ than this.

There's the bride/bridegroom thing. It's a different kind of knowledge. Paul touches on this deeper knowledge in the next verse when he writes, "I want to know Christ—yes, to know the power of his resurrection and participation in his sufferings, becoming like him in his death, and so, somehow, attaining to the resurrection from the dead" (Philippians 3:10–11).

I love those words "to know." Scholars explain that in this passage "to know" implies learning about someone through a deep, personal experience. It's the same sort of intimacy alluded to in the book of Genesis, where it says that Adam "knew" his wife, Eve (Genesis 4:1 KJV). Theirs was a deep, personal experience.

A level of relationship that went beyond head knowledge. It is also a physical illustration of the level of spiritual intimacy that God desires with us, something even deeper and more personal.

God covers His end of the relationship when He positions us in Christ. Positioning is His responsibility in factoring us into heaven. We cover our end of the relationship on earth as we experience the depths of knowing God. Experiencing is our responsibility in fitting ourselves for heaven. It's what wise virgins do while they wait.

Right now, the Bridegroom is absent. But, oh, I can hardly wait for the day when I break through to see the face of Jesus and once and for all *know* Him: To pass through Him, be united with and receive Him, "to participate in the divine nature" (2 Peter 1:4). To be overpowered, enraptured, and caught up in Someone grand and glorious beyond myself. To be swept and wrapped up in His joy. To no longer be hidden with Christ in God, but be turned inside out, and appear face forward with Him. For time to stand still in a heavenly ecstasy in which I forget myself and yet find myself. Like Elijah's chariot carrying me away to the wedding banquet! To embrace the words of the psalmist:

> As the deer pants for streams of water,
>   so my soul pants for you, my God.
> My soul thirsts for God, for the living God.
>   When can I go and meet with God?
> PSALM 42:1–2

THE WEDDING GIFT

It's common practice for newlyweds to give gifts to each other. I suppose when I finally see my Savior, my gift to Him will be whatever bits and pieces of earthly obedience I've done as evidence of my love. He said, "Anyone who loves me will obey my teaching" (John 14:23), and I'm sure these bits and pieces will sparkle and shine like diamonds.

But what will He give to us?

He will give the joy of heaven. Isaiah 35:10 is a peek at the gift: "They will enter Zion with singing; everlasting joy will crown their heads. Gladness and joy will overtake them, and sorrow and sighing will flee away." To have my head crowned with everlasting joy is one of those earthly images that looks askew, but I don't mind. People caught up in ecstasy don't worry about such things. Suffice it to say, it's a gift. A crowning gift.

Look at the gift with me for a moment. Joy is an aspect of the fruit of the Spirit (Galatians 5:22), and that means it has in it the essence of eternity. When joy grips us, it always appears new, like a surprise. At the same moment, it seems ancient, as though it had always been there. Joy always has in it a timeless, eternal element. Pleasure and happiness may come and go, but joy seems to remain. Happy feelings have nothing of that air of eternity about them that joy has. That's because joy, in its essence, is of God. He is the Lord of joy.

Whether experienced in shadow here or in light there, joy is dynamic. It cannot stay stagnant or bottled up. Joy flows. Actually, it overflows. It floods back to God in gratitude, out to others like a fountain, and rushes through our own hearts in a torrent. This is why people weep for joy. We human beings, all finite and compacted, cannot contain the overflow. We are too small for how big joy is, and so we must weep. This also explains why joy breaks our heart. For like love, joy cannot be contained. Remember when I said that lovers "in love" find themselves enveloped by something gloriously larger than themselves? Joy is the same. It will *overtake* us, Isaiah 35:10 says. This will be heavenly ecstasy.[7]

As an artist, I see something else about joy. It happens whenever I look at a certain painting that hangs on the office wall opposite my desk. It is a rendering of Mary the mother of Jesus and Gabriel the angel. Whenever my mind is at rest and my desk clear of work, I find myself drawn into that painting. I lose myself in it.

This may happen to you, if not with a painting, then with a great symphony. You're sitting in a symphony hall with your eyes closed, and then the music swells and surrounds you, and before you know it, you are lost. You're gone. You have become one with the sounds of the orchestra. There are times when I have listened to Robert Schumann's *Romance* in F-sharp major, op. 28, no. 2, that I would say I've "become one" with the music. A friend once discovered me crying in my art studio as I was listening to *Romance.* I looked up with wet eyes and said, "This music is me." Have you experienced this? A Brahms melody that breaks your heart? A Mendelssohn concerto that fills your eyes with tears?

Or if you're a left-brained person who isn't into art or music, how about that exhilarating moment when, during the 1980 Winter Olympics, the US hockey team pulverized the Russians? Whether in front of the television, in the stands, or on the ice, we all became "one" in the euphoria of victory. My strong, he-man father once told me about a time he was standing on the edge of a cliff overlooking Yellowstone Falls. With tears in his eyes, he described how he became one with the deafening roar of the water.

If you have experienced any of this, it's an inkling of the joy that will overtake us when we take just one glance at the Lord of joy. We will lose ourselves in Him. We will become one with Him. We will be "in Christ" (2 Corinthians 5:17) and will have "put on the Lord Jesus Christ" (Romans 13:14) at the deepest, profoundest, and most exhilarating level. The Lord's wedding gift to us will be the joy of sharing totally in His nature without us losing our identity; no, we will receive our identity. Thanks be to God for His indescribable gift!

This is why heaven is more than just a place of pleasure and happiness. If it were simply that, heaven would be boring. Pleasure is always seeking satisfaction. Happiness is finding satisfaction. But whether reached through pleasure or happiness, there is still something inert about satisfaction. It's a little too "still." That's why joy is satisfaction that is always moving. It bursts beyond pleasure and happiness; it calls for rejoicing out of sheer generosity. It is the real energy of praise. If we are to be praising God for all of eternity, which we will do, then joy will be the dynamic. Peter Kreeft writes:

> This state of mind is like light: traveling faster than matter, yet making no sound, no perturbation. Pleasure is the restless mind moving along a line, never reaching the end. Happiness is the mind resting at the end. Joy is the mind eternally moving *at* the end, motion at a point: the cosmic dance. Pleasure is moving; happiness is still; joy is moving while still. Pleasure is like work, happiness is like sleep, joy is like play. Pleasure is like action, happiness is like rest, joy is like contemplation. Pleasure is a river running to the sea; happiness is the full, calm sea; joy is a great and glorious storm on the sea.[8]

I like Kreeft's comment that "joy is like play." It happened to me earlier this year at another one of our Joni and Friends Family Retreats.

One night during the evening ice cream social, I powered my chair over to little red-haired Nicole in her wheelchair. Her friend Tiffany was there, along with Rachel, who was standing next to her in her leg braces. After we commented about the ice cream, we were soon playing a game of tag. Wheelchair tag. Before long, a kid in a walker joined us with his sister. And then a child with Down syndrome and her brother. Weaving in and out around the legs of the adults, we giggled and screamed as our foot pedals clunked together, bumping and bouncing like bumper cars.

After the ice cream began to melt, John, our retreat director, looked at his watch and began to gently invite the families to head back to their cabins. But we kept playing. We were so caught up in the game that I lost all track of time. Only after we waved good night to each other, exhausted, did I realize that our time together had been like heaven. It was a taste of heaven because of the play and the joy and the sense of timelessness. Right before I entered my cabin, I looked up to the stars and thanked Jesus for the sneak preview of heaven's joy. I had to smile at His answer from Matthew 19:14: "Let the little children come to me . . . for the kingdom of heaven belongs to such as these."

As I lay in bed that night, the entire experience of joyful play kept echoing. *The kingdom of heaven belongs to giggling, happy, carefree children.* I kept thinking and straining my ears—or was I trying to open the eyes of my heart—to hear or see more. I *knew* there was much more than just play in that experience. I had touched a moment of great happiness and wisdom. I didn't realize it then, but I had touched eternity in time. Months later, I came across another quote by Peter Kreeft that nailed it:

> When we touch eternity in time, we smell the salt air of the sea even here, far upstream in time's river. Whenever we touch wisdom or love, we swim in salt water. Earth is God's beach, and when we are wise and loving, we are infants splashing happily in the wavelets of "that immortal sea." But when we are spiritually full grown, we will buoyantly plow its breakers of wisdom and be borne up by its bottomless depths of love. Boredom, like pain, will be remembered only as a joke when we are "drenched in joy."[9]

THE BRIDEGROOM COMETH!

And so now we wait. We wait for our Bridegroom. With the psalmist, we say, "I wait for the LORD, my whole being waits, and in his word I put my hope. I wait for the Lord more than watchmen wait for the morning, more than watchmen wait for the morning" (Psalm 130:5–6). We lean on the windowsill of eternity, look to the sky, and whisper, "Come quickly, Lord Jesus, come quickly."

Oh, *when* will He come?

And every once in a while, when our heart grows weary of waiting, the Lord revives us with snatches of joy, such as the kind I experienced at that Family Retreat. It is a preview of the joy that will overtake us when, finally, "the Lord himself will come down from heaven, with a loud command, with the voice of the archangel and with the trumpet call of God, and the dead in Christ will rise first. After that, we who are still alive and are left will be caught up together with them in the clouds to meet the Lord in the air. And so we will be with the Lord forever" (1 Thessalonians 4:16–17).

And it will all happen in the twinkling of an eye.

Before we realize it, if we are blessed to be living at the time of His return, we will find ourselves in the embrace of our Savior at the wedding supper of the Lamb. Heaven will have arrived. The Lord's overcoming of the world will be a lifting of the curtain of our five senses, and we will see the whole universe in plain sight. Life and immortality will no longer be dim thoughts, but vivid and strikingly real. At first, the shock of joy may burn with the brilliant newness of being glorified, but in the next instant, we will be at peace and feel at home, as though it were always this way, that we were born for such a place. At that moment, earth will seem like a half-forgotten dream, pleasant enough, but only a dream.[10]

I imagine great multitudes of people rushing from jungles of roses, down banks of violets, pulsing with light and songs of birds and the voices of angels.

"Are all here?" someone will shout.

There will echo, "Yes, we are all here!"

Now, enjoy an unseen divine reality. Rev up your heart and picture yourself taking a seat at the wedding supper. Open the eyes of your heart and marvel at the crystal-clear glory, the dazzle of light that just *is*. The Holy City, the new Jerusalem, sparkling like a prism. And a banquet hall resplendent with banners and color and stunning with jewels and light and joy-filled music. The celebration will kick off with a loud and resounding "Hallelujah! For our Lord God Almighty reigns. Let us rejoice and be glad and give him glory! For the wedding of the Lamb has come, and his bride has made herself ready" (Revelation 19:6–7).

As you pull up a chair to the banquet table, take a look at what's on the menu:

> On this mountain the LORD Almighty will prepare
>   a feast of rich food for all peoples,
> a banquet of aged wine—
>   the best of meats and the finest of wines.
> On this mountain he will destroy
>   the shroud that enfolds all peoples,
> the sheet that covers all nations;
>   he will swallow up death forever.
> The Sovereign LORD will wipe away the tears
>   from all faces;
> he will remove his people's disgrace
>   from all the earth.
>   The LORD has spoken.
>   ISAIAH 25:6–8

There's no mistaking. This is a real banquet. And a specific one too. They won't be serving bologna or Spam. It won't be USDA-approved meat; it will be "the best of meats." And the beverage selection will not be Kool-Aid or cheap wine, but "aged wine . . . the finest of wines."

I get a charge just thinking about it! I wonder who will sit next to me or across from me. I glance down the table, and there's my friend, Verna Estes, mother of seven, swapping baby stories with Susanna Wesley, mother of seventeen. There's Verna's pastor-husband, Steve, getting the lowdown on Romans 6 from the apostle Paul. There's Moses toasting Martin Luther. Billy Graham doing a do-si-do with a Sunday school teacher. My husband, Ken (whose lifelong ambition was to fly an F-14 fighter), cornering astronaut James Irwin. Saint Augustine giving a bear hug to that jungle missionary who labored long and hard, unknown and unnoticed. At the other end of the table, Fanny Crosby is doing harmony on one of her hymns with the widow who faithfully played the rickety piano at the nursing home every Sunday. As for me, as soon as I see my friends who spent years getting me up in the morning—Carolyn, Francie, Judy, Jay, Bev, and Irene—I jump up and grab a platter of meat. I just can't wait to serve them something.

Then I'll look up, and walking toward me will be Dad. And Mother. He'll give me his ole thumbs-up and a wink; my mother will start giggling. Before you know it, we'll break into uncontrollable laughter. We will laugh and cry with the kind of tears that never flowed on earth. We will wipe our eyes and try to stop, and then we'll crack up again, crying and laughing and pointing at everybody. "Look at this! Can you believe this? We're here! They are here! I knew it was true, but not this true!"

Since we always sang together as a family on earth, I'm sure we'll break into song right there around the table, harmonizing through our tears.

When we shall say good-bye to earth
We'll gather with the family round the throne,
We will burst with joy at our Father's welcome
"Glad to be at home!"
We'll praise the Father; praise the Son,
We'll praise the Spirit three-in-one,
We will celebrate that on this date
"Forever" has begun![11]

Now stop the music. Stop the moving picture and let's retrace an earlier question. Will there be plates, knives, and forks at the Lamb's wedding banquet? Will someone be back in the kitchen, shuffling pots and pans to cook stuff in? Will there be mixers and trash compactors? And what about the meat? Certainly there won't be slaughterhouses in heaven! Will people from Arab lands use their fingers to eat? Will people from Asian lands use chopsticks? Will people in hell do cleanup duty?

These questions seem ridiculous now. In light of the glorious celebration, who cares? I'm sure it'll be made plain. All I care about is that it is real.

A real streamers-and-confetti celebration that death has died.

A real ticker tape parade announcing victory over sin.

The whole earth will join in the party and "will go out in joy and be led forth in peace; the mountains and hills will burst into song . . . and all the trees of the field will clap their hands" (Isaiah 55:12). Christ will open our eyes to the great fountain of love in His heart for us, beyond all that we ever saw before. It will hit us that we, the church, are His bride. Not just individually, but together. United. One with each other, and one with Him. Suddenly, our joy is multiplied a millionfold.

Most poignantly, when we're finally able to stop laughing and crying, the Lord Jesus will really wipe away all our tears. And then, we'll join hands around the banquet table, and "in that day

[we] will say, 'Surely this is our God; we trusted in him, and he saved us. This is the LORD, we trusted in him; let us rejoice and be glad in his salvation'" (Isaiah 25:9).

And the party is just beginning!

CLIMBING HIGHER

When I wrote my book on heaven in 1995, I'd only been married for thirteen years. Now with more than thirty-five years behind me, the whole bride-bridegroom way of looking at heaven glows with so much more richness and depth. Those thoughts came to mind recently when I heard John Piper speak about the love that Jesus has for us. In his talk, he quoted Isaiah 62:5: "As a bridegroom rejoices over his bride, so will your God rejoice over you."

Just for a moment try to wrap your mind around that thought.

Jesus loves you in the same way a bridegroom rejoices over his bride.

In other words, when the Bible talks about God's love toward us, it's not like a reluctant judge who shows kindness to a criminal whom he finds despicable. *"Okay, I'm dismissing charges against you. Now please get out of my sight. I don't want to see you in this courtroom again."* No, it's not like that at all. It's like a brand-new husband who shows uncontainable affection to his beautiful bride.

Sometimes we joke about newlyweds and say something like, "Oh, there you go, the honeymoon's over!" Everybody knows very well that a man and a woman can't possibly sustain the passion and level of intense affection they experienced on their honeymoon. You know what I mean—exchanging tender glances over a candlelight dinner, enjoying long moments holding hands and not even talking, laughing, and hanging on each other's every word.

Sooner or later (usually sooner), the bubble will burst; feelings will be bruised; and husbands and wives will settle into a more realistic world—a world where there will be arguments, disappointments, and conflicts between the two.

That's how it is with us.

But that's not how it is with God.

He makes it clear that His joy over you is like a bridegroom over a bride. But somehow, the honeymoon never ends! He doesn't mean it starts out that way and then fades.

Piper insists that God really is talking about honeymoon intensity, pleasures, energy, excitement, enthusiasm, and enjoyment. God seeks to impress upon us—to reach us at the deepest level—that He rejoices over us with all His heart.

These truths must have dawned on David at some point, when he penned: "How precious it is, Lord, to realize that you are thinking about me constantly! I can't even count how many times a day your thoughts turn toward me. And when I waken in the morning, you are still thinking of me!" (Psalm 139:17–18 TLB).

In Jeremiah 32:41, the Lord says, "I will rejoice in doing them good . . . with all my heart and soul." And then there's Zephaniah 3:17, where it reads, "The LORD your God is with you, the Mighty Warrior who saves. He will take great delight in you; in his love he will no longer rebuke you, but will rejoice over you with singing."

Don't you love it that the honeymoon never ends when it comes to Jesus and you?

Even in heaven. *Especially* in heaven.

Remember, God is infinite in His power and wisdom and creativity. And that leaves no room for boredom or drifting interest and affections for the next trillion ages.

Love like that is undeniable. Irresistible. Always exhorting and wooing us to His side. You can't help but feel the magnetic pull, as well as the passion. Who in the world wants to refuse—or even casually respond to—love like that? Such love demands an equal response, one of heavenly hunger and communal craving. *I desire You, Jesus.* "*Strengthen me with raisins, refresh me with apples, for I am faint with love*" (Song of Songs 2:5).

Friend, we are His ransomed bride; we have captured His heart. And may our hearts be captured with a honeymoon devotion.

A lasting desire for Him.

FIND YOUR TRAIL

1. Look up Revelation 2:4–5 and 3:15–16. We know that our Lord's honeymoon love toward us never changes, but what do these verses say about what can happen to our love for Him if we don't stay vigilant?
2. Read the tender conversation between the resurrected Lord Jesus and Peter in John 21:15–19. Peter was still feeling crushed because he had let the Lord down. How did Jesus specify that Peter could show Him love? In what specific situations could this apply to you today?

A HIKER'S PRAYER

Lord Jesus, I do love You. But too often it seems like the pain and pressures of daily life draw my focus away from You. Sometimes I just feel empty. I reach for You, and it seems like You are busy in another galaxy, somewhere far, far away. Lord, these are times when I remember and repeat Your promises, just like a bride remembers the long-ago vows of her groom. Thank You that You are the very definition of faithfulness, and that Your Word is true and constant, even when I am not. Restore my heart and rekindle my love. I ask it in Your strong name.

Seven

AT HOME WITH
Our King

This is how it will be.

> *Holy, holy, holy! all the saints adore Thee,*
> *Casting down their golden crowns around the*
>   *glassy sea;*
> *Cherubim and seraphim falling down before Thee,*
> *Who wert, and art, and evermore shalt be.*[1]

Above all, it will be Christ's coronation day.

I'm thrilled that we will enjoy the marriage supper of the Lamb, with its feast of rich foods and the finest of wines, and we will delight in our reunion with loved ones. And yes, it will be exhilarating to reign over angels and rule the earth, with new bodies to boot. But I have to keep remembering it will not be *our* celebration; it will be *His*.

I could never dare keep those crowns for myself. Could you?

We will press in line with the great procession of the redeemed passing before the throne, an infinite cavalcade of nations and empires, age following age—Europe, Asia, Africa, North and South America, all standing shoulder to shoulder, the people of the islands of the seas in one happy parade, generations of the redeemed from both before and after the cross, all carrying their diadems before God Almighty.

Then as Jesus rises from His throne before this great host, all crowns are lifted, all chimes ringing, and all hallelujahs hailing until the vocabulary of heavenly praise is exhausted. We will press our crowns against our breasts, look at one another, and say, "Now?"

"Now!" all will shout. Together we will raise our voices, not in four-part harmony, but perhaps in twelve-part, with the twenty-four elders as "they lay their crowns before the throne" (Revelation 4:10–11), and sing:

> *Crown Him with many crowns, the Lamb upon His*
> *throne:*
> *Hark! how the heavenly anthem drowns all music*
> *but its own!*
> *Awake, my soul, and sing of Him who died for thee;*
> *And hail Him as thy matchless King through all*
> *eternity.*[2]

If, indeed, we are given literal crowns, make no mistake about it—the diadems will be His. The judgment seat of Christ may have been center stage where Jesus showered praise on the believer, but all of heaven will turn the spotlight on the Lord to give Him back the glory. The universe will bow its knee and hail Jesus as King of kings and Lord of lords when He raises His sword in victory over death, the devil, disease, and destruction.

In a breathless moment—an infinite moment—we will comprehend that the whole plan of redemption was merely the Father's way of securing for His Son . . .

- a bride
- a family

- an army
- an inheritance

But the crowning purpose of His plan will be to secure for the Son a grand chorus of eternal worshipers.

This is what I was made for. This is the answer to all the times I asked on earth, "Why has God chosen *me*? Why not someone else?" The response is simply, *I am the Father's gift to the Son.* Ephesians 1:11–12 will then make perfect sense, for "in him we were also chosen . . . in order that we . . . might be for the praise of his glory." I will be the flashing and iridescent gift for the Son whom Zechariah admired: "They will sparkle in his land like jewels in a crown. How attractive and beautiful they will be!" (Zechariah 9:16–17).

This explains why I feel so beautiful when I sing that old Sunday school song. I *like* the idea of being a jeweled gift for Jesus:

> *When He cometh, when He cometh*
> *To make up His jewels,*
> *All His jewels, precious jewels,*
> *His loved and His own.*
>
> *Like the stars of the morning,*
> *His bright crown adorning,*
> *They shall shine in their beauty,*
> *Bright gems for His crown.*[3]

Earth was one big diamond mine in which I was chiseled from the dirt, cleaned, polished, and fitted for a King's crown. Can you now understand why I want to win as many crowns as possible while on earth? True, greater rewards will enhance my service in heaven, but they will also magnify the glory Jesus will receive. The more crowns, the merrier God's praise. My motive in gathering a truckload of diadems is not to hoard them, but to have more to cast at Jesus' feet.

You and I were chosen to praise Him. It's that simple. What a shame that on earth we made it so complicated.

In the early days of my paralysis when I first learned about heaven, I zeroed in on it because it was the place where I would receive new hands and feet. Heaven was the place I'd be freed from the pain, and so it became an escape from reality. A psychological crutch. At times, heaven was so me-centered that I felt as though the whole point of it was to get back all it owed me, all I had lost. And so heaven became a death wish.

Time passed, and with it I gained a little more spiritual maturity. It gradually dawned on me that the Day of Christ would be just that . . . the Day of Christ, not the day of Joni. Glorified hands and feet, as well as reunions with loved ones, began to look more like fringe benefits compared to the honor of simply being on the invitation list to the coronation party.

You'll agree. The privilege of casting your crowns at the feet of Jesus will be enough of an honor. Ruling the earth and reigning over angels, becoming pillars in God's temple and co-heirs of heaven and earth, are almost incidental. What we become, receive, and do in heaven won't be the highlight of heaven. To be there and to be "for the praise of his glory" (Ephesians 1:12) will be enough.

It will be Jesus' day.

Christ's Coronation Day

We should have known it all along. But it never sunk in. Oh, we understood it on paper, but how often did we live—really live—with the focus off ourselves and fixed on Christ as King of kings? It takes heaven to force us to fully comprehend what should have been plain on earth all along. If only we had stopped and read—really read—that "the God who made the world and everything in it is the Lord of heaven and earth" (Acts 17:24).

Jesus is the Lord of heaven and earth.

We said it in our prayers and sang it in our songs, and we would have sworn we believed it with a capital B. But it never really clicked for us. That's because "we" kept getting in the way. All those years when earthly trials hit hard, we burned rubber in our brains trying to figure out what it meant to us. How problems fit into God's plan for us. How Jesus could be conformed in us. Everything was always "for us." Even Sunday worship service focused on how we felt, what we learned, and if the hymns were to our liking.

Why, oh why, didn't we take the hint from Acts 17:24 and switch our attention off us and onto Him? Why didn't we appreciate that God gave every trial, heartache, and happiness to show us something about Himself?

That we might appreciate His grace?

That we were being polished for the praise of His glory?

That we might see that everything fit together in order that we might know Him?

We always marvel that God shows an interest in us, but in heaven it will be clear that every earthly thing happened so that we'd show an interest in Him. In every trial, happiness, and heartache, God wanted us to think about Him. We will finally be convinced that the One whom we lauded with our lips as King truly did have supremacy in all things.

His kingdom came.

His will was done, on earth as it is in heaven.

His word went forth and accomplished His purposes.

He was sovereign Lord over all.

While on earth, you never could have convinced us. We acted more like His kingdom sort of came, but not really. We behaved like His will was done, on earth as it is in heaven, mainly to benefit our jobs and relationships. And whenever we talked about heaven, it was more along the lines of an eternal playground where we would receive lots of new toys while God, like a granddaddy, would nod and smile to see us enjoying ourselves.

What a shame that on earth we acted as though we did God a big favor by accepting Jesus as Savior! We pitied Jesus because His reputation could never quite be vindicated. We felt sorry for God because it seemed like His justice was never quite served; in fact, at times we were embarrassed for our "King" as we scrambled to defend Him over earthly holocausts and horrors. Jesus never appeared to flex His kingly muscles and thus never got credit, much less glory.

We weren't the only shortsighted ones. Even the disciples had a small-minded view of God. They too failed to recognize the King in their midst. Occasionally the fog lifted from their thinking, and once, toward the end of Jesus' ministry, they rose to a heavenly perspective of their King and said, "Now we can see that you know all things." For a brief moment, their focus was off the kingdom on earth and fixed on the kingdom in heaven. It was a rare flash of revelation, and Jesus was moved enough to exclaim, "Do you now believe?" (John 16:30–31).

Those words of Jesus rip at my heart. All Jesus wanted from us was, at last, that we would believe. So why were our times of drastic obedience and absolute trust only flashes, brief moments, of illumination? Why did we always have such a hard time acting like Jesus was King?

THE KING WHO WON
AGAINST ALL ODDS

Perhaps because on earth, He never acted like a king.

Or at least not like one would think a king should act. Jesus, however, had a good reason for cloaking His majesty under the robe of weakness, shame, and humility. It has to do with His glory in heaven. When the Father designed the plan of salvation, He initiated a scheme that would ultimately bring the highest and brightest glory to His Son, the King of the cosmos. It was a plot that almost reads like an adventure story.

The plan was put into effect when the evil villain Lucifer enslaved the citizens of the kingdom of earth through treachery and deceit. He usurped the authority of the rightful Ruler and set up his own rival government. The good Ruler sent His most skilled servants to try to recapture the occupied territory, but with few exceptions, the villain seduced and defeated them. Finally, the Ruler sent His only Son, the rightful Prince, to invade Lucifer's territory, set the captive subjects free, and retake the kingdom under the family banner.

But the battle tactics of the Son were odd, to say the least. In fact, the manner in which He fought seemed to ensure defeat. At one point, when Lucifer had the Prince pinned, the Son merely yielded to the deathblow. All appeared lost, and the people's hearts fainted in despair. Little did they realize that the best and final part of the plan was just about to be set in motion. It was called the resurrection, and it was the only battle tactic that could deliver the killing blow to the enemy and his hordes of evil rulers.

Now any struggle between a hero and the bad guys is interesting enough, but when the hero is disadvantaged, a new element is introduced. Now the hero is in far more danger and appears to have less chance of winning. But if in his weakness he overcomes against all odds, he ends up twice as much the hero. When weak heroes outmaneuver strong villains, the victory is awe-inspiring.

And so the Prince of Peace, the Lamb who let Himself be slain, will be glorified, not because He employed brute force against Satan, but because He didn't.

THE KING WHO WON
through WEAKNESS

There's another aspect of the Father's plan that positions His Son as less than kingly, yet guarantees Him greater glory. It involves defeating the strong villain by using his own dark powers against him.

It's kind of like judo.

My husband, Ken, could tell you all about it. Every once in a while, he gets into his martial arts mode and starts jumping around the living room like a cat on catnip, pouncing helter-skelter, punching the air with his fists, and kicking toward the ceiling with the side of his foot. I always watch with distracted feminine interest.

Ken tells me that judo has its uses. It's the art of using the power of your enemy to defeat him, and although Ken may appear passive and even weak in a judo match, the secret is simply to wait for that moment when the opponent's full strength can be used to defeat him. When my husband is attacked, he simply judos his assailant and sends the guy flying over his shoulder.

Jesus appeared passive and weak. People kept looking for His diadem. We kept hoping He would behave as a monarch should and make the lives of His subjects happy, healthy, and free from trouble. But Jesus had other plans for earth—plans that involved greater praise for the believer and glory for Himself.

He kept doing judo. Especially against the devil. And most specifically at the cross. At the exact moment the devil thought he had Christ cornered and pinned down in defeat, he unleashed his full satanic fury to finish Him off. But it was Christ's weakness and vulnerability that enabled Him to judo Satan into slitting his own throat.

James Stewart, the Scottish theologian, put it this way:

> The very triumphs of His foes . . . He used for their
> defeat. He compelled their dark achievements to subserve

His ends, not theirs. They nailed Him to the tree, not knowing that by that very act they were bringing the world to His
feet. They gave Him a cross, not guessing that He would
make it a throne. They flung Him outside the gates to die,
not knowing that in that very moment they were lifting up
all the gates of the universe, to let the King come in. They
thought to root out His doctrines, not understanding that
they were implanting imperishably in the hearts of men the
very name they intended to destroy. They thought they had
God with His back to the wall, pinned and helpless and
defeated: they did not know that it was God Himself who
had tracked them down. He did not conquer *in spite of* the
dark mystery of evil. He conquered *through* it.[4]

Something glorious happened when the world's worst murder
became the world's only salvation. When the cross, a symbol
of torture, became a symbol of life and hope, it meant triple
the glory.

Jesus ends up triple the hero in heaven because He won using
weapons of warfare that were spiritual, and not carnal. His triumph was assured using divine judo. He won using perfect timing
and patience. "At *just the right time*, when we were still powerless, Christ died for the ungodly" (Romans 5:6, emphasis added).
He won through waiting, yielding, and submission. Philippians
2:7–9 reads like "The Basic Principles in Martial Arts" because
the weaker that Christ became, the greater was His victory, and
the greater the victory, the more glorious the honors: "He made
himself nothing . . . he humbled himself by becoming obedient to
death—even death on a cross! Therefore God exalted him to the
highest place and gave him the name that is above every name."

If we pitied Christ's life on earth or felt badly that His justice
seemed aborted, we wasted our time. If we were embarrassed for
His sake over so much senseless suffering, we would have done

better to take a few lessons in the martial arts. Jesus *did* flex His muscles as King on earth; it's just that our unskilled eyes, hearts, and minds weren't trained to see it. He wore a crown; it just wasn't the crown we expected. Not one of gold, but of thorns.

Up in heaven, we may be tempted to smack our foreheads and exclaim, "Oh bother! How did we miss it?" But there will be no room for remorse. We won't berate ourselves for not having seen it. No, our King of kings will be too gracious to allow us such regrets. It will be obvious why His medals of monarchy were hidden. It was all engineered to help us exercise faith, develop trust, and demonstrate obedience, as well as to teach us timing and patience, waiting and yielding. The King overcame the cross so that we might have power to parlay a bullying devil and thus accept our thorns, share our burdens, and carry our own crosses, while all the time turning tragedy into triumph and heartaches into victories.

With good grace, Jesus will not scold us for being so me-centered. He will assure us He knew how we were formed and remembered that we were but dust (Psalm 103:14). We will realize that on earth we were worse than we thought, but the Lord's grace went deeper than we thought, and so in heaven we will do better than we thought.[5]

The Lord Jesus will be sloppy with His kindness, letting it spill out and splash over everything. Even our regrets. And *that*, dear friends, will compel us to love, praise, and rejoice in Him all the more. At that point, God's glory in heaven will open up exponentially to the hundredth power.

I get so happy for Jesus when I picture this moment. For He will show Himself as He is, no longer the weak and suffering servant, but the Mighty Sovereign of time and space. His reputation will be vindicated. He will receive all the credit due Him, plus triple the glory. Most of all, His justice will be served.

And it won't look very nice. At least to some.

THE GREAT *and* TERRIBLE
DAY *of* THE LORD

All this stuff about weakness and humility grates on the nerves of some people. They don't buy a God who would let Himself be mocked, kicked, and spit on, all for the sake of justice. Especially justice on their behalf. How dare this weak, powerless God assert that they need to be saved—and from their sin, no less!

On earth, they pushed their own kind of justice. And first on their agenda was to defame and defrock Jesus. Setting themselves up at the center of their own moral universe, they thought they had the power to put God on trial. They arraigned and indicted Him, accused and banished Him, as some impotent, third-rate deity. They kicked Him out of school classrooms and erased His mark from the public square. Profaning His name, they neutered God and tamed Him so He would bless their lusts and passions.

But in heaven, the record will be set straight. God will vindicate His holy name and dispense His pure and perfect justice. For a great many people, it will be terrifying.

What a shock when they behold this Jesus whom they tried to shove back into a Sunday school room! Horror will strike their hearts as the scene in Revelation 19:11–16 unfolds, and they'll weep.

> I saw heaven standing open and there before me was a white horse, whose rider is called Faithful and True. With justice he judges and wages war. His eyes are like blazing fire, and on his head are many crowns. He has a name written on him that no one knows but he himself. He is dressed in a robe dipped in blood, and his name is the Word of God. The armies of heaven were following him, riding on white horses and dressed in fine linen, white and clean. Coming out of his mouth is a sharp sword with which to

strike down the nations. "He will rule them with an iron scepter." He treads the winepress of the fury of the wrath of God Almighty. On his robe and on his thigh he has this name written: KING OF KINGS AND LORD OF LORDS.

These symbols aren't clunky at all; they're frightening! As an artist, not only could I not paint it, but I would never want to. Eyes like blazing fire? A robe dipped in blood? This is no senile Benevolence that drowsily wished human beings well while they were on earth, a God to be pitied or to feel sorry for. This is the great and terrible Lord, the consuming fire Himself, the God described by Isaiah: "See, the LORD is coming with fire, and his chariots are like a whirlwind; he will bring down his anger with fury, and his rebuke with flames of fire. For with fire and with his sword the LORD will execute judgment on all people, and many will be those slain by the LORD" (Isaiah 66:15–16).

This is not a pretty sight, for "it is a dreadful thing to fall into the hands of the living God" (Hebrews 10:31). The same mouth that spoke peace and reconciliation will one day emit the sharp sword of judgment. The same eyes that glowed with compassion will one day blaze with fire. Is this the Rose of Sharon, the Lily of the Valleys, my Bridegroom? Yes, this same Jesus into whose loving hands I first fell is the dreadful living God.

Lover and Avenger? He is perfectly one and the same. He is altogether loving in His justice, and just in His love. And because He is perfect, His justice is pure.

HOW WILL IT FEEL *on* THAT TERRIBLE DAY?

Once in heaven, we will know in every fiber of our being, beyond a shadow of a doubt, that whatever the Judge declares about us is true. As He says we are, so we are. No more, no less. Maybe we will even realize, in a dim, hazy way, that this was our actual deep-down self on earth all along. If the Judge rules that we are righteous in Christ, then, "Hallelujah! I knew it all along." If He declares us unrighteous, wicked, and steeped in selfishness, then, "Curse me! I knew it all along." The self-evident truth about you or me will be clear to everyone.

This fact is especially humbling to believers. Remember when I said that Christians will not have their sinful past replayed before everyone like some awful R-rated movie? Don't worry, I'm not throwing you a curveball. It's true we won't have to bear that shame because God has separated us from our sin as far as the east is from the west.

But if it were not so, if, say, our secret closet sins *are* exposed, I'm convinced there's not a single righteous soul who would protest. You and I would wholeheartedly agree with the Judge and say, "Jesus, You are absolutely right. Your justice is perfect. I was a manipulator on earth, always fudging the truth and faking it with everybody around me. That was my true, deep-down self all along!"

In fact, I can picture myself tugging at His robe and saying, "Wait, Jesus, I have some other ugly hidden things about me that I want you to expose. I want everyone to know how vast and far-reaching Your grace was to me. I don't want to cover up my sins. I want everyone to see how rotten to the core I was, so they know how deeply cleansing was Your grace!"

Jonathan Edwards takes this thought a step further when he says that sinners "will have so much the more admiring and joyful sense of God's grace in pardoning them, that the remembrance of their sins will rather be an indirect occasion of joy."[6]

If—and I say if—our gruesome pasts are to be replayed, it will serve to bring God greater glory for such great grace.

That's why, as strange or absurd as it may seem to us now, we won't cringe or cower on the great and terrible day of the Lord.

Oddly, we will rejoice. This sounds insane, because our human sense of compassion abhors the idea of justice being executed with unbridled sound and fury. On earth, justice is served as prisoners are quietly escorted from their cell on death row to chambers where hushed groups of people sit behind soundproofed windows and, without emotion, watch death happen.

But not in heaven.

There, judgment is full of emotion.

Smack-dab in the middle of the apocalypse, as bowls of wrath are being poured out with smoke and fire, we are found singing and rejoicing while watching the judgment. This parenthesis of incredible praise is squeezed between the rage of God in Revelation 18 and what looks like Armageddon at the end of Revelation 19. In the mighty praise chorus of 19:1–10, we are numbered among the angels, the elders, and "the roar of a great multitude in heaven shouting: 'Hallelujah! Salvation and glory and power belong to our God, *for true and just are his judgments*'" (emphasis added).

Why will we happily agree with Jesus as He treads the winepress of the fury of the wrath of God Almighty? Will it be because the tables will finally turn on the bad guys? No. We will accompany the judgment with choruses of praise because we will love purity and hate the perniciousness of evil. We will desire truth deeply and despise lies and wickedness. With perfect minds and devout hearts, we will joyfully accent all of God's judgments with a hearty "Yes!" And we'll do it as He's treading His grapes of wrath.

The Day of Christ will be a great and terrible day. Great for the righteous, and terrible for the unrighteous. C. S. Lewis reminds us, "In the end that Face which is the delight or the terror of the universe must be turned upon each of us either with one expression or with the other."[7]

I'm just grateful that Scripture speaks of that time as only "a day." It may mean the Great Judgment will be swift. After all, writes Lewis, "There are only two kinds of people in the end: those who say to God, 'Thy will be done,' and those to whom God says, in the end, '*Thy* will be done.' All that are in Hell, choose it."[8]

For all the people who insisted, "My will be done!" God will not dissuade. He will no longer strive with them, either by pointing to His glory in creation or by preaching to them the gospel. For those who turn their backs on Christ, there is no heaven.

"ALL THAT ARE *in* HELL, CHOOSE IT"

Yes, there is a hell.

It's unthinkable to talk about heaven without at least mentioning hell. Please note I didn't refer to it as "heaven's counterpart." Heaven has no counterpart. It has no opposite. Just as Satan is not God's opposite (for the devil is merely a created being—and a fallen one at that!), neither does heaven have an opposite. In the vastness of God's infinite, as well as cleansed and purified, universe, hell may end up being only a speck. A trash heap. A garbage dump.

Outside of Jerusalem, the Holy City, there was a junkyard where the Jews took their garbage to burn. In earlier times, pagan tribes, and wayward Jews themselves, had used this area called *Gehinnom* for performing rituals and sacrifices; that's why God's people considered it to be just a place fit to set fire to their waste. They ended up calling it *Gehenna*, and that became the biblical term for hell.

The actual hell will be the trash compactor of the universe. Peter Kreeft writes:

> God makes no garbage, but we do; and a good cosmos
> must eventually purify itself of spiritual garbage like egotism,

hate, greed, cowardice, or lust . . . We can even rejoice that it exists, for we should want our spiritual garbage burned away, if we do not identify ourselves with that garbage. If we do, *we* are burned eternally . . . God cannot allow that garbage into heaven; and if we do not want to throw it away, if we clutch our garbage so close that we become garbage, there is only one place for us.[9]

Hell will not pollute the purified universe, nor will it be a festering boil in the side of the new heaven, an ugly sore spot that forever seeps and demands someone's attention. It may well be too small for that. I don't mean hell will be smaller than heaven in terms of population statistics, but in terms of its importance in the new heaven and new earth. Nobody pays much attention to smoldering junk heaps.

Since I brought up the subject of numbers, however, I'm reminded of Jesus' words in Matthew 7:13–14: "Enter through the narrow gate. For wide is the gate and broad is the road that leads to destruction, and many enter through it. But small is the gate and narrow the road that leads to life, and only a few find it." No doubt about it. The world, for the most part, chooses the path to hell. Not many choose Christ and His heaven.

But I wonder, will hell have greater numbers than the repentant residing in heaven? What about the redeemed who number more than the grains of sand on the beach or stars in the sky? Revelation 7:9 claims there is to be a multitude in heaven that no one can count.

There's no contradiction between Jesus' words in Matthew and His words in Revelation. C. H. Spurgeon reconciles it this way:

I believe there will be more in heaven than in hell. If you ask me why I think so, I answer, because Christ, in everything, is to "have the pre-eminence" [Colossians 1:18], and I cannot conceive how he could have the pre-eminence if there are to be more in the dominions of Satan than in paradise. Moreover, it is said there is to be a multitude that no man can number in heaven; I have never read that there is to be a multitude that no man can number in hell. *But I rejoice to know that the souls of all infants, as soon as they die, speed their way to paradise. Think what a multitude there is of them!*[10]

Rather than debate the census figures of heaven and hell, it is simply sufficient to say that hell exists. It's horrible; you don't want to go there; and you want to do everything in your power to keep others from choosing it. Jesus' teaching about hell, with its weeping and gnashing of teeth (Matthew 13:42), is meant to strike terror in our hearts, warning us that if heaven is better than anything we could dream of, hell will be worse than we can imagine.

Hell warns us to seek heaven.

It is its own best deterrent.

I know this firsthand. At the time of my injury, doctors pumped me up with powerful drugs to get rid of the infection that was raging through my paralyzed limbs. My body was on fire with pain. When nurses turned me facedown on the Stryker frame, I could only see the floor and people's feet. Horrified, I saw the ugly cloven hooves of demons where there should have been the shoes of nurses. The feet of friends were webbed with claws. I screamed at the nurses not to flip me faceup, fearful that I would see ugly monsters. But when they turned me over, I was shocked to find everything to be normal.

What a hell! Looking back, I know my terror was drug-induced. But those frightening images remained with me, even through subsequent years of backsliding and bitterness. In fact, during those years when I teetered on the brink of rejecting Christ entirely, scary cloven hooves would flash in my mind. For me, it was a warning.

My teen years were full of warning. I recall reading Jonathan Edwards's sermon "Sinners in the Hands of an Angry God" while studying American Literature in tenth-grade English. My hands trembled as I held the book! I wish public high school students were still required to read Edwards, one of America's greatest thinkers, but times have changed. Few read such cautions like this summary of Edwards's doctrine of hell written by John Gerstner, a notable authority on Edwards:

> [Sinners] too, at times, see God in his essence . . . But what they see is God's essence as a consuming fire. The same God whom the saints see as their supreme lover, sinners see as the enemy of their souls. The divine and supernatural light of the saint is the divine and supernatural darkness of the sinner . . . As the redeemed see God as the source of every blessing that heaven affords, the impenitent see God as the source of every curse of hell . . . For the saint, heaven is God. For the wicked, hell is God. Cursed are the impure in heart for they too shall see God![11]

Does this seem unfair? Does it seem cruel that unbelievers "will be thrown outside, into the darkness, where there will be weeping and gnashing of teeth" (Matthew 8:12)? Our human sense of justice may think so, but remember, God owes this utterly rebellious planet absolutely nothing. Were it not for God's quickening grace, we would all remain dead in our trespasses. Plus, were it not for His grace, this planet would have ripped itself apart at the seams long ago in hatred and violence. That the human race has survived this long is a demonstration of God's compassion. The question is not, "How could God let so many people go to hell?" but should be "How could God be so generous and save as many as He does?"

Human fairness is not the point; the justice of God is. If there's no judgment and subsequent hell, then it makes more sense to eat, drink, and be merry, for tomorrow we die and . . . period. Nothingness. It's all over. But there *is* a hell. As well as a judgment: "I saw the dead, great and small, standing before the throne, and books were opened. Another book was opened, which is the book of life. The dead were judged *according to what they had done* . . . Anyone whose name was not found written in the book of life was thrown into the lake of fire" (Revelation 20:12, 15, emphasis added).

That's the one verse in the Bible that makes my hair stand on end. Apocalyptic verses about signs of the times, earthquakes, floods, and pestilence don't do it. Not even word pictures about snarling beasts and ten-horned creatures or the heavens rolling up as a scroll and the mountains fleeing into the ocean. The worst verse in the Bible is the one about dead people being judged. That's because some of those dead will be my neighbor down the street, my elementary school teacher, the woman at the dry cleaning shop, or even those Muslim young men who work at the Shell station near my house (not to mention millions of others worldwide).

When I pray, "Come quickly, Lord Jesus," I utter that word *quickly* with caution. Do I really want Jesus to return soon? Yes! And no.

HOLDING OFF *the* DAY
of GOD'S WRATH

The day dawned quietly over Nazareth, except for the crowing of a rooster and the barking of a few dogs. The hour was still early, but the sun was high, the air dry and hot. Any other morning, the streets of Nazareth would have been bustling with hawking vendors and women chatting on their way to the well. But this was no ordinary day. This was the Sabbath. And this was no ordinary Sabbath. Jesus had come home, and He was going to be in the synagogue.

No one was sure how long He'd been gone. Two, maybe three months? Rumor had it that one morning, Jesus just hung up His carpenter's apron and headed off to the Jordan River to find John the Baptist. Then something strange happened. When Jesus was baptized, there was a thunderous voice, followed by a dove. Next, He vanished. Some say Jesus headed off into the wilderness. Others reported His whereabouts later on in Capernaum. That's when rumors really got weird. Sick people getting healed? Something about water becoming wine?

And now He was back in Nazareth.

The air in the synagogue was hot and close. The attendant handed Jesus the scroll of Isaiah. He quietly unrolled it, found the verse He was looking for, and began to speak with the voice of uncommon authority: "The Spirit of the Lord is on me, because he has anointed me to proclaim good news to the poor. He has sent me to proclaim freedom for the prisoners and recovery of sight for the blind, to set the oppressed free, to proclaim the year of the Lord's favor" (Luke 4:18–19).

He stopped in the middle of the verse. Just like that, Jesus left it unfinished and sat down. The eyes of everyone were fastened on Him. Little wonder, they had never heard Isaiah 61 read in such a way, like the words were His own. Finally Jesus broke the silence: "Today this scripture is fulfilled in your hearing."

The rest was a blur. The crowd started demanding tricks, a magic show, shouting, "Do here in your hometown what we have heard that you did in Capernaum!" Jesus reminded them that crowds demanded the same performance from Elijah and Elisha, but like the prophets of old, He would do no miracles among faithless, stiff-necked, prideful people. A scuffle broke out and then a town riot. They drove Jesus out of the village and took him to the brow of the hill to throw Him down the cliff. The story abruptly ends there, with Jesus escaping and going on His way.

This incident in Luke 4 records the formal announcement

of Jesus' ministry. From the very moment He embarked on His earthly mission, He made clear His motives and intentions. He had come for heaven's sake. But why wasn't the crowd satisfied with His mission statement?

Perhaps it wasn't so much what He said as what He didn't say. Jesus did not read the entire verse from Isaiah 61. He announced He had come to proclaim the year of the Lord's favor, but He failed to finish the sentence. He did not say what the people were hoping He would say: that He had come "to proclaim . . . the day of vengeance of our God." It was obvious to the people gathered in that synagogue that Jesus had no intention of executing the wrath of God on their Roman oppressors. And everybody thought that's what the Messiah was supposed to do—execute wrath and judgment.

He left off the most terrifying part of the second verse of Isaiah 61 because He did not come to condemn or destroy; He came to seek and save the lost (Luke 19:10).

This threw everybody into confusion. Especially John the Baptist, who was poised for the judgment. John had been paving the way for Jesus, proclaiming, "Repent, for the kingdom of heaven has come near" (Matthew 3:2). He preached the coming hellfire and warned that the vengeance of God was at hand. Little wonder that John the Baptist was stymied. He had risked his life saying angry things against Herod, as well as pointing the finger at hypocritical religious leaders. When Jesus failed to crush evil and castigate sinners, John was confused and disappointed. He got himself thrown into prison for the sake of the coming judgment, yet Jesus didn't lift a finger to release him from jail.

Jesus made it clear that His agenda was not to execute the wrath of God, but to bear in His own body that same wrath. I'm heartbroken by that statement: Jesus, precious Savior, did not come to execute the wrath of God, but to *bear in His own body* God's fury. All of the Father's white-hot anger against my sin was poured out on the cross. Because of Jesus, the Father has no anger left for you and me.

Instead, He's storing up His anger for the day His Son will come back.

One day, Jesus is going to return and consummate the verse from Isaiah 61.

He will judge the living and the dead. He will crush the wicked. Punish rebellious, impudent evildoers. Upset nations and overthrow kings and rulers. He will institute the day of vengeance of our God.

This is what tempers my pleas for the soon return of Christ. Yes, I pray, "Come quickly, Lord Jesus," but in the same breath, I remember the high school girl in the white-sequined dress whom I prayed for at the prom, the ten-year-old Asian girl at the Hair and Nail Shoppe, and a few aunts and uncles who, unless they come to profess Christ as Savior, will end up getting trampled with all the grapes of God's wrath.

Please hold off a bit longer that great and dreadful day of the Lord!

Still, I need to remember that God's timing is perfect. You and I have a job to do, just as the disciples were reminded when they asked Jesus when He would come back. The Lord said to them, "It is not for you to know the times or dates the Father has set by his own authority. But you will receive power . . . and you will be my witnesses in Jerusalem, and in all Judea and Samaria, and to the ends of the earth" (Acts 1:7–8).

I need not bother myself with God's timing. I simply need to be bothered enough to witness. While Christ is in heaven, He is proclaiming through us the year of the Lord's favor. He is carrying out His agenda of compassion and forgiveness through you and me. He is still the tender, merciful Shepherd looking for more people to rescue, searching for lost men and women on whom He can gladly bestow salvation.

So when I begin to lean on the windowsill of eternity and pine for my Savior to fulfill His promise to return, I bite my lip and recall 2 Peter 3:9: "The Lord is not slow in keeping his promise, as some understand slowness. Instead he is patient with you, not wanting anyone to perish, but everyone to come to repentance." That's all the reminder I need to get away from that windowsill and to go rescue the perishing.

How patient of the Lord to hold His breath for almost two thousand years now and refrain from bringing down His vengeance. I don't mind the slowness of God, even if it means having to spend extra years in this wheelchair. God's slowness means more time and opportunity to increase heaven's numbers. More time for His inheritance to be enriched, His body the church to be made complete, His bride to be more beautiful, His army to be greater in rank, and the grand chorus of eternal worshipers to be louder and more thunderous in their praise. In short, it means more glory for Him.

I can sum up 2 Peter 3:9 with this paraphrase: "The Lord is not slow in finishing His sentences, as some understand slowness. He is holding off the last part of Isaiah 61:2, so that, heaven willing, my neighbor, my relatives, and the people who work in my community will come to repentance."

Oh, how gracious of Jesus, how patient. How kind of our God, how merciful. Until the King of kings and Lord of lords returns with eyes of blazing fire, robe of blood, and sword and fury, you and I will do well to get out there and proclaim the year of the Lord's favor.

CROWN HIM *with* MANY CROWNS

Is your blood pressure a notch higher, like mine is right now? Maybe you are feeling like me—awash in delight, yet reverent in fear. Tingling with joy, yet trembling with holy respect. Our God is an awesome God! That's why I wish we were huddled together against the cold night air right now, listening to my neighbor's whistling pine trees and gazing at a thin slice of the moon making a smile on the horizon. I wish we were standing together underneath a starry dome, feeling small and swallowed up and tuning into the faint and haunting melody of a hymn. A certain hymn striking a resonant chord in our souls.

It would be a moment of great happiness and wisdom. But this time, we wouldn't let it go. Nothing mundane or ordinary could drown it out, and we'd not only hold ourselves in that ecstatic state of listening to heaven's music, but we would lift our voices and sing along.

Crown Him the Lord of love;
Behold His hands and side,
Rich wounds, yet visible above,
In beauty glorified.
No angel in the sky
Can fully bear that sight,
But downward bends his burning eye
At mysteries so bright.

Crown Him the Lord of life,
Who triumphed o'er the grave,
Who rose victorious to the strife
For those He came to save.
His glories now we sing,
Who died, and rose on high,
Who died eternal life to bring,
And lives that death may die.

Crown Him the Lord of heav'n,
One with the Father known,

> *One with the Spirit through Him giv'n*
> *From yonder glorious throne.*
> *To Thee be endless praise,*
> *For Thou for us hast died;*
> *Be Thou, O Lord, through endless days*
> *Adored and magnified.*
> *Amen.*[12]

CLIMBING HIGHER

Whenever my afflictions entice me to throw in the towel, God shores up my spirits, time and again, in always new and refreshing ways. And the most stimulating way is found in the book of Hebrews. This invigorating epistle has a verse for every weary Christian, every tired soldier in the Lord's army. Here is how it reads: "For here we do not have an enduring city, but we are looking for the city that is to come" (Hebrews 13:14).

That's another way of saying, "Hey brothers and sisters, don't get so absorbed in the ups and downs of this present world. Save some of your energy, affection, and desire for the beautiful world just up ahead."

I'm reminded of a story I read years ago about a conquering general leading his victorious Italian army home after several great battles in northern lands. The campaign had stretched on for more than a year, and his men were homesick and bone-tired—almost dead on their feet. Their southward route led them through vast swaths of terrain, including rivers, plains, and deep forests. Finally they reached the foothills . . . of the Alps!

Now they had a mountain range to cross. As you might imagine, the ranks of war-weary soldiers began to falter as they marched on and on, through deep ravines and over mighty mountain passes. And then came the snow, wind, and freezing temperatures, sapping what little strength and will the exhausted warriors had in reserve. They were too cold, too tired, and too daunted by the climb to go on.

That's when the general knew he had to make the best speech of his life. As it turned out, it was also probably the shortest speech of his life. Stopping on a precipice where he could look back at all his men and be heard by them, the general pointed upward and shouted, "Men, just beyond those mountains lies *Italy*!"

Really, that was all that needed to be said. Thoughts of home swept through the ranks like a warm, fragrant wind. Italy! Waving fields of grain, beautiful orchards, sparkling fountains in the town squares. Mothers and fathers, wives and children and sweethearts! *Home!*

That one timely reminder changed everything. Fainting hearts revived. Tired muscles found new strength. The army got to its feet and pressed on, surmounting every obstacle until they crossed the summit and marched down the other side, reaching home at last.

To me, that's like the book of Hebrews in the New Testament. It was originally written to a group of Jewish converts to Christ who were undergoing all kinds of harsh persecution. A number of them must have been ready to quit. This new life in Christ was just too hard. Bruised and battered, many of them thought about returning to Judaism and the old, familiar ways of seeking God.

The book of Hebrews was a rallying cry—like the general standing on the precipice trying to encourage his exhausted army. The writer uses words like, "Don't turn back now. You're almost Home! Heaven is right around the corner. Jesus is waiting with open arms. You will be richly rewarded for all your toil and tears."

Jesus has already conquered death for you. (2:9)
Jesus will help you defeat temptation. (2:18)
Jesus is a High Priest who knows what you've been through. (4:15)

Jesus will give you mercy and grace in time of need. (4:16)
An eternal inheritance awaits you. (9:15)
The day you enter heaven is almost at hand. (10:25)
Don't throw away your confidence. Your rewards will be
  rich! (10:35)
The heavenly city is just over the horizon. (11:10)
The Better Country is coming into view. (11:16)
The finish line is just ahead. (12:1–2)
The kingdom is yours! (12:28)
Look . . . look for the city up ahead. Here it comes! (13:14)

Talk about refreshment for the weary soul! Friend, if you
are tired of constant setbacks and disappointments, remember
that we are in a race . . . and that the finish line is very near!
This world isn't our home. The nations and cities of earth will
soon be lost to memory. So many of the contemporary issues that
dominate the headlines and seem like such a big deal now will
fade in the morning sunlight like a vaguely disturbing dream. We
are really heading to the land we were born for, the City of the
great King. As the writer of Hebrews put it:

> But you have come right up into Mount Zion, to the
> city of the living God, the heavenly Jerusalem, and to the
> gathering of countless happy angels; and to the church,
> composed of all those registered in heaven; and to God who
> is Judge of all; and to the spirits of the redeemed in heaven,
> already made perfect; and to Jesus himself, who has brought
> us his wonderful new agreement.
>
> HEBREWS 12:22–24 TLB

Remember, you are a citizen of a heavenly kingdom, and you
will soon walk through gates of pearl into your eternal home,
where there will be no more war, no more pain, and no more

sorrow. The victory will be settled, once and for all, and your Savior will open the curtain on rewards beyond anything you could imagine in a score of lifetimes.

Take heart, no matter where you are in the battle.

Heaven is so much closer than you think.

FIND YOUR TRAIL

1. Hebrews 12:1 in the Living Bible speaks about "a huge crowd of men of faith watching us from the grandstands," cheering us on as we finish our race on earth. Whom do you picture in those grandstands—and how does that thought motivate you to stay in the race?
2. Look again at Hebrews 13:14. As you look at the world around you, listen to pessimistic news headlines, and even look in the mirror, what reminds you that "here we do not have an enduring city"? How can these thoughts spur you on to think about this "city that is to come"?

A HIKER'S PRAYER

Dear Father, the world seems like such a frightening place sometimes, with hurricanes, earthquakes, fires, and terror attacks. Sometimes we feel so small, insignificant, and out of place in the big events that sweep across our planet. Remind our hearts today that we are children of Almighty God, sons and daughters of the King of kings. Remind us of Jesus, our Brother, Friend, and Advocate, and the Holy Spirit, our Counselor, Helper, and inseparable Companion. Remind us of our indestructible inheritance waiting for us just over the horizon in Your very own house.

PART THREE

The Journey Home

I wouldn't dare speak it aloud, but years ago, my eternal estate just wasn't that big a deal. Heaven seemed like such a "long time ago in a galaxy far, far away" proposition that I couldn't get worked up about eternal logistics. Back then, I was simply glad to be numbered in the back of the pack. I was just "happy to get there"—and didn't have a clue as to how high the cosmic stakes really are.

This nonchalant view of heaven reveals itself in the way we live life on earth. We say the Sinner's Prayer and keep our nose clean, and when we get to the other side of our tombstone, we just hope God will be merciful. We take a ho-hum attitude toward obedience, toward the call to "be holy, because [He] is holy" (1 Peter 1:16).

Well, the longer I live with chronic pain and quadriplegia, the more serious these cosmic stakes become. Suffering has a way of doing that. It makes you take God's Word more seriously. You take *obedience* more seriously.

When you suffer—and suffer hard—time ticks by slowly. Which, in turn, makes each moment, each response to affliction, each ounce of patience, *precious*. Every hard effort generously faced, every sacrifice cheerfully submitted to, every word spoken under difficulties—in other words, every drastic bit of obedience—raises those who suffer to a higher level.

In the final two chapters, we will think together about trip preparation for heaven. You can't pack your bags for that final journey, but you can get ready. In fact, it may be the most important thing you ever do.

Eight

GETTING READY
for Heaven

"File this, Francie, and make copies of this letter, would you," I said to my secretary without looking up from my desk. "And, oh yes," I sighed, "would you please pull out the sofa bed one more time?"

"Are you serious? Again?"

"Again." With that, my face flushed and my eyes became damp. For the fourth time that day, I needed to be lifted out of my wheelchair and laid down. I had to undress to readjust my corset—shallow breathing, sweating, and a skyrocketing blood pressure were signaling that something was either pinching, bruising, or sticking my paralyzed body. My secretary tissued away my tears and unfolded my office sofa bed.

As she shifted my body, examining my legs and hips for any telltale pressure marks or red areas, I stared vacantly at the ceiling. "I want to quit this," I mumbled.

We couldn't find anything wrong. She put my clothes back on, hoisted me into my chair, and stepped back.

I looked sheepish. "Where do I go to resign from this stupid paralysis?"

Francie shook her head and grinned. She's heard me say it scores of times. It's nothing new. My disability is, at times, a pain.

As she gathered the pile of letters off my desk and got ready to leave, she paused and leaned against the door. "I bet you can't wait for heaven. You know, like Paul said, 'We groan, longing to be clothed instead with our heavenly dwelling'" (2 Corinthians 5:2).

My eyes dampened again, but this time they were tears of relief and hope. "Yeah, it'll be great." I couldn't return to my dictating. The verse kept sticking with me, and I whispered a prayer: "Yes, Lord, I do look forward to being whole, to having a body that will never know pain. But to be honest, what I really want is a new heart that doesn't want to resign or quit."

I sat and dreamed what I've dreamed of a thousand times: the hope of heaven. I jerked my will right side up, refocused my emotions, and realigned my thoughts. I mentally rehearsed a flood of other promises and fixed the eyes of my heart on unseen divine realities and future divine fulfillments. I zeroed in on a few heavenly coordinates to lift my sights above my physical pain:[1]

When Christ appears, we shall be like Him.
The perishable must clothe itself with the imperishable, and
    the mortal with immortality.
That which is sown in weakness will be raised in power.
He has given us an inheritance that can never perish, spoil,
    or fade.
If we suffer with Him, we shall also reign with Him.

It was all I needed. I opened my eyes and said out loud with a smile, "Come quickly, Lord Jesus."

The scene I described can sometimes happen two or three times a week. Physical affliction and emotional pain are, frankly, part of my daily routine. But I only stay me-centered long enough to release a few tears and blubber a few gripes, and that's it.

I learned long ago that self-pity can be a deadly trap, and so I avoid it like the plague. I quickly move onward and upward.

Hardships are God's way of helping me to get my mind on the hereafter. And I don't mean the hereafter as a death wish, psychological crutch, or escape from reality. I mean it as the true reality. And nothing beats rehearsing a few time-honored, well-worn verses of Scripture if you want to put reality into perspective.

Every time my corset wears a wound in my side or I'm faced with a four-week stint in bed or I feel the stab of someone else's pity, I look beyond the negatives and see the positives.

I recall that foreigners aren't supposed to feel at home on earth.

I set my heart and mind on things above and wait on the Bridegroom.

I remember the promise of a new body, heart, and mind.

I dream about reigning on earth and ruling in heaven.

I think about crowns and rewards and casting them all at Jesus' feet.

When these Scriptures strike that resonant chord in my heart, I tune into the melody and hold myself in the state of listening to heaven's music. Before I know it, the song lifts me, and I'm soaring on Spirit wings, breathing celestial air. I'm in heaven. It's a glorious vantage point from which to look down on my pain and problems. The soul that mounts up to heaven's kingdom cannot fail to triumph.

It's odd that it took a wheelchair—something that bolts me to earth—to make me see the futility of fighting spiritual battles on the earthly plane. When I attempted to live on the same low level as my bolts, gears, wheels, and leather, I made blunder after blunder. I was powerless there until I shifted to a higher battleground and chose a different perspective.

Looking down on my problems from heaven's perspective, trials looked extraordinarily different. When viewed from its own level, my paralysis seemed like a huge, impassable wall, but when viewed from above, the wall appeared as a thin line, something that could be overcome. It was, I discovered with delight, a bird's-eye view. It was the view of Isaiah 40:31: "Those who hope in the LORD will renew their strength. They will soar on wings like eagles; they will run and not grow weary, they will walk and not be faint."

Eagles overcome the lower law of gravity by the higher law of flight, and what is true for birds is true for the soul. Souls that soar to heaven's heights on wings like eagles overcome the mud of earth that keeps us stuck to a temporal, limited perspective. If you want to see heaven's horizons, as well as place earth in your rearview mirror, all you need to do is stretch your wings (yes, you have wings, and you don't need larger, better ones; you possess all that you need to gain a heavenly perspective on your trials) and consider your trials from heaven's realms. Like the wall that becomes a thin line, you are able to see the other side, the happier outcome.

That's what happened to me that day in my office. I was able to look beyond my "wall" to see where Jesus was taking me on my spiritual journey.

Although paralysis has aided me in my pilgrimage, it has not made me automatically holy. You could say the same about your own suffering. Pain and problems do not make one instantly obedient. For me, it has taken time. Time, in more ways than one.

THE VIEW FROM *the* END *of* TIME

Scripture mainly presents us with a view of life from the eternal perspective. Some call it "the heavenly point of view." I like to refer to it as the "end-of-time view." This perspective separates what is transitory from what is lasting. What is transitory, such as physical pain, will not endure, but what is lasting, such as the eternal weight of glory accrued from that pain, will remain forever. Everything else—numbing heartache, deep disappointment, circumstances that seem topsy-turvy—everything else, no matter how real it seems to us on earth, is treated as inconsequential. Hardships are hardly worth noticing.

The apostle Paul had this perspective when he said, "For our light and momentary troubles are achieving for us an eternal glory that far outweighs them all" (2 Corinthians 4:17). And regarding his own problems, he added, "I consider them garbage" (Philippians 3:8).

Wait a minute. Did he say, "Troubles, light"? "Hardships, garbage"?

The apostle Peter had this perspective too when he wrote to Christian friends being flogged and beaten, "In all this you greatly rejoice, though now for a little while you may have had to suffer grief in all kinds of trials" (1 Peter 1:6).

Rejoice? When you're being thrown to lions? The Christians to whom Peter was writing were suffering horribly under Nero, the Roman emperor. Peter expected them to view their problems as lasting . . . *a little while*? What sort of wristwatch was he using?

This kind of nonchalance about gut-wrenching suffering used to drive me crazy. Stuck in a wheelchair and staring out the window at the fields of our farm, I wondered, *Lord, how in the world can You consider my troubles light and momentary? I will never walk or run again. I will never use my hands. I've got a leaky leg bag. I smell like urine. My back aches. I'm trapped in front of this window. Maybe You see all of this as achieving an eternal glory, but all I see is one awful day after the next of life in this stinking wheelchair!*

I did not buy the heavenly point of view. My pain screamed for my undivided attention, insisting, "Forget the future! What's

God going to do *now*?" Time does that. It rivets your attention on temporal things and makes you live in the moment. And suffering doesn't make it any easier. It tightens the screw on the moment, making you anxious to find quick fix-its or escape hatches. That's what it was like as I pitied myself in my chair. When I read the call in Romans 5:3 to "glory in our sufferings," my first thought was, *Sure, God, I'll rejoice the day You get me out of this thing! And if You don't, what's going on? Are You poking fun at my paralysis? Trying to convince me that I'm in spiritual denial? That my hurt and pain are imaginary?* When it came to my afflictions being light and momentary, God was obviously using a different dictionary.

Years later, the light dawned. The Lord hadn't used a different lexicon when He picked words like "light and momentary" to define earthly troubles. Even if it meant being sawn asunder, torn apart by lions, or plopped in a wheelchair for the rest of one's life. The Spirit-inspired writers of the Bible simply had a different perspective, an end-of-time view. Tim Stafford writes, "This is why Scripture can seem at times so blithely and irritatingly out of touch with reality, brushing past huge philosophical problems and personal agony. That is just how life is when you are looking from the end. Perspective changes everything. What seemed so important at the time has no significance at all."[2]

It's a matter of perspective. "Therefore we do not lose heart," 2 Corinthians 4:16–17 reads. "Though outwardly we are wasting away, yet inwardly we are being renewed day by day. For our light and momentary troubles are *achieving for us an eternal glory that far outweighs them all*" (emphasis added). What could possibly outweigh the pain of permanent paralysis? The coordinates of the new perspective are found in the next verse: "So we fix our eyes not on what is seen, but on what is unseen, since what is seen is *temporary*, but what is unseen is *eternal*" (emphasis added). The greater weight of eternal glory is clear:

- the healing of that old ache
- joy, eternal and ecstatic
- being beautifully robed in righteousness
- knowing Christ fully, my King and co-heir
- the final destruction of death, disease, and the devil
- the vindication of Christ's holy name
- the restoration of all things under Christ

These things outweigh thousands of afternoons of sweats and high blood pressure any day. They outweigh a lifetime of not feeling or moving. Mind you, I'm not saying that my paralysis is light in and of itself; it only *becomes* light in contrast to the far greater weight on the other side of the scale. And although I wouldn't normally call three decades in a wheelchair "momentary," it *is* when you realize that "you are a mist that appears for a little while and then vanishes" (James 4:14).

Scripture is constantly trying to get us to look at life this way. Our life is but a blip on the eternal screen. Pain will be erased by a greater understanding; it will be eclipsed by a glorious result. Something so superb, so grandiose, is going to happen at the world's finale that it will suffice for every hurt and atone for every heartache. It also helps to know that the state of suffering we are in here is necessary to reach the state we want (more accurately, God wants!) in heaven.

This is why Jesus spent so much energy emphasizing the end-of-time perspective. The Lord had come from heaven, and He knew how wonderful it was. Thus, He was always focusing on end results—the harvest of the crop, the fruit from the tree, the close of the day's labor, the profit from the investment, the house that withstands the storm. He knew if we were to glory in our sufferings, our fascination with the here and now would have to be subdued. How else could He say to those who mourn, "You are blessed"? How else could He tell the persecuted to be happy?

How else could He remind His followers facing torture and death to "count it all joy"?

Nothing more radically altered the way I looked at my suffering than leapfrogging to this end-of-time vantage point. Heaven became my greatest hope. In fact, I wondered how other people could possibly face quadriplegia, cancer, or even a death in the family without the hope of heaven. It meant no more wallowing away hours by the farmhouse window, scorning Romans 8:28, and muttering, "How can it say all things fit together into a pattern for good in my life!" God's pattern for my earthly good may have smelled like urine and felt painful, but I knew the end result in heaven would exude a fragrant and glorious aroma: Christ in me, the hope of glory.

It's all a matter of time. "God has made everything beautiful in its time," reads Ecclesiastes 3:11. And for many, they won't see the beauty until the end of time. Time solves the dilemma of Romans 8:28, as well as all the other problems of evil, suffering, and pain.

THE CONNECTION *between* HARDSHIP *and* HEAVEN

You may not be paralyzed with a broken neck, but you might be paralyzed by other limitations. A broken heart. A broken home. A broken reputation. These things that presently scream for your undivided attention may close the doors to earthly satisfaction, but they can swing windows wide open to a spirited hope of heaven.

Mind you, the closed doors—many of which have slammed in your face and crunched your fingers—are no accident. God wishes to instill within you a deep desire for your inheritance that can never perish, spoil, or fade, but in order to grip your heart, He will take drastic measures. You may not appreciate His modus operandi at first, but later, with an end-of-time perspective, you can be grateful for it. The nineteenth-century minister Edward Payson described the connection between heaven and hardships this way:

> If God had told me some time ago, that he was about to make me as happy as I could be in this world, and then had told me that he should begin by crippling me in all my limbs, and removing me from all my usual sources of enjoyment; I should have thought it a very strange mode of accomplishing his purpose. And yet, how is his wisdom manifest even in this! for if you should see a man shut up in a closed room, idolizing a set of lamps, and rejoicing in their light, and you wished to make him truly happy, you would begin by blowing out all his lamps; and then throw open the shutters, to let in the light of heaven.[3]

That's exactly what God did for me when He sent a broken neck my way. He blew out the lamps in my life that lit up the here and now and made it so captivating. The dark despair of total and permanent paralysis that followed wasn't much fun, but it sure made heaven come alive. And one day, when our Bridegroom comes back—probably when I'm right in the middle of lying down on my office sofa for the umpteenth time—God is going to throw open heaven's shutters. There's not a doubt in my mind that I'll be fantastically more excited and ready for it than if I were on my feet.

Suffering is no failure of God's plan. True, it is part of the curse, along with death, disease, and destruction. But before God comes back to close the curtain on suffering, it is meant to be redeemed. Our miracle-working God can reach down into what otherwise looks like awful evil—terrible evil—and He and He only can pull out of it positive good for us and glory for Himself.

So what is this connection between heaven and our hardships?

SUFFERING MOVES OUR
HEARTS *toward* HEAVEN

Suffering makes us want to go to heaven. Broken homes and broken hearts crush our illusions that earth can keep its promises, that it can really satisfy. Only the hope of heaven can truly move our passions off this world—which God knows could never fulfill us anyway—and place them where they will find their glorious fulfillment.

When I was on my feet, it would have been nice had I focused on heaven purely for Christ's sake, but forget that. Altruistic, yes. But realistic? No. I was healthy, athletic, distracted, and not the type to get hyped-up about heaven for anyone's sake other than my own. Who wants to think about heaven when you've got things to do and places to go here? Besides, you have to die in order to get there. I did not want to think about that at the age of seventeen.

It's the nature of the human beast. At least this beast. Some people have to break their necks in order to set their hearts on heavenly glories above, and I happen to be one of them. It was only after the permanency of my paralysis sank in that heaven interested me.

Thank heavens, you don't have to break your neck to get grabbed. When you come to *know* that the hopes you have cherished will never come true, that your loved one is gone from this life forever, that you will never be as pretty or successful or famous as you had once imagined, your sights are lifted. You long for and look forward to the day when your hopes will be fulfilled and your heartache will vanish. The glorious day when you will be whole becomes your passion as you realize that, once and for all, earth can never meet your deepest longings.

My hopes of running through earthly meadows and splashing my feet in a stream will never come true—but it will in the new heaven and new earth. My dream of hugging a loved one and actually *feeling* his or her embrace will never come true—but it will when we stand together before Jesus.

You can appreciate this, especially if earth has broken your heart. You may be a mother who lost her child in an accident, a son who lost his father to cancer, or a husband whose wife has passed on to glory. These dear ones take with them a part of your heart that no one can replace. And since the pursuit of heaven is an occupation of the heart anyway, don't be surprised if you find yourself longing for heaven after you leave the graveside. If your heart is with your loved ones and they are home with the Lord, then heaven is home for you too.

A broken heart leads to the true contentment of asking less of this life because more is coming in the next. The art of living with suffering is the art of readjusting our expectations in the here and now. There are simply some things I will *never have* because of this wheelchair. Such longings heighten my loneliness here on earth. The psalmist tried to wrap words around this loneliness in Psalm 73:25–26: "Whom have I in heaven but you? And earth has nothing I desire besides you. My flesh and my heart may fail, but God is the strength of my heart and my portion forever."

Larry Crabb writes, "Godly people . . . nobly endure hard things. An anorexic daughter, a layoff, betrayal by a friend. They know that their existence is meaningful and that they are destined for unlimited pleasure at the deepest level [in heaven]. Because they keenly feel that nothing now quite meets the standards of their longing souls, the quiet but deeply throbbing ache within them drives them not to complaint, but to anticipation and further yieldedness."[4]

But asking less is not a loss, and readjusting expectations is not a negative. It's good. When I was on my feet, big, boisterous pleasures provided only fleeting satisfaction. In a wheelchair, satisfaction settles in as I sit under an oak tree on a windy day and delight in the rustle of leaves or sit by a fire and enjoy the soothing strains of a symphony. These smaller, less noisy pleasures are rich because, unlike the fun on my feet, these things yield patience, endurance, and a spirit of gratitude, all of which fit me further for eternity.

It is this yieldedness that gains you the most here on earth. You enjoy "a sincere heart and . . . the full assurance that faith brings," as it reads in Hebrews 10:22, which in turn gives conviction to unseen divine realities and future divine fulfillments. You enjoy a new degree, a new release, of energy at every point in your life as the eye of your soul is strengthened and spiritual understanding is quickened. A greater assurance of faith shows you that in all things God is indeed working for your good, and you realize without a doubt that the smallest of kind deeds done in Christ's name will result in a greater capacity to serve God in glory.

Suffering hurries the heart homeward.

Suffering Prepares Us *to* Meet God

Just think. *Suppose you had never in your life known physical pain.* No sore back, twisted ankle, or decayed molars. What if you never had to use those crutches or that walker? How could you appreciate the scarred hands with which Christ will greet you?

Yes, Jesus will be the only One in heaven who will bear the scars of life on earth, the imprint of nails in His hands. We know this because on His throne, the risen Christ appears as "a Lamb, looking as if it had been slain" (Revelation 5:6). And when we touch His scars, God will give us at least a partial answer to the "Why?" questions about our suffering, commenting to us, "Why not?"

If Jesus went through so much suffering to secure for us that which we don't deserve, why did we complain when we endured on earth only a tiny fraction of what He went through on our behalf? But if, instead, we stifled complaints and rejoiced in the privilege of participating in the sufferings of Christ, we will be overjoyed when His glory bursts onto the scene. For "we share in his sufferings in order that we may also share in his glory" (Romans 8:17).

In a way, I wish I could take to heaven my old, tattered Everest & Jennings wheelchair. I would point to the empty seat and say, "Lord, for decades I was paralyzed in this chair. But it showed me how paralyzed You must have felt to be nailed to Your cross. My limitations taught me something about the limitations You endured when You laid aside Your robes of glory and put on the indignity of human flesh."

At that point, with my strong and beautiful glorified body, I might sit in that old wheelchair, rub the armrests with my hands, look up at Jesus, and add, "The weaker I felt in this chair, the harder I leaned on You. And the harder I leaned, the more I discovered how strong You are. Thank You, Jesus, for learning obedience in Your suffering . . . You gave me grace to learn obedience in mine."

Not only will I appreciate the scars of Christ, but also the scars of other believers. There I will see men and women who were cut in pieces, burnt in flames, tortured and persecuted, eaten by beasts, and drowned in the seas—all for the love they had for the Lord. What a privilege it will be to stand near them! But what a shame it would be if, in conversing with them, we could only shrug our shoulders and prattle, "Me? Suffer? Well, there was that time I had to endure the most insipid color of yellow on my living room walls—and, uh, oh yes, my gallbladder surgery. Do you want to see my scars?"

Forgive me for being flippant, but perhaps we would bite our complaining tongues more often if we stopped to picture the scene in heaven. The examples of other suffering saints are meant to inspire us upward on our heavenly journey home. This is why I love reading the biographies of missionaries like Amy Carmichael or J. Hudson Taylor, people who considered it a privilege to bear their sufferings with grace so they might share in Christ's glory.

Suppose you had never in your life known emotional pain. No stained reputation. No bruised feelings. No pangs of guilt. What if no one had ever offended you deeply? How could you adequately express your gratitude when you approach the Man of Sorrows who was acquainted with grief?

If you were never embarrassed or felt ashamed, you could never grasp how much He loved you when He endured the spit from soldiers, the spinelessness of His disciples, the callousness of the crowd, and the jeers from the mob. All for the love of you.

He took your shameful sins and made them His. You will be able to say, "Lord, I'm grateful that I felt the piercing stab of guilt. I can better appreciate how You were wounded by sin on the cross!"

Lastly, suppose you had never in your life known the struggle against sin. There's a distinct connection between heaven and this struggle. The apostle John tightened the connection when he wrote in 1 John 3:2–3, "We know that when Christ appears, we shall be like him, for we shall see him as he is. All who have this hope in him purify themselves."

It is rare to find believers who, for the sake of heaven, purify themselves. But I want to be one of them, don't you? I want to sweep my conscience clean and jerk open every closet in my heart that hides a skeleton. It's painful to sit this close to self-scrutiny and cut away every sin that entangles, and I don't like cutting off a hand or gouging out an eye any more than you do. But it's the kind of drastic dealing with our sin that the Lord requires if we are to possess a lively anticipation of seeing Him face-to-face (Matthew 18:8–9). All who purify themselves have a heavenly hope, and all who possess this hope will purify themselves.[5]

I want to be as happy as possible in heaven. Bishop J. C. Ryle is on target when he warns, "Heaven is essentially a holy place; its inhabitants are all holy; its occupations are all holy. To be really happy in heaven, it is clear and plain that we must be somewhat trained and made ready for heaven while we are on earth . . . Our hearts must be somewhat in tune. To reach the holiday of glory, we must pass through the training school of grace. We must be heavenly-minded, and have heavenly tastes, in the life that now is."[6]

Yes, you want to be happy in heaven. And, yes, you'd like to feel at home with King David and the apostles Paul and John. Then live a life in agreement with the things they spoke about. Could we enthusiastically greet the apostle Paul, who said, "Submit to one another out of reverence for Christ" (Ephesians 5:21) if we made it a practice of stepping on others to get ahead?

Could we look forward to hours alone with the apostle John, who said, "Whoever lives in love lives in God, and God in them" (1 John 4:16) if in truth we settled for a halfhearted, ho-hum devotion to our Lord Jesus? Would we really feel comfortable with David, who said, "I cry out to God Most High, to God who fulfills his purpose for me" (Psalm 57:2 ESV) if we opted to ignore God when troubles came?

How could we be thrilled to meet the Lord face-to-face after clinging on earth to the very sins for which He died? It is impossible to hold on to sinful habits while at the same time holding on to the desire to touch the nail-scarred hands of Christ. No one can hope for heaven while consciously clutching on to sins he or she knows to be offensive. True, holy living is rugged and demanding, but its heavenly rewards are precious. It is heavenly-minded people who nail their sin to the cross; who desire, like John, to lean on Christ; who abandon themselves, like Paul, to be caught up into a third heaven; who wish, like David, to sit at the feet of His Lord.

Yes, it's a struggle. And all of Romans 7 assures us that holy living will always be a struggle. But think of it as the best way of showing your love to Christ! "Of all the things that will surprise us in the resurrection morning, this, I believe, will surprise us most: that we did not love Christ more before we died."[7]

I don't know about you, but that's one surprise I want to avoid. I want to cut away every sin that entangles.

A curious thing will happen if you view your suffering this way. Once you see your affliction as preparation for meeting God, you won't be quick to call it "suffering" again. Even though I have rough moments in my wheelchair, such as the one in my office with high blood pressure and pain, for the most part I consider my paralysis a gift. Just as Jesus exchanged the meaning of the cross from a symbol of torture to one of hope and salvation, He gives me the grace to do the same with my chair. If a cross can become a blessing, so can a wheelchair.

I'm inspired by Madame Guyon, who, although locked away in the depths of a French dungeon for many years, wrote, "I have no desire that my imprisonment should end before the right time. I love my chains."[8] And I'm also inspired by Amy Carmichael, the missionary to India, who wrote from her bed of affliction:

> *Before the winds that blow do cease,*
> *Teach me to dwell within Thy calm:*
> *Before the pain has passed in peace,*
> *Give me, my God, to sing a psalm.*[9]

Madame Guyon and Amy Carmichael would say something else. They would expect me to never dare say I was "suffering" paralysis. Once a gift, always a gift. The wheelchair is, in a sense, behind me now. The despair is over. There are now other crosses to bear, other "wheelchairs" in my life to be exchanged into gifts.

When you meet Jesus face-to-face, your loyalty in your

hardships will give you something tangible, something concrete, to offer Him in return. For what proof could you bring of your love and faithfulness if this life were to leave you totally unscarred?

WHEN SUFFERING SEEMS INSURMOUNTABLE

Over the phone, I could hear the puffing and wheezing of Lisa's ventilator as she labored to speak between breaths. "Joni, I don't . . . see why God . . . is putting me through . . . all this suffering . . . Why doesn't He just . . . take me home . . . now?"

I leaned my head against the receiver and wondered, for the thousandth time, what to say. Lisa was a twenty-one-year-old woman who became severely paralyzed as a result of an accident two and a half years earlier. In that time, she had been shifted from one hospital to another. The doctors had done all they could, and now they were deliberating over where to send her next. Her parents couldn't take her in. Independent living centers for people her age were overcrowded, and they had long waiting lists. The only option? A nursing home.

I'd had many years in a wheelchair—Lisa, only a few. How could I expect her to grasp the things that had taken me ages to understand? What could I give her or say to her to help?

"I'm a Christian," Lisa continued, interrupting my thoughts. "Why do I . . . have to go through all . . . this?"

I used to ask myself that many times. *Okay, I'll accept this connection between hardship and heaven, but what if the hardship is insurmountable? Overwhelming? Unbearable?* I'm paralyzed from the shoulders down, but Lisa is paralyzed from the neck down. She can't even breathe on her own. How can one deal with so much frustration and affliction? Questions such as these lose their academic tone when wrapped around the struggles of someone like her. This young ventilator-dependent quadriplegic is thrust out into a no-man's-land, way ahead of the frontline trenches where most of us suffer.

As we talked on the phone, I sensed that her questions were not the "why?" of the clenched-fist sort, but the "why?" of a searching heart. Bitterness was not her nemesis. Lisa was actually wondering how to live, how to view her affliction as meaningful. I knew that if she could rise above her circumstances to see her suffering from a heavenly end, she'd be in the enviable position of gaining more than most.

"You mean I've got more to gain than you?" she breathed into the phone.

"Yes, I believe you do," I answered gently.

"I'm ready . . . I want to understand . . . I don't want to live my life . . . in vain."

For the next hour, I slowly tried to lift her sights beyond the impassable wall of her hospital room. I began with the basics (which are really not so basic) and shared how her paralysis could become the best place from which to know God. "'Be still, and know that I am God,' it says in Psalm 46:10. Lisa, the hours you spend in that bed of yours are a way of being still before the Lord. A large part of you doesn't move. Literally. It is always quiet. This built-in stillness can help you understand things about the Lord that most people never grasp," I explained.

Perfect stillness is not always available to those who would appreciate it most, and often it's not appreciated by those who have it. Lisa had a long way to go before she could learn how to be comfortable in her enforced stillness, but the softness in her voice assured me she was on her way. She will learn that it's not merely an absence of noise and fidgety movement, but a spiritual alertness, a receptivity. Jim Elliot, the missionary who was speared to death in Ecuador by members of the Huaorani tribe, wrote in his diary, "Wherever you are, *be all there*. Live to the hilt every situation you believe to be the will of God."[10]

"Enough has been wasted in your life, Lisa," I said. "Don't waste any more of it. And don't worry about finding answers. I don't think they would satisfy you at this point anyway. Just use the time you've got, the stillness you're experiencing—use it to get to know God."

"But how?"

I smiled at her question because I knew the answer was going to sound so simple that it would seem sophomoric. "Talk to Him in prayer, and let Him talk to you in His Word."

"That's it?"

"That's it."

Lisa told me she would start doing just that, especially when I told her that the faintest prayers of those who suffer reach more deeply into God's heart. At that point, I imagined angels in heaven kicking up their heels and rejoicing. This ventilator-dependent quadriplegic who will lie in bed and spend long moments in prayer may not realize it, but she will be doing the work of angels. After all, there are angels in heaven who do nothing but praise God, such as the seraphim who proclaim day and night before the Lord, "Holy, Holy, Holy is the LORD Almighty!" (Isaiah 6:3; Revelation 4:8).

She has an arduous road ahead, but when hurting people like her give God an inch, He always takes a mile. He wants those who suffer greatly to receive even greater glory.

Look at how Douglas Kaine McKelvey describes it:

The clock has stopped.
The universe has flashed and cracked.
The flood has swept the dam.
Bright angels sift like gold dust from the gash,
heralding invitations of the lamb:
"Arise ye hobbling, tattered, orphaned, blind;
ye maimed in spirit, measured without merit,

by men cast off as useless.
Rise and find the crown, the throne, the birthright to
    inherit.[11]

THE GREATER *the* SUFFERING, *the* GREATER *the* GLORY

There is a direct relationship between earth's suffering and heaven's glory. I'm not glorifying suffering here. There's no inherent goodness in Lisa's spinal cord injury. There's nothing applaudable about the agony. Problems are real, and I'm not denying that suffering hurts. I'm just denying that it *matters* in the grander scheme of things. It is light and momentary *compared* with what our response is producing for us in heaven—yes, suffering is pivotal to future glory. This places Lisa in that enviable position I mentioned earlier.

Let me explain. The greatest suffering that ever occurred happened on the cross. And the greatest glory ever given in response to suffering was the glory ascribed to Christ when He ascended. He suffered "death on a cross. *Therefore* God exalted him to the highest place" (Philippians 2:8–9, emphasis added). There is a direct correspondence between suffering and glory.

When the mother of James and John approached the Lord and asked if her sons could please enjoy a position of prominence in the kingdom of heaven, Jesus replied, "You don't know what you are asking." Then He said to her sons, "Can you drink the cup I am going to drink?" When they answered, "We can," Jesus replied, "You will indeed drink from my cup" (see Matthew 20:20–23).

The Lord inferred that if His followers were to share in His glory, they would also have to share in His sufferings. And the deeper the suffering, the higher the glory. This is why the apostle Peter could say that to the degree one suffers, keep on rejoicing: "*Rejoice* inasmuch as you participate in the sufferings of Christ, *so that you may be overjoyed* when his glory is revealed" (1 Peter 4:13, emphasis added). We rejoice on earth . . . so that we may be overjoyed in heaven.

Does this mean that those who suffer greatly, yet nobly, will have a bigger halo? A shinier face? No, but it does mean that they will enjoy a greater capacity to serve God in heaven. Those who suffer beyond comparison will, if they honor Christ with an uncomplaining spirit, be glorified beyond all comparison.

I'm sure there will be times when Lisa will smirk—like I did—as she reads Romans 8:18: "I consider that our present sufferings are not worth comparing with the glory that will be revealed in us." Like me, she will go through cycles, thinking, *Is the Bible being flippant about my lot in life?* But as long as she keeps focused on the basics—being still and knowing God through prayer and Scripture—she will remain on the high road home. She will be more devoted to the future than the present. More devoted to the spiritual than the physical. And more devoted to eternal realities than temporal ones.[12]

DON'T GO *to* HEAVEN YET!

There's another cycle Lisa will have to go through. I still deal with it, and I bet you do too. The firmer my heart becomes anchored in heaven, the more I want to go there. *Now.*

It has nothing to do with being tired of sitting down or getting a crick in my neck from holding up my head all day. It's just that less of my heart is here, and more of it is there. I identify with the apostle Paul, who wrote in Philippians 1:21–24, "For to me, to live is Christ and to die is gain. If I am to go on living in the body, this will mean fruitful labor for me. Yet what shall I choose? I do not know. I am torn between the two: I desire to depart and be with Christ, which is better by far; but it is more necessary for you that I remain in the body."

Like Paul, I often debate the pros and cons of life. But also like him, my earthly life is meant to be one of discontentment. I am torn between the two. I desire to depart. Since my heart has already gone ahead, I long to follow it home. But it is more necessary that I—as well as Lisa and thousands like us—remain in the body. For others.

I touched on why at the close of my phone conversation with Lisa. "If you remain faithful, despite the odds, it helps people like me more than you'll ever know."

"But it's hard . . . to think of others . . . when you're hurting."

"I know." My voice was nearly a whisper. "But it is more necessary for you to remain in the body. It is more necessary for me and many more who know you better. A fellow with a disability once wrote in 2 Corinthians 1:5–6, 'For just as we share abundantly in the sufferings of Christ, so also our comfort abounds through Christ. If we are distressed, it is for your comfort and salvation; if we are comforted, it is for your comfort, which produces in you patient endurance of the same sufferings we suffer.'"

There was a long pause at the other end.

"The fact that you hang in there does something for the rest of us Christians. I'm not talking about you being an inspiration. It's more than that—it's a mystery. God somehow strengthens others by your faithfulness. You may feel like a burden to others, but God thinks the opposite. He thinks it's necessary that others take care of you. You will be doing more for their spiritual well-being than you can imagine. What's more, it's all being credited to your account. The apostle Paul said so in Philippians 1:25–26, when he said to a group of fellow believers who were inspired by his example, 'I will continue with all of you . . . so that through my being with you again your boasting in Christ Jesus will abound on account of me.' Did you get that part about 'on account of me'? If good things happen to others because of your example, God chalks it up to your record."

Lisa threw a curveball: "But I don't . . . see others any-more . . . Everyone . . . has gone away . . . I may help you . . . but nobody else."

At that point, she pointed me to another reason that God hasn't taken her to heaven yet. She must endure not only for the benefit of others, but for the purpose of teaching the unseen powers, the rulers, and the authorities in the heavenly realms about her powerful and all-sustaining Lord.

"You see," I explained, "I had a friend named Denise when I was in the hospital. She lay in bed for eight years, blind and paralyzed. Much worse than you or me. She hung in there, despite the odds."

There was another long silence on the other end, and I knew Lisa was listening intently.

"Denise died after eight years in that bed. My human logic said, 'God, You should have taken her home to heaven sooner. What did all her striving accomplish for the handful of nurses who happened to know her?' But then I read a verse in Ephesians 3:10 that tells us that God uses our lives like a blackboard on which He teaches lessons about Himself. And He does it for the benefit of angels and demons—maybe not for people, but for quadrillions of unseen beings."

Something dynamic is happening in heaven right now. Angels and demons are learning new things about God. It happens when believers allow their painful circumstances to be the platform from which their souls rise to heavenly heights. Every day we go on living in these bodies means fruitful labor—for us, for others, for the glory of God, and for the heavenly hosts.

ONWARD *and* UPWARD

Suffering does this. It always drives us in deeper and up higher. Always onward and upward into the heart of heaven.

Lisa and I said good-bye and continued to keep in touch. She settled into a living situation with a friend and began to attend a local college. She got involved with her church and started going to a Bible study. After five years, we lost contact. I wasn't worried about her, though, because she seemed to be on a steady path.

This year, however, I got the shock of my life when, after I finished speaking at a conference, a young woman hooked up to a ventilator wheeled up to me with a confident smile. I knew immediately who she was. The light in her eyes assured me this was the same young woman. She was happily heading for home and making the most of every day on the way.

Had Madame Guyon been able to reach across the centuries to Lisa (confined in her own set of bolts and bars), she would congratulate her with these words penned from her dark dungeon:

> What gain has been made compared to the little that has been lost! You will have lost "the creature" in order to gain "the Creator." You will have lost your nothingness in order to gain all things. You will be boundless, for you will have inherited God! Your capacity to experience His life will grow just a little more. Everything that you once had, and lost, will return to you in God.[13]

Lisa and I have seen the future, and the future is us. A glorious future for those who, for Christ's sake, suffer valiantly.

Yours is a glorious future too. God has placed suffering in your life to remind you that heaven is not only for the future; it is for now, for this present moment. Heaven is meant to bless your path and be a source of strength in your suffering today. Valiantly welcome it and greet it.

In her book *Grace Grows Best in Winter*, Margaret Clarkson quotes these powerful words of the fifteenth-century Italian painter Fra Angelico:

No heaven can come to us unless our hearts find rest in it today. Take heaven. No peace lies in the future which is not hidden in this precious little instant. Take peace. The gloom of the world is but a shadow. Behind it, yet within our reach, is joy . . . Life is so generous a giver, but we, judging its gifts by their coverings, cast them away as ugly or heavy or hard. Remove the covering, and you will find beneath it a living splendor, woven of love, and wisdom, and power. Welcome it, greet it, and touch the angel's hand that brings it.

Everything we call a trial, a sorrow, a duty: believe me, that angel's hand is there, the gift is there, and the wonder of an overshadowing Presence. Our joys, too: be not content with them as joys. They, too, conceal diviner gifts. Life is so full of meaning and purpose, so full of beauty beneath its covering, that you will find earth but cloaks your heaven. Courage, then, to claim it, that is all! But courage you have, and the knowledge that we are pilgrims wending through unknown country our way home.[14]

CLIMBING HIGHER

A few pages ago, my eye caught that section heading—"The Greater the Suffering, the Greater the Glory." It was so easy to write when I originally penned it decades ago. But as chronic pain and the encroachments of age try to erode my joy, I keep my eye on the finish line . . . when God calls me Home . . . when He sends His angels to reap a rich harvest while bringing in the sheaves.

If you grew up in church in the 1950s, as I did, you might remember the old gospel song, "Bringing in the Sheaves."

In Sunday school, our teacher would have us kids stand and march around the room singing the chorus. Written generations ago, the song spoke about plowing and working the soil until harvest time. "Sheaves" are the bundles of ripe grain, bound up and carried by the harvesters.

The song was penned in 1874 by Ohio evangelist Knowles Shaw, drawing from Psalm 126:6: "Those who go out weeping, carrying seed to sow, will return with songs of joy, carrying sheaves with them."

The harvest described in the song speaks of heaven and that glad, glorious, golden season when we will present the fruits of our earthly labors to Jesus, the Lord of the harvest. In the meantime, however, working the ground and tending crops down here on earth can be difficult, heartbreaking work at times. Galatians 6:9 (TLB) is meant to give encouragement: "And let us not get tired of doing what is right, for after a while we will reap a harvest of blessing if we don't get discouraged and give up."

Don't get discouraged . . . Don't give up.

Over the years of pressing on and persevering through many afflictions, I have often straightened up from my labors, leaned on my hoe, gazed at the horizon, and longed for harvest time . . . for that Better Country. When I'm feeling overwhelmed by life's trials, I keep reminding myself that they have a purpose—and an end in view. That purpose is beautifully expressed in a Puritan prayer I have often whispered to the Lord, sometimes through tears. Here is an excerpt:

> Give me a deeper trust,
>> that I may lose myself to find myself in thee,
>>> the ground of my rest,
>>> the spring of my being.
> Give me a deeper knowledge of thyself
>> as saviour, master, lord, and king . . .
> Plow deep in me, great Lord, heavenly husbandman,
>> that my being may be a tilled field,
>>> the roots of grace spreading far and wide,

until thou alone art seen in me,
thy beauty golden like summer harvest,
thy fruitfulness as autumn plenty.[15]

I think you can see why I love this prayer. Because I don't want to throw down the hoe, frustrated that harvest time seems too far in the distance. So I pray, *Plow deep in me, Lord.*

I'll be honest with you. It's a risky prayer. We are asking for a deeper knowledge of our Savior, a deeper holiness, or a deeper power in prayer. We are asking God to take His plow—the sharp, cutting edge of His will—and run our lives through and furrow us, unearthing parts that need to be tilled, places in our souls that have been too long in the dark. We're asking Him to turn those places upright to the sunshine of God's love and the showers of His mercy.

Plow deep in me, Lord.

It's a risky prayer because it's an invitation into our Lord's school of suffering.

Here's the bottom line. No one goes to Christ's heaven unless they take up their cross daily and follow in His steps. God shares His joy on His terms, and those terms call for us, in some measure, to suffer as He did. No, not in the degree He did, but rather in the manner in which He approached His cross.

But oh, the unspeakable intimacy and sweetness of knowing Christ through your suffering—the pleasure of knowing the Man of Sorrows in this deeply personal way. It is worth it.

And when harvest time finally comes? "Those the LORD has rescued will return. They will enter Zion with singing; everlasting joy will crown their heads. Gladness and joy will overtake them, and sorrow and sighing will flee away" (Isaiah 35:10).

And they will be bringing in their sheaves.

By the way, that's how the author of that gospel song entered heaven. Knowles Shaw, the Ohio evangelist, was a happy, upbeat man who delighted his listeners with his wit, charisma, and knowledge of Scripture. Through his brief ministry, he led to Christ and baptized more than eleven thousand men and women. At the age of forty-four, he died in a train wreck in McKinney, Texas. Before he passed, however, struggling in the wreckage with terrible injuries, he managed to save the life of a fellow minister.

His last words were, "It's a grand thing to rally people to the cross of Christ."[16]

With that, he stepped into the final harvest.

> *Sowing in the sunshine, sowing in the shadows,*
> *Fearing neither clouds nor winter's chilling breeze;*
> *By and by the harvest, and the labor ended,*
> *We shall come rejoicing, bringing in the sheaves.*[17]

FIND YOUR TRAIL

1. Read Ephesians 3:10. How is God using each of our lives like a blackboard to teach lessons to countless heavenly beings—as well as to those who watch our lives on earth? How does that motivate you as you face a difficult season of trial?
2. Jesus said in Luke 9:23, "Whoever wants to be my disciple must deny themselves and take up their cross daily and follow me." To the best of your understanding, what do these words mean in your life, in your exact situation—this very day?

A HIKER'S PRAYER

Dear Lord, help us not to lose our focus and our true purpose and reason for living today. Pain turns our thoughts inward. Frustrations push us into dark and negative places. The pressures of daily responsibilities lead us to focus on check marks on a to-do list. The songs and sentiments of the world around us draw us into their empty promises and fevered dreams. Lord and King, Savior and Friend, lift our vision again to the path You have given us to walk today, and let us glimpse the glow of heaven and Home, just beyond sight but not beyond reach.

Nine

Homeward
BOUND

The glowing sunset behind the coastal mountains stopped me in my tracks as I left the Joni and Friends office. I sat by my van in the parking lot and watched the hues shift and deepen from vivid lilac to pink and then a fiery red. A show-off sunset it was, a sassy kaleidoscope, teasing me, inviting me to follow it over the horizon. It was another one of those heaven-inspired moments wooing me not only over the horizon, but Home. I knew I couldn't follow. For now, I could only sit and enjoy.

"Good night, Joni," a couple of coworkers said with a smile as they headed toward their cars.

"G'night," I said dreamingly. I roused and added, "Hey, girls, wait. Can you believe that sunset?"

My friends paused, and together we stood, quietly, face-on into the color. It washed us in its glowing tone, touching us like the finger of Midas and making our group a single and silent statue of gold. We were bound together in a timeless moment that we knew was slipping away, even as we tried to hold on to it. *Drink it all in*, we seemed to understand. *This won't last forever.*

As the colors peaked, golden rays shot up from behind the

mountain just as the last vestige of sun slid beneath its crest. Then it was gone. Finished.

We watched the sky darken and threaten as fog from the ocean crept up over the hills. I shivered, and we said good-bye and went our separate ways. Getting into my van, I remembered a favorite line from Amy Carmichael: "We shall have all eternity to celebrate the victories, but we have only the few hours before sunset in which to win them."[1]

Amy Carmichael knew a lot about the Christian life—and a lot about sunsets. She knew the colors of the fading sun mesmerize us with their beauty, making us stand still and almost believe in timeless moments. Then in the next second, the lingering pink and gold vanish.

Why am I always surprised at how fast sunsets disappear? How fast my days disappear?

Then again, I'm always amazed at how fast *life* disappears. I watch a sunset, get in the van, drive away, stop at the gas station or the market, help Ken fix dinner, and then collapse in bed long after dark. The next morning, I'm up and at it again. My life will be gone in a flash, in the twinkling of an eye. Suddenly—just like that—it will be over. Finished. The fading beauty of all the good things in life will disappear.

Drink it all in. This won't last forever. Soon, much sooner than I realize, I will follow that sunset over the horizon and step into the other side of eternity. And if I'm able to look over my shoulder at earth, I know I'll be stunned that life went by so rapidly. But in heaven, there will literally be no time to think about it.

So I must think about it now.

That's why God gives us timeless moments in the here and now, striking that resonant chord in our hearts that echoes eternity. He woos us away from this world with that heavenly haunting, and it happens when we're enfolded in the arms of the one we love. Or watch a baby break into a giggle. Or savor a Scripture that springs to life in our heart. Or cry when a choir sings a triumphant hymn. Or watch a sunset or gaze at the stars.

Timeless moments are those that send our hearts on ahead to heaven. Moments when we demonstrate drastic obedience, choose patience over complaint, or honor God when it's hard. Amy Carmichael calls this "celebrating victories" in the few hours we have before sunset.

"Be very careful, then, how you live—not as unwise but as wise, making the most of every opportunity, because the days are evil," Ephesians 5:15–16 echoes. Days are fleeting; hours are fading. And before we know it, we will no longer have the chance to prove our love to Jesus with our obedience. We won't have the time to get back on track. To build with gold, silver, and precious stones.

The sun will have set.

TWILIGHT: APPROACHING *the* PASSAGE *to* HEAVEN

No one appreciated sunsets like my mother. Lindy, as her friends called her, was like me in that she would put everything on hold to watch a sassy sunset. During the summer, her early evening ritual included pulling up a chair and sipping coffee on the back porch of her condominium to watch the sun disappear below Sinepuxent Bay on the eastern shore of Maryland. Then she would watch the twilight give way to a thousand twinkling stars that stretched from horizon to horizon. She loved looking up and always called me to remind me when there was a full moon.

Mother was aware of how short the days were. By the time she took her last breath in 2001, she had seen many thousands of sunsets and understood that even the brightest day was sure to have its twilight. As she grew older, the shadows were falling longer, thicker, and faster, and the warmth was going out of the air. Her strongest hours of building with gold, silver, and precious stones were waning as the afternoon of her life passed. Lindy knew she was approaching twilight. But even in her twilight, even though Mother seemed grand and old, she was so . . . *young*!

I'm convinced it's because she kept looking up and focusing on something far beyond her many birthdays and blocked arteries. Heaven was literally nearer to her, and such a focus would always infuse youth into the heart. After all, to live in the heavenlies is to live in a kind of timelessness. People who look up and see beyond the encroaching years enlarge their souls with eternity. They have about them the air of something eternal, not temporal. They know that every year draws them closer to heaven, which, in turn, instills more youth into their hearts.

You didn't have to convince my mother, and you didn't have to twist the arm of my friend, Alice McIntire. Alice—who, when I knew her, was beyond my mother's years—enjoyed looking up as the shadows fell longer and faster. For years her heart had beaten in rhythm with her Savior's, and every once in a while, she seemed to tilt her head as if catching the strains of heaven's celebration. I wouldn't have been surprised if she did. She had an ear for things festive. She lived and looked the part, even after eight decades. Alice knew she would have all of eternity to celebrate the victories, so she made the most of the moments in her sunset years. She taught a women's Bible study, and she did it in St. John's knits with silk blouses and bows, earrings, and jeweled pumps.

Her Bible studies wouldn't have been complete without the best china and linens for coffee and cookies afterward. Her spunk, humor, and style amazed me, and I once said to Alice, "You must be really looking forward to heaven," to which she replied, "Oh, honey, yes, but I hope I stay around for Jesus' return. I never like to miss a good party."

Alice kept looking up. That's why she stayed so young (as did my mother). Every Christian who keeps looking up stretches his or her heart's capacity for heaven. They don't seem old; they are young.

Dr. Sherwood Wirt, who was editor emeritus of *Decision* magazine, was closing the ranks behind Alice McIntire and, like her, carried about him the air of youth. As he made his way into his eighties, he wrote, "People speak of the 'transitions' that age brings, usually in terms of externals such as thinning hair and hearing aids. I am now eighty-three years old and wish to testify that inside, where I live, age means nothing. I am the same person that I was at twenty-one, or forty-six, or sixty-five."[2]

I'm not ninety or in my eighties, but I identify. I feel so young inside, somewhere around the age of twelve or thirteen. As though I were a little girl. A girl like my mother, who still bundled up to run outside and gaze at the moon. Or Alice, who selected the latest designs off the petite rack. Or Dr. Wirt, who disarmed you every time with that twinkle in his blue eyes. We feel young when we forget the temporal and focus on the eternal—that's what children do who have no concept of time, and the kingdom of heaven belongs to such as these (Luke 18:16).

People such as these understand that time is not their natural environment. They realize they are spiritual beings who have a short stint in a physical experience. Time, for them, doesn't seem quite so much a stalking enemy as a passage—albeit a difficult one—into a brighter, better eternity.

WHEN *the* PASSAGE IS PAINFUL

It may be brighter at twilight, but not necessarily easier.

That final passage for our loved ones may be swift and sweet, but there's no guarantee. For many, the passage is ugly and painful.

It was this way for Billie Barrows, the wife of Cliff Barrows. For more than forty years, they labored together with Billy Graham, full of zest for life and zeal for the good fight. That zeal buoyed Billie during her last nine years as she wrestled courageously against breast cancer, which spread into her liver, bones, and finally her brain. She chose the high road and kept a joyful outlook, building up her body with the medicine of a happy heart, as well as a regimen of vitamins, various teas, and beet and carrot juice. But even with five chemotherapy treatments, Billie could not stave off the disease.

Surrounded by a loving family, boosted by prayer, and bolstered by a fighting spirit, hers should have been the model passage—wonderfully serene with chariots swinging low as the angels quietly came to carry her home. It wasn't that way. It was a knock-down-drag-out fight in the center ring, with time bullying and battering and showing no mercy.

On five different occasions, her sons and daughters flew from the far corners of the country to join their dad at Billie's bedside. *Surely this time God will take Mother home*, they reasoned. But it was not her appointed time. During the last two weeks of her life, Billie's joy, which had been such an inspiration to Cliff, friends, doctors, and the family, was silenced by the ticking of each painful minute that failed to bring release.

The deathbed was not a place of blessing for Billie. But it did become a place of blessing for the family. Cliff and his sons and daughters, in-laws, and grandchildren discovered a deeper, richer blessing in being together. Not around a holiday table with laughter and lighthearted moments, but around a bed of affliction that poignantly offered moments of love and reconciliation. Although Billie couldn't communicate, the large tears that rolled down her cheeks right before she died said it all. Finally, blessed release came. She left the land of the dying for the land of the living.

Not long after Billie's funeral, I called her daughter Bonnie. We talked about the wrenching agony of those last days. "Joni, Christians shouldn't glamorize death. Death is Satan's last-ditch effort, and he's going to make it as awful as he can."

There was a long pause.

"But God has the last word. Resurrection. And at the grave-side, we were able to sing—actually, we kept singing it every day:

> *'Soar we now where Christ has led, Alleluia!*
> *Foll'wing our exalted Head, Alleluia!*
> *Made like Him, like Him we rise, Alleluia!*
> *Ours the cross, the grave, the skies. Alleluia!'* [3]

I could hear the smile in Bonnie's voice, and it wasn't hard to imagine that same smile through tears as she and her family left the graveside singing that glorious hymn of victory, "Christ the Lord Is Risen Today."

As I hung up, I thought of Corrie ten Boom, the Dutch woman who was sent to a Nazi concentration camp for hiding Jewish families. Decades after Tante Corrie's release, I had a chance to sit by her bedside when Corrie was old and stroke-stricken. Watching her mind and body waste away to a thin shadow of her former self, I wondered—much like Billie's family—why the Lord didn't take Tante Corrie home sooner. But after the funeral of my elderly friend and as I was driving home with Ken, I reflected, "Every day Corrie lived was a victory over the devil. He would have had her die fifty years earlier in Ravensbrück, but just the act of living, without doing a thing, just breathing life in and out, was a triumph. If her final years had not influenced any person on earth and if the only reason the Lord allowed her to remain on earth was to make a silent daily statement to the principalities in heavenly places that 'Jesus is victor,' then it was an important silence, for sure."

Was something of eternal value actually being accrued to Billie Barrow's account just by her surviving a few extra months or weeks? Were unseen divine realities at work? Realities that the Barrows family was unable to detect through the blinding veil of suffering? Perhaps God's glory will ultimately be more golden because of family faith forged at her bedside—a victory that will be credited to Billie. The days of her dying may have been evil, but she labored on the best she could. Her body obeyed the impulse of God-given life. And perhaps that—no glamour intended—was a victory.

In all their suffering, neither Tante Corrie nor Billie was diminished.

Luther F. Beecher, a nineteenth-century New England preacher, wrote these words:

> I am standing upon the seashore. A ship at my side spreads her white sails to the morning breeze, and starts for the blue ocean. She is an object of beauty and strength, and I stand and watch her until she hangs like a speck of white cloud just where the sea and sky come down to meet and mingle with each other. Then someone at my side says: "There! She's gone!" Gone where? Gone from my sight— that is all. She is just as large in mast and hull and spar as she was when she left my side, and just as able to bear her load of living freight to the place of her destination. Her diminished size is in me, and not in her.
>
> And just at that moment when someone at my side says: "There! She's gone!" there are other eyes that are watching for her coming; and other voices ready to take up the glad shout: "There she comes!"
>
> And that is—"dying."[4]

I look at my own degenerating body and wonder how I will approach that final passage. Will it be short and sweet? Or long and agonizing? Will my husband be able to take care of me? Or will my quadriplegia better suit me for a nursing home? It's not so much that I'm afraid of death, but it's the uncertainty of the dying that gets to me.

Whether it's painfully prolonged or a peaceful passing in the night, I'm strangely comforted by the thought that a servant shouldn't expect to suffer less than his or her Master. There is no holy peace with death. Theologian Alexander Schmemann wrote in his classic *For the Life of the World*, "Only if Christ is Life is death what Christianity proclaims it to be, namely the enemy to be destroyed, and not a 'mystery' to be explained."[5] Even earth will convulse in upheaval in its final birth pains before the new heaven and the new earth. All seeds—whether a plant, a person, or a planet—must die. But then, the harvest.

BETWEEN DEATH *and* THE RESURRECTION

Until the harvest, Billie Barrows and Tante Corrie are not diminished while they are presently in heaven. They gained immeasurably the instant they crossed from the land of the dying to the land of the living. Second Corinthians 5:8 explains that "to be away from the body [is to be] at home with the Lord." Billie and Tante Corrie are not present with the Lord in some soul sleep right now; they are "at home" with Him in the best sense of the word. They are alive, awake, aware, and full of the joy of having come home. Home where they fit and feel warm and welcomed, a place where they belong. Who can begin to measure the fullness of the meaning of that word *home*!

There's another way that departed saints are not diminished, and the clue is given in Luke 16:19–31. Jesus relays not a parable, but an amazing real-life occurrence after the deaths of a beggar named Lazarus and a rich man. The rich man was very conscious of his hellish surroundings, as well as the condition of his brothers who were still on earth, and he wanted desperately to warn his family. He felt, saw, prayed, remembered, and desired. My point? If lost souls can feel and care, how much more can those who have died in the faith!

Tante Corrie and Billie presently reside with the Lord of glory, the Lord of love. How deeply they must feel and pray and see! How fervent must be their love! Could it be that our loved ones in glory are able to love us now? Pray for us now? Love does not die; it *cannot* die because it cannot fail. Love is a part of a departed saint's being—not their body, but their person. I'm convinced that Billie now loves her husband, Cliff, with a purer, holier, and more intense love than ever known on earth. And even if she is able to observe the mistakes, blunders, and tears of her loved ones on earth, she has the benefit of an end-of-time view. She is able to see the bigger, better picture.

In heaven, we do not lose, for "to die is gain" (Philippians 1:21). We aren't less; we're more. When we die, we're not in some soul sleep of a stupor, not in some kind of purgatory, and we're certainly not unconscious. We are at home with the Lord. Home!

THEN *the* RESURRECTION *and* REST

Then one day, the resurrection: "But your dead will live, LORD; their bodies will rise—let those who dwell in the dust wake up and shout for joy—your dew is like the dew of the morning; the earth will give birth to her dead" (Isaiah 26:19).

The veil over this unseen divine reality was pulled back for me one particular Sunday afternoon. My mother-in-law had recently purchased a family grave plot at a cemetery called Forest Lawn. She would not sign the papers, however, until Ken and I looked at the lot and gave our approval. "Do I have to?" I whined at Ken. I could think of better things to do with our Sunday afternoon.

Playing the submissive wife, I trekked to Forest Lawn with Ken, looked at my gravesite located in a section called "Murmuring Pines," and listened to the realtor (that's what she was actually called) remind me, "Well, with your head *here* and your feet *there*, you'll have a grand view of the valley and the distant mountains."

"That's important," I said. I also told her I did not have plans to stay there very long.

While the realtor and my mother-in-law conferred over the papers, I looked around at the hundreds of tombstones. It suddenly struck me that I was sitting on the exact spot where my body will rise, should I die before Christ comes. Resting on that grassy hillside did more to ignite the reality of the resurrection than hearing sermons or reading essays on the subject. One day, actual beings will return to actual graves and reunite to rise.

And then, heaven.

Then, rest.

Not the rest of inactivity, but rest from the pain, the weariness, and the disappointment. I've already passed through middle age, but like many of my friends who have toiled for years, I'm ready for a rest. No more wrestling against sin. No more prying the world's suction cups off my heart. No knock-down-drag-out fights with the devil. No collapsing in bed after an exhausting day only to snatch a few hours before you're up and at it again. "There remains . . . a Sabbath-rest for the people of God" (Hebrews 4:9).

This thought alone makes the earthly toil not only bearable, but lighter. I can remember how, after hours of riding my horse to check gates and fences, my weary mount would be wet with sweat, her head hanging low. I had to urge her to put one tired hoof in front of another. Then as soon as she caught a whiff of home or recognized the fences of her own pasture, her ears would pick up and her pace would quicken. The nearer we came to the barn, the more eager her trot became. After a quick unsaddling, she would joyfully roll around in the dirt and take long, deep drinks from the trough. How good it feels for a beast to be home, to be able to rest.

How good it will feel for us to rest, to be at home.

Maybe the writers of the Bible—some who had scars on their bodies from stonings, others whose joints were stiff from chains that chafed—had this sweet rest in mind, a rest that perked them up and quickened their pace. They wrote vigorous encouragements like, "Let us, therefore, make every effort to enter that rest" (Hebrews 4:11), and "Be very careful, then, how you live . . . making the most of every opportunity, because the days are evil" (Ephesians 5:15–16). The weary labor for them seemed light as a feather compared with the glorious rest into which they were about to enter.

SEIZE *the* DAY!

The sun is setting. There are only a few hours left in which to gain heavenly victories.

I believe we are in the twilight of our hardships, as well as in the twilight of the world's history. I believe the time is short. My closing words for you are these: "Make the most of every opportunity" (Colossians 4:5). It is what my mother, Alice McIntire, and Sherwood Wirt did, and it is what Billie Barrows and Tante Corrie did in the last painful years of their lives. If we could hear it from the lips of Amy Carmichael herself, perhaps we would sense the urgency of winning triumphs for Christ in these last few hours before the sun disappears.

I tried to drive home this end-of-time perspective to Kim, a young Christian woman with Lou Gehrig's disease who was trying to decide whether to go on a ventilator. She wasn't sure if a ventilator was something that would sustain her life or simply prolong her dying. We talked about how the impact of her decision would affect not just her but a wide circle of family and friends. We discussed the facts of her disease and whether she was, indeed, imminently dying. We talked about the difference between selfishness and selflessness.

I breathed a quick prayer, asking God to help me to be as sensitive as I could, and then I said to Kim, "If you can resolve these questions with a Spirit-controlled conscience, then I don't think you can make a wrong decision. But between the two, there may be a better choice. And to guide you, let me read this powerful verse from 2 Peter 3:8.

"It begins, 'But do not forget this one thing, dear friends.' You probably know from your days in Sunday school that what Peter is about to say is ultra-important, like Jesus saying, 'Very truly I tell you!' And Peter continues, 'With the Lord a day is like a thousand years, and a thousand years are like a day.'"

I explained to Kim why that verse is so key. We all recognize the old adage that God looks at the last two thousand years as only a couple of days gone by, but how many of us ever consider the second half of the verse? The part about seeing each day as like a thousand years? It's a little like divine geometry, a mathematical formula assuring us that each day is a chance to invest in a thousand years' worth of eternity. God gives us a twenty-four-hour slice of time in which to make the most of every opportunity—opportunities that will have eternal repercussions.

The way we spend—the way Kim spends—the hours and moments counts. It counts far more than we realize. I suggested to Kim that she ought to smile and say thank you to her mother when she syringes liquid lunch into her G-tube. It's a way of making the most of an opportunity, and it could resound to 359 years of eternal benefit to her and her mother, and glory to God. Kim gave a little laugh when I told her this. "And when you bite your tongue from complaining about something, it could shake out to five hundred years of eternal bliss, benefit, and glory!" What a way for this young woman to live out her remaining days. If Kim were to live only two more weeks with this heavenly perspective, it pans out to be fourteen thousand years in heaven. If she were to live a month, that adds up to thirty thousand years of eternal investment.

I'm not saying that every day here exactly equals one thousand years there. Remember, heaven has a different kind of time. Time just *is* in heaven. My purpose in using 2 Peter 3:8 was simply to give heavenly meaning to Kim's earthly hours.

Little wonder that Psalm 90:12 reads, "Teach us to number our days, that we may gain a heart of wisdom." *This* is the kind of wisdom God wants you to apply to your twenty-four-hour slices of time. This is the kind of wisdom that sends your heart on ahead to heaven.

Oh, if we could only realize how short life is. James 4:14 reads, "What is your life? You are a mist that appears for a little while and then vanishes." And if we need another nudge, Isaiah 40:6–7 reads, "All people are like grass . . . The grass withers and the flowers fall, because the breath of the LORD blows on them. Surely the people are grass."

Therefore make every effort. The days are evil.

Make the most of your moments.

COME HOME!

Yes, the older I get, the younger I feel. The faster time flies, the more precious my hours become. On some days, I feel as though I might be called Home any moment.

I had this "let's go home" feeling when I used to play in the woods beyond our backyard. As soon as I got home from elementary school and while Mom was preparing dinner, I'd put my things in my room and race out the back door to play tag with Kathy and a few neighborhood kids. We would call out to each other, and our shouts would echo through the tall oak trees. Everything echoed—the chatter of birds, the distant clatter of an old lawnmower, the slamming of screen doors. Our play was so much fun that an hour would go by and I'd hardly realize it. I barely noticed the rays of the sinking sun cutting long shadows through the trees. Kathy and I knew that soon Mother would call us home.

Funny, I rarely took it upon myself to go home unless I was called. I rather enjoyed hearing the sound of Daddy's or Mom's voice through cupped hands, shouting my name. No sooner did I hope they'd call when I would hear the familiar "ding ding a ling ding" of the dinner bell by the back door.

"Supper's ready. Time to come home!"

It's odd how I can still hear Mother's voice. It almost makes me cry now; it just about made me cry when I was a child. The echo of the bell . . . the haunting sound through the woods . . . the joy about to break open my heart for the love of home . . . the warmth of family—not to mention fried chicken and mashed potatoes by a glowing fire in the dining room. And often in the summer, after the table was cleared and dessert was over, we'd sit in the backyard and watch the sun go down.

"There it goes."

"It's almost gone . . . just a little tip of light left."

Our family would vie for who'd be the last one to see the sun set.

And then, we'd wait until the stars came out, singing hymns and counting the constellations. It was all I could hope for as a kid. And here I am, an adult who is still looking beyond Ursa Major, singing heaven's melodies, and winning victories until earth's twilight gives way to the dawn of eternity.

Most of the things that have deeply possessed my soul have been echoes that have died away as soon as they caught my ear. But the echo of that dinner bell, now, many years later, has not died but is swelling into the sound itself.

When that happens to any of us, when those tantalizing glimpses, those promises never quite fulfilled, find broader, more complete fulfillment in our maturing years, then we know we've found what we longed for. Beyond every shadow of a doubt, we would say, "Here at last is the thing I was made for. This is the healing of the old ache."

That's why for me, the echoes are getting louder. They resonate with the rich, full, and deep tones of Someone calling just a short distance away.

> *Softly and tenderly Jesus is calling,*
> *Calling for you and for me;*
> *See, on the portals He's waiting and watching,*
> *Watching for you and for me.*
>
> *Come Home, come Home,*
> *Ye who are weary, come Home;*
> *Earnestly, tenderly, Jesus is calling,*
> *Calling, "O sinner, come Home!"*[6]

CLIMBING HIGHER

Where does it all end? "In the face of all this, what is there left to say?" (Romans 8:31 Phillips). Yes, we know the cosmic stakes are high, but how high? Here on earth we are given this one chance to believe in and follow Christ—belief and actions that will impact our eternal estate a billion years from now. And that's just for starters.

The apostle writes, "Live life, then, with a due sense of responsibility, not as men who do not know the meaning and purpose of life but as *those who do*" (Ephesians 5:15 Phillips, emphasis added). According to this Scripture, you already understand what this life is about. You already get it. If we have committed to follow Jesus through time and into eternity, we have at least a tentative grasp on why God put us here. But in another sense, I think we are all in kindergarten—in nursery school, in the maternity wing—when it comes to grappling with *God's ultimate purpose for us*.

Think for a moment about the Trinity, each Person mutually indwelling the other. None lesser than the other. All equal.

All giving away glory to the other without being diminished in any way.

We know that God is love, and that the very nature of love is to give. What "love gift," then, could each member of the Trinity possibly give to the other? (What do you give to Someone who has everything and knows everything?)

Are you ready for the answer?

Look in a mirror.

I'm not being irreverent or flippant here. In Christ, you, as a redeemed, bought-and-paid-for son or daughter, become part of a gift exchange that we can only begin to fathom. It would be like saying you understand the heavens because you caught a glimpse of the moon through a toy telescope.

- As adopted sons and daughters, we are a gift that Jesus and the Spirit give to the Father.
- As a bride, we are a gift that the Father and the Spirit give to the Son.
- As a temple and a dwelling place for God, we are a gift that the Father and Son give to the Spirit.

Listen in, just for moment, on a prayer between Jesus Christ—the Son of God—and God the Father: "I have revealed you to those whom you gave me out of the world. They were yours; you gave them to me and they have obeyed your word . . . I pray for them . . . for those you have given me, for they are yours. All I have is yours, and all you have is mine. And glory has come to me through them" (John 17:6, 9–10).

What wonder is this? Jesus and His Father are having a conversation about you and me! We have been gifted to the Father from the Son, and gifted to the Son from the Father. And some way, somehow—though it strains comprehension—this gift of ourselves brings God's Son glory.

And if that isn't enough, Jesus opens His great heart to His Father with this special request: "I want those you have given me to be with me where I am, and to see my glory" (John 17:24). In other words, *I want to take My gifts home with Me. I want them to be with Me forever.*

We will *see* His glory, and then . . . we will *share* in His glory (see Romans 8:17).

This is holy ground. This is "take off your shoes, catch your breath" terrain. We are God's gift that He gives to Himself, and the gift exchange will be finalized when we're finally Home, together at last.

In the meantime, if I'm a gift to God, if I'm a wrapped-up-and-ribboned package for Jesus, I want to be the *best* gift He enables me to be. Why should I arrive on the other side dented, stained, and dog-eared like a package lost for six months in the mail? We glorify God when we keep ourselves holy—obedient, pure, and sanctified.

I want to be an obedient child, so that my Father takes pleasure in me.

I want to be a pure bride, so that the Son takes pleasure in me.

I want to be a clean-and-cleansed temple, so that the Spirit will take pleasure living inside of me.

So as all this giving is going on, I guess the first order of business is to give myself to God every morning as I get out of bed, whether I feel like it or not. Paul calls that being "a living sacrifice" (Romans 12:1).

I call it my reason to breathe.

FIND YOUR TRAIL

1. Read Romans 12:1–2. What steps does Paul describe in these verses that will help you become the kind of gift God would love to give to Himself?
2. We've probably all read what Moses prayed in Psalm 90:12: "Teach us to number our days, that we may gain a heart of wisdom." It's a very good request to bring to God—for all of us. But how might the Lord answer a prayer like this in your life?

A HIKER'S PRAYER

Lord, Your Word says that "when David had served God's purpose in his own generation, he fell asleep" (Acts 13:36). Help us not to second-guess what Your purposes are for each life in each generation. Some live longer with terrible suffering than we would hope or wish for. Others seem to leave us way too soon, with so many possibilities and so much potential unfulfilled. Lord, we acknowledge once again that You are the Lord of time, Lord of life, and Lord of eternity. Help each one of us to serve Your good and far-reaching purposes for our lives during the time You allow us in this passing world. In Jesus' strong name.

EPILOGUE

I recently attended a funeral to pay respects to Boris Vujicic, the sixty-two-year-old father of my friend and world-renowned speaker, Nick Vujicic. His beloved dad had died from pancreatic cancer. No one would choose to go to many funerals, but this graveside service lifted my heart—for more than one reason. We sang hymn after hymn about heaven, and if you know me, you'll know that's one of my all-time favorite things to do. And given that many of Nick's relatives were Christians from Eastern Europe, they sang with a robust passion, clearly convinced of the Better Country to which we are all heading.

As I began to wheel away after the service, Michelle, Nick's twenty-year-old sister, ran up and stopped me. Dabbing her eyes and with an unsteady voice, she shared a conversation she'd had with her dad the day before he passed away.

She explained that her father had been very restless that day, unable to rest, unwilling to let go. When she asked him why he seemed so agitated—even anxious—he sighed and hoarsely whispered, "Oh, honey, I grieve that I won't be here to walk you down the aisle."

Mustering every effort to console her precious father, Michelle replied, "Oh, Daddy, please don't let that bother you. After all, you are a man of Hebrews 11. You are heading for a Better

Country. There's *nothing* to miss about my earthly wedding. My dress will fade and become torn. My wedding photos will yellow with age. My body will grow old and turn to dust. But everything in heaven will last forever, and I will meet you at the *real* wedding on the other side!"

Immediately, Boris relaxed, and a smile came over his face. They both knew very well that what she had said was true, and the next day he let go of his grip on this world and peacefully entered heaven.

Before I wheeled away, Michelle told me, "And you know what, Joni? I meant everything I said to him. I *meant* it. Heaven will be that good."

Michelle, heartbroken as she may have been, was so right. Heaven is *that* good, because God is *that* good. Heaven is a Better Country—not because of its location, its terrain, its scenery, its climate, its cities, its rewards, its duration, or all of the wonders that no eye has seen nor ear heard nor heart imagined. Heaven is a Better Country because of the One who will open the gate for us and welcome us home, the One who waits for us at this very moment. *Savior. God-with-us. Advocate. Counselor. Redeemer. Friend of Sinners. Alpha and Omega. Pioneer and Perfecter. Desire of Nations. Good Shepherd. Lamb of God. True Light. Prince of Peace. Bright Morning Star.* Just for a moment, set aside the visions of a continent-sized new Jerusalem, descending like a multidimensional, spectral star. Set aside the crystal sea, shot through with living flames. Set aside the river of life and the rustle of healing leaves on the magnificent trees lining its banks. Set aside your made-just-for-you residence in the safety and splendor of the Father's house.

As I said in the introduction, heaven is about Jesus.

That's what makes the Better Country better.

If you can imagine it even for an instant, what if there were no heaven as the Bible describes it, and Jesus called us to be with

Him in some desolate valley on the backside of nowhere? What then? Well, if God's Son is there, and if that's where He wants to spend forever, that's where I would want to be too. Heaven is heaven because of Him.

Do you know Him?

The first step in the right direction home begins with a prayer, honest and from the heart. If you want to be certain that you're homeward bound to heaven, then let the following prayer be your guide as you express your own heart to the Lord:

> *Lord Jesus, I realize I have lived my life far from You, and I see now how my sin has separated me from You. Please come into my life—my heart, mind, and spirit—and make me the person You want me to be. Forgive me for living away from You all these years and help me to turn from my old ways to Your new and righteous ways. I invite You to be Lord of my life, and thank You for the difference You will make. Amen.*

If that is your prayer, then I have a strong hunch that you and I will meet face-to-face, if not here, then there. It may take a few thousand years, but hey, that's no time at all! How will you know me? Somehow, I don't think that will even be an issue. But just in case, look for the radiant young woman who never stops running, leaping, and dancing—and never lets Jesus out of her sight for even a minute.

Joni Eareckson Tada
Joni and Friends
P.O. Box 3333
Agoura Hills, CA 91376
818-707-5664
www.joniandfriends.org

NOTES

INTRODUCTION: WHAT'S SO GREAT ABOUT HEAVEN?

1. These ideas were suggested to me by my reading of chapter 1 in A. W. Tozer, *The Knowledge of the Holy* (San Francisco: HarperSanFrancisco, 1961).

2. This idea is found in the writings of Nathaniel Hawthorne; see, for example, his *The Marble Faun: or, The Romance of Monte Beni* (New York: Crowell, 1902), 87.

3. C. S. Lewis, *The Weight of Glory and Other Addresses* (1949; repr., New York: HarperCollins, 2001), 111.

4. C. S. Lewis, *Miracles: A Preliminary Study* (1947; repr., New York: Macmillan, 1978), 149.

5. See C. S. Lewis, *The Problem of Pain* (New York: Macmillan, 1962), 144–54.

6. C. S. Lewis, *Letters to Malcolm: Chiefly on Prayer* (1963; repr., San Francisco: HarperOne, 2017), 116.

7. Geoffrey Keynes, ed., *Blake: Complete Writings* (Oxford: Oxford University Press, 1966), 184.

CHAPTER 1: WHO ARE WE IN HEAVEN?

1. *The Book of Common Prayer* (Philadelphia: Reformed Episcopal Publication Society, 1932), 512.

2. See Robert L. Sassone, *The Tiniest Humans*, 2nd ed. (Stafford, VA: American Life League, 1995), viii.

3. C. S. Lewis, *The Weight of Glory and Other Addresses* (1949; repr., New York: HarperCollins, 2001), 45.

4. *Book of Common Prayer*, 5.

5. This idea was suggested to me by my reading of C. H. Spurgeon.

6. C. S. Lewis, *The Four Loves* (1960; repr., New York: Harcourt, Brace, Jovanovich, 1991), 89.

7. A. A. Hodge, *Evangelical Theology* (Carlisle, PA: Banner of Truth, 1976), 400.

CHAPTER 2: WHAT WILL WE DO IN HEAVEN?

1. C. S. Lewis, *The Weight of Glory and Other Addresses* (1949; repr., New York: HarperCollins, 2001), 39.

2. C. S. Lewis, *The Great Divorce* (New York: Macmillan, 1946), 36–37.

3. C. S. Lewis, *The Last Battle* (New York: HarperCollins, 1956), 228.

4. E. L. Mascall, *Grace and Glory* (New York: Morehouse-Barlow, 1961), 68–69.

5. Lewis, *Great Divorce*, 19, 21–22.

6. Quoted in Dave Browning, *What Leaders Do: A Leadership Primer* (Bloomington, IN: iUniverse, 2009), 45–46.

CHAPTER 3: WHERE IS HEAVEN AND WHAT IS IT LIKE?

1. John M. Templeton, *The God Who Would Be Known* (San Francisco: Harper & Row, 1989), 25.

2. Robert Jastrow and Malcolm Thompson, *Astronomy: Fundamentals and Frontiers* (Santa Barbara, CA: Wiley, 1977), 4, 12.

3. This idea was suggested to me in a personal letter from David Parrish.

4. Jonathan Edwards, *The Works of Jonathan Edwards*, vol. 2 (1834; repr., Edinburgh: Banner of Truth, 1974), 646.

5. See Jonathan Edwards, "Spiritual Appetites Need No Bounds," in *Jonathan Edwards: Containing 16 Sermons Unpublished in Edwards' Lifetime*, ed. Don Kistler (Morgan, PA: Soli Deo Gloria, 2004), 223–35.

6. Margaret Clarkson, *Grace Grows Best in Winter* (Grand Rapids: Eerdmans, 1984), 187.

CHAPTER 4: WHY DON'T WE FIT ON EARTH?

1. Albert E. Brumley, "This World Is Not My Home" (Glendale, CA: Praise Book, 1951), 111. Used by permission.

2. Malcolm Muggeridge, *Jesus Rediscovered* (New York: Doubleday, 1979), 47–48.

3. Peter Kreeft, *Heaven: The Heart's Deepest Longing* (New York: Harper & Row, 1980), 39.

4. This idea was suggested to me in Kreeft's book *Heaven*, 39–40.

5. Arthur Bennett, ed., *The Valley of Vision: A Collection of Puritan Prayers and Devotions* (1975; repr., Edinburgh: Banner of Truth, 2005), 203.

6. Sheldon Vanauken, *A Severe Mercy* (San Francisco: HarperSan Francisco, 1977), 200, 202.

7. C. S. Lewis, *A Grief Observed* (New York: Seabury, 1961), 23.

8. Kreeft, *Heaven*, 42.

9. Joni Mitchell, "Woodstock" (Siquomb, 1969). Used by permission. All rights reserved.

10. Kreeft, *Heaven*, 49–50.

11. George MacDonald, "The New Name," www.george-macdonald .com/etexts/new_name.html.

12. See C. H. Spurgeon, "Jesus Admired in Them That Believe," Sermon No. 1477, delivered on June 1, 1879, *Metropolitan Tabernacle Pulpit*, www.spurgeongems.org/vols25-27/chs1477.pdf.

13. Jonathan Edwards, *Six Occasional Sermons*, vol. 3 of *The Works of President Edwards* (New York: Leavitt and Allen, 1857), 630.

14. Kreeft, *Heaven*, 50.

15. A. W. Tozer, *The Knowledge of the Holy* (San Francisco: Harper SanFrancisco, 1961), 47.

16. Elizabeth Barrett Browning, *Aurora Leigh: A Poem in Nine Books* (New York: Crowell, 1883), 265.

17. George W. Robinson, "I Am His, and He Is Mine." Public domain.

18. Jeanne Guyon, *Spiritual Torrents* (Sargent, GA: SeedSowers, 1989), 98–99.

19. C. S. Lewis, *Mere Christianity* (New York: Macmillan, 1960), 118.

CHAPTER 5: HEAVEN HAS OUR HEART'S DESIRE

1. The idea for this imagery comes from Harry Blamires, *Knowing the Truth about Heaven and Hell* (Ann Arbor, MI: Servant, 1988), 111.
2. Jerry Leiber and Mike Stoller, "Is That All There Is?" (Jerry Leiber and Mike Stoller Music, 1966). All rights reserved. Used by permission.
3. Peter Kreeft, *Heaven: The Heart's Deepest Longing* (New York: Harper & Row, 1980), 24.
4. C. S. Lewis, *The Weight of Glory and Other Addresses* (1949; repr., New York: HarperCollins, 2001), 42.
5. The ideas in these three paragraphs are derived from C. S. Lewis, *The Four Loves* (1960; repr., New York: Harcourt, Brace, Jovanovich, 1991).
6. Sharalee Lucas Sherman, "I See Jesus in You" (Nashville: Rambo-McGuire Music, 1986). Used by permission.
7. Lewis, *Weight of Glory*, 45.
8. This idea is from Augustine, *Enarrationes in Psalmos* 127.9.
9. Augustine, *Confessions*, I.I.
10. William Herbert Carruth, "Each in His Own Tongue." Public domain.
11. Clara T. Williams, "Satisfied." Public domain.
12. A. W. Tozer, *The Knowledge of the Holy* (San Francisco: HarperSanFrancisco, 1961), 10.
13. Charles Wesley, "Love Divine, All Loves Excelling." Public domain.
14. John MacArthur Jr., *Heaven* tape series (Panorama City, CA: Grace to You, 1987).
15. C. S. Lewis, *The Problem of Pain* (1940; repr., San Francisco: HarperSanFrancisco, 2001), 116.

CHAPTER 6: HEAVEN: THE HOME OF LOVE

1. The idea for this opening portion of chapter 6 comes from the Rev. Louis Lapides, Beth Ariel Fellowship, Sherman Oaks, CA; sources: Maurice Lamm, "The Jewish Marriage Ceremony," in *The Jewish Way in Love and Marriage* (San Francisco: Harper & Row, 1980), 145–68; Alfred Edersheim, *Sketches of Jewish Social Life in the Days of Christ* (Grand Rapids: Eerdmans, 1974), 148.

2. This idea is found in Tim Stafford, *Knowing the Face of God: Deepening Your Personal Relationship with God*, rev. ed. (1989; repr., Eugene, OR: Wipf & Stock, 2005), 182.

3. Horatius Bonar, "Here, O My Lord, I See Thee Face to Face." Public domain.

4. George W. Robinson, "I Am His, and He Is Mine." Public domain.

5. George Matheson, "O Love That Wilt Not Let Me Go." Public domain.

6. This idea is suggested by the writings of Andrew Greeley.

7. This idea is found in Peter Kreeft, *Heaven: The Heart's Deepest Longing* (New York: Harper & Row, 1980), 77–101.

8. Kreeft, *Heaven*, 89–90.

9. Kreeft, *Heaven*, 58.

10. These ideas are borrowed from C. S. Lewis, *Till We Have Faces* (New York: Harcourt, Brace, 1956).

11. Lynn Hodges and Joy MacKenzie, "Heavenly Praise" (SpiritQuest Music, 1994). Used by permission.

CHAPTER 7: AT HOME WITH OUR KING

1. Reginald Heber, "Holy, Holy, Holy! Lord God Almighty." Public domain.

2. Matthew Bridges, "Crown Him with Many Crowns." Public domain.

3. William Cushing, "When He Cometh." Public domain.

4. James S. Stewart, *The Strong Name* (London: Hodder & Stoughton, 1941), 59–60, emphasis original.

5. This idea comes from Dr. Jack Miller, who was professor of practical theology at Westminster Theological Seminary for many years.

6. Jonathan Edwards, *The Works of Jonathan Edwards*, vol. 2 (London: Ball, 1839), 621.

7. C. S. Lewis, *The Weight of Glory and Other Addresses* (1949; repr., New York: HarperCollins, 2001), 38.

8. C. S. Lewis, *The Great Divorce* (New York: Macmillan, 1946), 69, emphasis original.

9. Peter Kreeft, *Heaven: The Heart's Deepest Longing* (New York: Harper & Row, 1980), 75, emphasis original.

10. C. H. Spurgeon, "Heavenly Worship: A Sermon (No. 110),"
    December 28, 1856, www.romans45.org/spurgeon/sermons/0110
    .htm, emphasis added.
11. John H. Gerstner, *Jonathan Edwards on Heaven and Hell* (Grand
    Rapids: Baker, 1980), 91.
12. Bridges, "Crown Him with Many Crowns." Public domain.
    Second stanza written by Godfrey Thring.

CHAPTER 8: GETTING READY FOR HEAVEN

1. See 1 John 3:2; 1 Corinthians 15:53; 15:43; 1 Peter 1:4;
   2 Timothy 2:12.
2. Tim Stafford, *Knowing the Face of God: Deepening Your Personal
   Relationship with God*, rev. ed. (1989; repr., Eugene, OR: Wipf &
   Stock, 2005), 221.
3. Quoted in Asa Cummings, ed., *Memoir, Select Thoughts and
   Sermons of the Late Rev. Edward Payson*, vol. 1 (Portland, OR:
   Hyde, Lord & Duren, 1846), 411.
4. Larry Crabb, *Men and Women: Enjoying the Difference*, rev. ed.
   (1991; repr., Grand Rapids: Zondervan, 2013), 91.
5. This idea is suggested in the writings of Bishop J. C. Ryle.
6. J. C. Ryle, *Holiness (Abridged): Its Nature, Hindrances, Difficulties,
   and Roots* (Chicago: Moody, 2010), 59, 98.
7. Ryle, *Holiness*, 246.
8. Thomas C. Upham, *Life, Religious Opinions and Experience of
   Madame de la Mothe Guyon* (London: Sampson Low, 1858), 146.
9. Amy Carmichael, *Rose from Brier: A Priceless Treasury of Helpful
   Thoughts for Those Who Are Ill* (1933; repr., Fort Washington,
   PA: CLC Publications, 2006), 16. Used by permission.
10. Quoted in Elisabeth Elliot, *Through Gates of Splendor* (1956;
    repr., Wheaton, IL: Tyndale, 1986), 20, emphasis original.
11. Douglas Kaine McKelvey, *Cattail, Fishscale, and Snakeskin*
    (Chicago: Cornerstone, 1994), 38. Used by permission.
12. These ideas are found in John MacArthur Jr., "Secrets to
    Endurance" message (Panorama City, CA: Grace to You, 1994).
13. Jeanne Guyon, *Spiritual Torrents* (Sargent, GA: SeedSowers,
    1989), 80.

14. Margaret Clarkson, *Grace Grows Best in Winter* (Grand Rapids: Eerdmans, 1984), 191–92.
15. Arthur Bennett, ed., *The Valley of Vision: A Collection of Puritan Prayers and Devotions* (1975; repr., Edinburgh: Banner of Truth, 2005), 75.
16. Quoted in *The Ecclesiastical Observer*, vol. 31 (London: Hall, 1878), 196.
17. Knowles Shaw, "Bringing in the Sheaves." Public domain.

CHAPTER 9: HOMEWARD BOUND

1. Amy Carmichael, *Things as They Are: Mission Work in Southern India* (New York: Young People's Missionary Movement, 1906), 158.
2. Sherwood Wirt, "Remembering the Joy," *Decision*, December 1994.
3. Charles Wesley, "Christ the Lord Is Risen Today." Public domain.
4. Luther F. Beecher, "What Is Dying?" *Northwestern Christian Advocate*, vol. 52, July 6, 1904, 14.
5. Alexander Schmemann, *For the Life of the World: Sacraments and Orthodoxy* (Crestwood, NY: St. Vladimir's Seminary Press, 2004), 99–100.
6. Will L. Thompson, "Softly and Tenderly." Public domain.